Organization Design:
The Collaborative Approach

Organization Design: The Collaborative Approach

Naomi Stanford

Routledge
Taylor & Francis Group

LONDON AND NEW YORK

First published by Butterworth-Heinemann
This edition published 2011 by Routledge
2 Park Square, Milton Park, Abingdon, Oxon OX14 4RN
711 Third Avenue, New York, NY 10017, USA

First published 2005

British Library Cataloguing in Publication Data
A catalogue record for this book is available from the British Library

Library of Congress Cataloguing in Publication Data
A catalogue record for this book is available from the Library of Congress

ISBN 0 7506 6367 7

Typeset by Charon Tec Pvt. Ltd, Chennai, India
www.charontec.com

Contents

*'The importance and value of a systematic design plan cannot be
underestimated.'*

> Carter, L. et al. (2001). *Best Practices in
> Organization Development and Change.* Jossey-Bass.

*'You can still be in a fog when surrounded by databases, information
systems, knowledge sharing, learning environments, and people full of
wisdom.'*

> Jensen, B. (2000). *Simplicity.* Perseus Publishing.

*'Leaders who take the same risks they ask of others – changing their
own behavior and giving up a measure of comfort and control – truly
inspire and energize others.'*

> Hesselbein, F. and Cohen, P. M. (1999).
> *Leader to Leader.* Jossey-Bass.

Contents

Chapter 3   Finding the right sponsor   35

*'In excellent companies, the role of the sponsor is not to supervise
the project manager but to make sure that the best interests of both
the customer and the company are recognized.'*
> Kerzner, H. (1998). *In Search of Excellence in
> Project Management.* John Wiley & Sons, Inc.

Chapter 4   Phase one – Preparing for change   47

*'Changing the formal organization is sometimes the most effective
way to influence the informal operating environment.'*
> David A. Nadler and Michael L. Tushman (1997).
> *Competing by Design.* Oxford University Press.

Chapter 5   Phase two – Choosing to re-design   73

*'People have to be grouped so that they can have the power, information,
knowledge, and rewards that allow them to coordinate their efforts
and cause them to feel collectively responsible for their performance.'*
> Lawler, E. (1996). *From the Ground Up.* Jossey-Bass.

Chapter 6   The communications plan   97

*'Inadequate description of change often results in implementation
breaking down at lower levels and employees questioning
management's knowledge of the details.'*
                    Timothyt J. Galpin (1996). *The Human Side of Change.*
                                            Jossey-Bass.

Chapter 7   Managing stakeholders   115

*'How companies define their stakeholders can make an enormous
difference in how they implement their business idea.'*
                    Schwartz, P. and Gibb, B. (1999). *When Good Companies
                    Do Bad Things.* John Wiley & Sons, Inc.

Chapter 8 Phase three – Creating the high-level design and the detailed design

'The roles design team members play during an event alternate between thinking and acting as participants and thinking and acting as a design team.'

Jacobs, R. W. (1997). *Real Time Strategic Change.* Berrett-Koehler Publishers.

Chapter 9 Risk

'It is not enough to identify and quantify risks. The idea is to manage them.'

Lewis, J. P. (1998). *Mastering Project Management.* McGraw Hill Professional Book Group.

Chapter 10 Project management

'A project is a unique set of coordinated activities, with definite starting and finishing points, undertaken by an individual or organisation to meet specific objectives within defined time, cost, and performance parameters.'

BS 6079 – 2:2000. Project Management. *Vocabulary.*

Chapter 11   Phase four – Handling the transition   205

'Neither fit nor commitment is sufficient by itself; both are needed.'
Jay R. Galbraith (1995). *Designing Organizations*. Jossey-Bass.

Chapter 12   The people planning   227

'Nothing is more crucial to the success of your transition than
how you select and treat people.'
David van Adelsberg and Edward A. Trolley (1999). *Running
Training Like a Business*. Berrett-Koehler Publishers.

Chapter 13   Phase five – Reviewing the design   247

'One of the most common reasons that re-designs fail is the all too
common assumption that the job essentially ends with the
announcement of the new design.'
David A. Nadler and Michael L. Tushman (1997).
Competing by Design. Oxford University Press.

Contents

*'There is a melt down of all traditional boundaries. Products and
services are merging. Buyers sell and sellers buy. Neat value
chains are messy economic webs. Homes are offices. No longer is
there a clear line between structure and process, owning and using,
knowing and learning, real and virtual. Less and less separates
employee and employer.'*

Davis, S. and Meyer, C. (1998). *Blur: The Speed of
Change in the Connected Economy.* Warner Books Inc.

Foreword

Contemporary organizations face constant pressure to enhance levels of service and productivity whilst also improving levels of cost efficiency. The volatility of external environment and the rapid pace of technological change increasingly demand innovative means of improving business performance and securing competitive advantage. Human resources (HR) are increasingly recognized as the prime source of competitive advantage and the need for effective people management is therefore more important than ever before.

The responsibility for effective people management is shared between senior managers, HR professionals and line managers but the challenges facing today's organizations provide an ideal opportunity for the HR function to demonstrate its ability to contribute to organizational performance at a strategic level. To take advantage of this opportunity it is necessary to not only recognize the changes that are required but also to identify the steps to ensure that they can be implemented effectively.

Whilst much has been written about strategic HR management and its contribution to organizational performance, real life examples of what works and what does not remain thin on the ground. We recognize that HR professionals and senior managers alike face a sometimes overwhelming pressure to follow trends or apply quick-fixes to a wide range of people management challenges and it can be difficult to get impartial advice about what to change and how to change it in order to create lasting results. We have therefore developed this series to bridge the gap between theory and implementation by providing workable solutions to complex people management issues and by sharing organizational experiences. The books within this series draw on live examples of strategic HR in practice and offer practical insights, tools and frameworks that will help to transform the individual and functional delivery of HR within a variety of organizational contexts.

This, the first book in the series, focuses on the constant need for organizational change faced by all contemporary workplaces. Organization design is one of the key areas of expertise through which HR professionals can significantly add value to their organization. Often narrowly interpreted to mean 'restructuring', organization design remains one of the secret levers of significant positive culture change. To achieve this requires an understanding of the mechanics of organization design together with a real understanding of the dynamics of the human workplace. The author outlines approaches to communication and stakeholder engagement, which should maximize the effectiveness and buy in to the new structures. As Michael Hammer, one of the 'fathers' of reengineering has recently noted, restructuring to achieve business process improvement has to take into account the needs of the people who are going to make the new structures work.

We are delighted to include Naomi Stanford's readable, practical book on organization design in this series. Naomi draws on her own experience in major organization and her writing reflects her understanding of the challenges for line managers and HR professionals trying to produce successfully redesigned organizations. She provides a step-by-step guide through the design process together with user-friendly tools, which practitioners can apply in their own organization. Naomi encourages strategic thinking with regard to what the design is meant to achieve and also asks some very straight questions about whether redesign is always the best option.

Applying the principals outlined in this book should not only lead to more successful organization design but will also will enhance the credibility of HR professionals as real business partners.

Julie Beardwell
Principal Lecturer in Human Resource Management
De Montfort University

Linda Holbeche
Director of Research
Roffey Park Institute

Acknowledgements

This book began its life as a training course in organization design I ran during the time I worked at British Airways. Much of the thinking behind it and the tools that come with it I developed in collaboration with colleagues there. So the core of this book is a collaborative effort on all our parts. To Neil Robertson, Sara Smart, Rick Wills, Peter Read, Silla Maizey, Gina Storey, Jacqui Fabian, and the many others with whom I worked my thanks and appreciation for the happy time I spent with them.

I would also like to thank colleagues at Marks & Spencer from whom I gained further skills, and learned more about the applications of organization design. Fiona Holmes, Mike Morley-Fletcher, and Mark Thomas all gave insights, support, and encouragement in my career there. Others helped me maybe more than they know; reading drafts, spurring ideas, and pointing out different approaches.

Kay Quam, Bill Hancy, and other new friends at SiloSmashers have smoothed my transition into a different working environment and I much appreciate their perspectives on organization design and systems thinking. Yvonne Mattocks has done a sterling job wresting the manuscript into shape.

My staunchest allies and, in their very different ways, most challenging and inspirational role models, are my family. Hannah Barugh, Rosa Barugh, Roger Woolford, Michael Stanford, Sonjia Stanford, Rosie Stanford, Patty Stratton, and Howard Benedict, from these people I learn every day. My love and thanks to them for all their support in this book endeavour.

I am donating all royalties from this book to The Medical Foundation for the Care of Victims of Torture. This is a human rights organization existing to enable survivors of torture and organized violence to engage in a healing process to assert their own human dignity and worth. Their concern for the health and well being of torture survivors and their families is directed towards providing medical and social care, practical assistance, and psychological and physical therapy. It is also the mission of the Medical Foundation for the Care of Victims of Torture to raise public awareness about torture and its consequences. Contact them at www.torturecare.co.uk.

Introduction

'*The importance and value of a systematic design plan cannot be underestimated.*'

Louis Carter, David Giber and Marshall Goldsmith (2001).
Best Practices in Organization Development and Change. Jossey-Bass.

Who would not agree with the quote above? And yet who has been invited to a meeting and been asked to help in a re-design project which must be accomplished in less than a month for reasons which no-one is quite able to articulate clearly? This book helps you to tackle this sort of assignment with confidence. Its purpose is to:

■ Provide the tools and techniques that human resource (HR) practitioners need to fulfil their emerging role as business partners, specifically in the area of organization design (OD).
■ Give line managers the insights they need in order to use the practical design process and available HR support on their projects.
■ Indicate how HR and the line can work most effectively together on design projects.
■ Provide the knowledge and method to handle the kind of recurring organizational change, that all businesses face and find troublesome – those which do not involve transforming the entire enterprise, but which necessitate significant change at the business unit, divisional, functional, facility or local levels.

The approach is strictly practical not an academic, top down 'architecture' approach. It explicitly covers areas often missing in the top down methods, that is:

■ How to actually *design* the softer aspects of organization at the same time as designing the structure. (The softer aspects include roles, culture, language, shape, style, communications, work/life balance, etc.)

- How to design the non-structural hard aspects, particularly the 'rules' that attempt explicitly to shape how people behave.
- How to agree and use the language – spoken, written, visual – to bring to life, describe, communicate, the design.
- How to clarify and work with the changing roles of the 'players' in the design as it unfolds. (For example, the HR practitioner might move from being an initiator of the re-design to being the coach of the manager.)
- How to ensure interface departments are kept involved and up-to-speed in the design process in order to adapt at the boundaries. (For example the information technology (IT) department may need to make some system changes.)

The method for design that the book aims to teach you is systematic but flexible. It is grounded in five underpinning beliefs:

1. That there is no one right way for doing organization design.
2. That organization design is an evolving iterative process which sometimes looks and feels messy and complicated.
3. That the design you come up with is not one which will last forever (or even for very long).
4. That the chosen design may be one of several which would work just as well to achieve your objectives (there is not necessarily a 'right' design).
5. That getting lost in the 'cottage industry' of designing, forgetting that the design is simply a means to an end, must be avoided at all costs.

With these in mind the book's first chapter discusses some of the key aspects of organization design, and subsequent chapters guide you through the five sequential phases you need to work through to successfully deliver the business benefits of an OD project. Figure I.1 summarizes the five phases.

This systematic approach may sound contradictory to the beliefs but it is not. The structure presented provides discipline and focus for successfully implementing a difficult assignment. It is similar in many ways to a game such as football where players need to know the boundaries of the pitch and the rules for playing. With these in mind they can then be alert to what's going on and respond accordingly. In the same way that there is not one right way to workout the moves and play a football match so

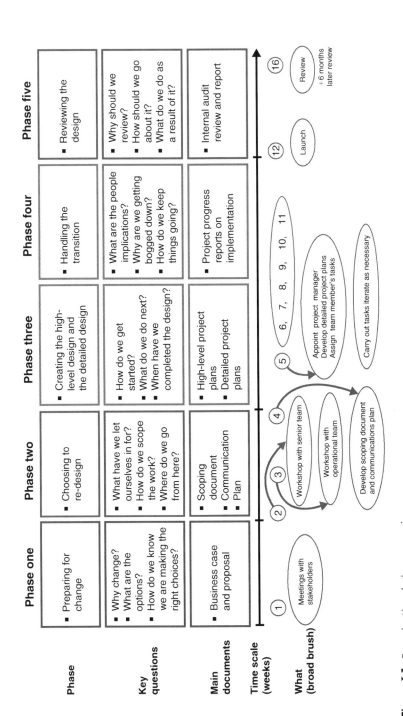

Phase

Phase one — Preparing for change

Phase two — Choosing to re-design

Phase three — Creating the high-level design and the detailed design

Phase four — Handling the transition

Phase five — Reviewing the design

Key questions

Phase one:
- Why change?
- What are the options?
- How do we know we are making the right choices?

Phase two:
- What have we let ourselves in for?
- How do we scope the work?
- Where do we go from here?

Phase three:
- How do we get started?
- What do we do next?
- When have we completed the design?

Phase four:
- What are the people implications?
- Why are we getting bogged down?
- How do we keep things going?

Phase five:
- Why should we review?
- How should we go about it?
- What do we do as a result of it?

Main documents

Phase one:
- Business case and proposal

Phase two:
- Scoping document
- Communication Plan

Phase three:
- High-level project plans
- Detailed project plans

Phase four:
- Project progress reports on implementation

Phase five:
- Internal audit review and report

Time scale (weeks)

1 ... 2 ... 4 ... 5 ... 6, 7, 8, 9, 10, 11 ... 12 (Launch) ... 16 (Review) +6 months later review

What (broad brush)

1 — Meetings with stakeholders

2 — Workshop with senior team

3 — Workshop with operational team

Develop scoping document and communications plan

5 — Appoint project manager
Develop detailed project plans
Assign team member's tasks

Carry out tasks iterate as necessary

Figure I.1 Organization design – overview

there is not one way of designing and delivering a new organization shape. But both need an underpinning discipline and framework to have the best chance of achieving successful results.

If you look at the overview map (Figure I.1) you will see that each phase of the process poses three key questions, lists the main tracking documentation associated with the phase and gives an approximate time line. The book describes and explains the phases of the method as follows:

■ An overview of the phase answering each of the three key questions in turn by explaining what you need to do in order to answer the question and why you need to do these things. This overview section closes with a discussion of the role each of you play during this phase of the project.
■ The overview section is followed by three sections discussing aspects of the OD project.
■ Then comes:
  – Useful tools – giving you some examples of the tools you can use.
  – Self-check – so that you can assess your skills and understanding.
  – Do's and don'ts – for the topic under discussion.
  – Summary – the bare bones of the chapter.

The book is addressed at two audiences working together – the HR practitioner and the line manager whose organization or part of the organization is being designed or re-designed. Ideally both parties should read the book so that they share a common understanding of the process.

If what you've read so far sounds daunting, be optimistic. If you've previously thought that an OD project was a gift from hell you'll change your mind after reading this book. With it in your hand you'll develop the know-how and confidence to get real business performance improvement from an OD project – the approach outlined is clear, it's simple, and it works. You'll get a wealth of useful tools, sample workshops, and action checklists to help you make your project stunning and you'll be delightfully surprised by how HR and the line can work brilliantly together on positive impact change.

1

What is Organization Design?

'You can still be in a fog when surrounded by databases, information systems, knowledge sharing, learning environments, and people full of wisdom.'

Jensen, B. (2000). *Simplicity.* Perseus Publishing.

Overview

This chapter describes organization design as a systems approach that is more than just structure. However, the first section of this chapter does outline some of the structural options that are open to you as you think about the design. Be cautious against deciding on a structure too early in the design process. As you read more about the systems approach you find out that if you change one part of your organization design it will affect other parts. The start-point is knowing your organization's business purpose and strategy and organization design starts from clarity on this.

The methodology this book describes is a five phase one that involves teams working at a high level and at a detailed level. In this chapter, you will learn something of how these operate as the design process proceeds. Later chapters explain the participative approach in more detail.

Essential to your design work is excellent communication to all those who are affected by any changes that you make. This chapter starts your thinking about the communication plan which is described in more detail in Chapter 6.

Enjoy your learning and assess how much you know by the end of the chapter where you will find a short do's and don'ts section, a self-check of your understanding, and a bare-bones summary.

Learn Something about Organization Design and Structure

Organization design specialists state that an organization will perform the way it is designed to perform and that the design must be able to realize specifically desired outputs. As evidence of this the Organization Design Forum – a US-based networking group for organization design practitioners – actively promotes the belief that highly effective, thriving, competitive businesses are *consciously designed* to achieve these ends.

A conscious organization design is more than its structure (defined as the under-pinning framework – the sort of thing you see on an organization chart). Nevertheless, it is useful to have an idea of what types of structures are commonly found in organizations in order to find a structure that will meet your overall design purpose. Consider an architecture analogy – if you know the types of structures commonly used for domestic dwellings for example, town-house, studio flat, block of flats, open plan, detached, semi-detached, terraced – you can then accept or reject structures that do not suit your purpose (a studio-flat structure would not be the best design option for family unit of one parent and two grown-up children).

Jack Kondrasuk and John Lewison in their paper *Organization Structures: a primer* describes the range of types of organizational structures. Chapter 14 extends the discussion on some of the newer organizational forms discussed below.

Functional structures are the form you are most likely to be familiar with. Usually they are organized on a departmental basis with skill or expertise within the function. Typically in an organization of this type you will see department heads of Marketing, HR, Sales, Product Development and so on. Each department has a specific function and is usually managed in a self-contained way giving rise to senior management statements like 'we must break down the silo mentality.' Co-ordination of the departments takes place at an executive level.

Process structures are best seen as an alternative to functional structures. In these, processes cut across an organization and represent the flow and transformation of information, decisions, materials, or resources to serve customers. Organizations structured in this way have the potential to quickly introduce new processes or make radical changes to existing processes. They are worth considering if you have a need to reduce process cycle times in your organization.

Product, market, or geographical structures start to evolve as a result of trying to get better cross-organization working. Business units are formed around a product, service and/or geography (e.g. Commercial Banking in Hong Kong, Retail Banking in the Americas) and there may be a sharing of corporate supports services like HR, IT, and finance. Whilst these structures may benefit from closer contact with customers than other structures, frequently there are replications of each of the core functions. So one organization might have several IT functions each one within a product business unit. When this happens you often hear statements like 'we must get rid of overlap and duplication.'

Matrix or project organizations combine aspects of both the functional and product structures. Typically employees deploy their technical skills on a project either full or part-time and report to a project manager on this while reporting to a line manager for the non-project aspects of their work. Some organizations are wholly structured on a matrix basis. In this case there may be 'embedded' functional/ product staff who report to the business unit head and to the functional head.

Boundaryless organizations have no discernable formal structure but rather are formed on a network basis to operate the business in an emerging way. There are organizations which aspire to this structure and some are close to operating it. Visa under the leadership of Dee Hock is one such example often mentioned.

Modular organizations are those which co-ordinate a range of suppliers whose products or services are integral to the end product. So, for example, Dell computers have Intel chips and Microsoft software. Airline catering is another example where the meals provided are integral to the service passengers get on airlines, but are not usually part of the core airline business – they are outsourced or sub-contracted. This type of organization has a certain designed in flexibility which can be advantageous.

Adopting this structure requires high attention to be paid to service level agreements and delivering on these.

Virtual organizations, partnerships, alliances – a bit of a catch-all category describing a variety of forms – some may have a short life span if they have been formed to deliver a particular one-off project which is then disbanded once that has been accomplished. Construction work frequently involves a number of organizations where each has a specific but autonomous role to play in the lifespan of the project.

Cellular organizations, networks or associations are typically self-organizing structures, attracting people who have similar interests and can benefit from some joint activity with little or no formal organization. 'Communities of practice' are examples as they are special interest groups. People can be members of many different associations and cells contributing to and gaining from each in a variety of ways.

One of your major organizational design choices is the basic structure. But you cannot start by deciding on the structure. The choice process begins with you having a clear understanding of your business strategy. By matching what is required by the strategy to what is done best by the various structures, you can start to come to a decision. Unfortunately, in the typical situation no one type of structure will necessarily best fit the business strategy. You need to go through a process to identify the various structural alternatives possible. Part of this includes considering what your business priorities are in relation to the strategy and where you most want the new design to make a difference.

However, structure is not the only consideration. Jay Galbraith (1995) describes a framework for organizational design consisting of a series of design policies that are controllable by management and can influence employee behaviour. He describes them in five categories and depicts them as a star model (Figure 1.1).

This model clearly demonstrates that changing the structure impacts on each of the other aspects of the organization. For things to work well you need to *design* not simply re-structure. This is why it is not a good idea to re-draw the organization chart, put people in their new places and expect performance improvements.

Thinking beyond structure into design additionally involves consideration of two inputs: customer requirements and environmental demands and opportunities (these lead to the identification of the business purpose and then to the business strategy). A somewhat different

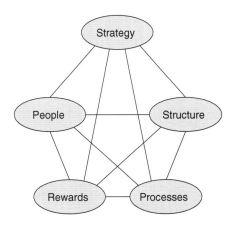

Figure 1.1 The star model

Inputs	Processing elements	Outputs
Customer requirements	People, work	Products/services
Environmental demands	Informal organization	
and opportunities	Formal organization	
	(working in balance/harmony)	

Figure 1.2 Input–output model

design model from Jay Galbraith's, presents designing as an input–output diagram where the structure and design decisions take place in the processing elements (people, work, formal organization, informal organization, see Figure 1.2) where you are working to get balance and harmony among these elements in order to produce the required outputs. This latter model starts the design process described in this book.

The challenge in trying to achieve a design that results in this balance is in being able to look beyond the 'structure' of your organization, whether it is hierarchy, matrix, network or something else, to the design that lies behind it. You need to be able to make sound judgements on what to change and what to leave – remembering that as soon as you change one element, it will affect all the other elements. To compound the challenge, you are trying to make this judgement in a context where customer requirements and environmental demands are constantly shifting.

None the less, the challenge is achievable if you are systematic about it. The overview, repeated in Figure 1.3, illustrates the five phases of the design process you will learn about in this book, together with the key questions you need to answer in each phase, the type of documentation it is

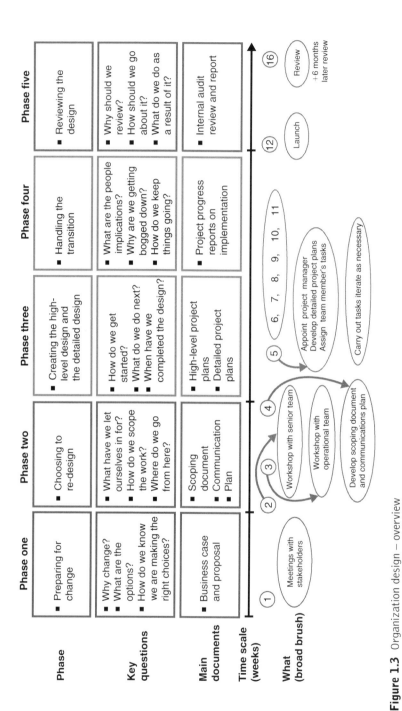

Figure 1.3 Organization design – overview

advisable to use, and a suggested timeline. Note that the timeline depends on the scale and complexity of the project. It could be a shorter timeline or a longer one. The timeline presented has worked, for example, for an internal department of about 120 people who were becoming an independent business unit (subsidiary). It has also worked for an IT rollout project from the UK into one country in Europe within the accounting department.

Know the Systems Approach to Organization Design

Events occur in organizations which precipitate the need to change the structures and operating processes quickly. Often there is a good and communicable reason for this: for example, you might be introducing a new computer system which changes the way work flows and this in turn forces consideration of the way people are organized to handle the work. Other times the events leading up to the decision of re-organization may be less obvious and less communicable to people, giving rise to this quote often shown in change management training.

> *We trained hard, but it seemed that every time we were to form up in teams, we would be re-organized.*
>
> *We tend to meet any new situation by re-organizating – and a wonderful method it can be for creating the illusion of progress … while producing confusion, inefficiency, and demoralization.*
>
> (Attributed to Petronius Arbitor Roman Governor of Bithynia, AD 60)

Your task is to keep abreast of the context that the organization is operating in, the pressures that it is being subjected to and the impact that these have on the business strategy and performance. This information will help you decide whether or not an organization design response is the right one for the situation you are facing.

This book takes as given that you need to change the ways your organization or part of the organization does things in order to increase productivity, performance, and profit. The problem lies in knowing what needs to change and how to change it. The design method we will be discussing looks at an organization as a system (defined as a set of inter-related elements where a change in one element affects the other elements).

Put simply, systems theory describes four major elements of organizations or departments (from now the two words are used interchangeably), Figure 1.4 describes each of the elements.

The work	The basic tasks to be done by the organization and its parts including the job roles and content, job design, number of positions, what work is done at what level
The people	The characteristics of individuals in the organization including their skills, capabilities, aptitudes, talents, demographic profile, length of service, and time in role
The formal organization – the 'architecture' which is the focus of organization design	The structures that are evident and can be described to a third party, including the organization hierarchy, the work-flow processes, the systems and methods that are formally created to get individuals to perform tasks. In organization design work your focus is on the formal organization
The informal organization	The implicit or emerging arrangements including variations to the norm, processes, and relationships, commonly described as the culture or 'the way we do things round here.' The informal organization also includes the 'shadow side' the way people 'decide' how to think and behave, the in-groups and out-groups, social routines, rites and rituals which reinforce the culture

Figure 1.4 Four elements of organization

The way these four elements relate, combine and interact affects productivity, performance, and profit.

Broadly each of the four elements work with each other to form six possible pairs as follows:

- People/work
- People/formal organization
- People/informal organization
- Work/formal organization
- Work/informal organization
- Formal organization/informal organization.

Generally speaking the more pairs that work well together, the more effective the organization will be. This becomes obvious if you think about the first pair (people/work). At a simple level the work makes skills, and knowledge demands on the individuals who do it. It is clear that if an individual's ability matches the demands of the work, his or her performance will be more effective than if there is a mismatch.

When you need to improve productivity, performance, and profit you need to improve the relationships and interactions among one or more of the pairs of components which make up your department.

Changing the relationship within any of the pairs will affect the relationship among the pairs. So, for example, if you train your people to use new skills to do the work this will not only affect the work but also the formal and informal organizations.

Your first step in knowing how to change requires you to survey and analyse where your change efforts will have maximum effect with minimum disruption. This research forms part of phase one – preparing for change and the method for doing it is described in Chapter 4.

When you have completed the analysis you will know where you are going to focus your efforts. If you decide to change your formal organization – to re-design it – or if you are setting up a new organization or part of an organization (i.e. designing from scratch as in a merger or new department) this book is right for you.

You may decide that a change is not necessary or right at this stage or that design is not the right response to the change. There are circumstances when it is absolutely the correct decision to sit tight, wait, and review the situation later – do not be afraid to do this.

Familiarize Yourself with the Five Phases of the Organization Design Method

Read through this whole book. You can read it at a skim read level in the first instance so that you understand the tone and approach, and start to get a feel for the OD project. The methodology described, which you will read about in detail as you go through the book comprises five phases (this whole 'What is Organization Design?' section that you are working through now is really the orientation programme). For the sake of clarity the five phases of the OD project are presented sequentially but in reality they are iterative, perhaps simultaneous, and often emerging. What you will recognize as you skim read is that whatever your design plan and desired outcomes are, you must go through each of the five phases if you are to reach a successful conclusion. Missing out one of the phases is likely to lead to confusion or worse.

The way it works is that two teams are formed during the first phase: the first a high-level design team of usually more senior people who are in a position to see and influence the bigger picture and who have the clout to lobby for and sanction change in their own and related organizations. The second team does the detailed-level design. Members of this are drawn from those who operate at the level of the practical daily work of the organization and can influence the way it is done. In practice there are usually several, rather than one, detailed-level design teams working on different aspects of the change process. But there is only one high-level team. (In larger projects you may have a governance structure which includes a steering group. In small projects you will need to have an organizational sponsor who will champion your change in the wider organization.)

The design teams work collaboratively to build a workable design. This approach works because the team members 'see' different parts of the organization and exchange and build on ideas as the work progresses. The high-level design team and the detailed-level design teamwork on an iterative basis. The result is a richly textured design which has the backing of people at all levels and in all roles. There is more about the teams and the iterative process in a later section, just now you need to start thinking whom you might involve as team members when the time is right. Note that members of the design teams do not usually work on the project full-time – it is an adjunct to a current role and is a good development opportunity for the right people.

As you read, aim to understand the approach the book takes. You already know this book is written for HR practitioners working with line managers and staff so the approach is not academic. Neither is it untested – it has worked well in several large UK organizations not only to transform a whole organization but also in out sourcing projects, alliance and merger situations, and in smaller-scale re-organizations of departments and working groups. It approaches organization design from the stance that organizations will perform the way that they are designed to perform. As you have already read organization design is not simply about 'structure' but the design principles that under-pin it. Remember architects follow a similar process when they sketch out a design for a specific type of building, for example, a hospital, domestic dwelling, or retail shopping mall. Before they begin the design they need to know what the inhabitants of the building will be using it for and then they design for that purpose. The form of the building is designed to accommodate the function of the occupants. So the design of the organization should facilitate the purpose of the organization. Anyone who has worked with a badly designed product will understand the frustrations of this. Similarly, a badly designed organization will not deliver the products or services in the optimum way.

You need to familiarize yourself with organization design and its methodology for a variety of reasons, the key one being so you know a bit about the possibilities and the route you are about to take, in order that you can prepare for it and then feel comfortable and confident you can last the course. What you are about to embark on, is a complex project which will impact the culture, the core work processes and the elements that feed into these (people, structure, measurement and reward systems, information and decision-making processes). As you are changing the organization you also need to be able to keep the business running on a day-to-day basis.

Start Planning Your Communications

A large part of the way you will succeed as you try to build commitment and involvement relates to the way you communicate with others. Good communication at all times is critical and at times of heightened organizational activity or change, it becomes crucial. You probably do not doubt the significance of communication in your project, but others before you have known this and done it poorly.

Guidelines for developing a communication plan are given in Chapter 6 but at this stage what you need to know is that communication is integral to your OD project so that as you skim read the book, start thinking about how you are going to herald your first action with a well thought through communication. Your communication will hit the mark if you recognize that the organization design approach advocated is one of participation, and collaboration with the people who will be working in the changed environment.

Useful Tools

Tool 1: Web sites

www.organizationdesignforum.org. 'The Organization Design Forum'. This is a US organization. (In the UK, you can contact: James Shillady

15

at Kiddy and Partners, jshillady@kiddyandpartners.com, to learn more about what is going on there.)

www.fastcompany.com is an excellent read on companies. It also comes out as a monthly magazine.

Tool 2: Books

At the head of each chapter you will see a quote from a book on organization design. Any one of those quoted would be useful to skim through or read in more detail. Jay Galbraith and David Nadler are well-known writers in the field and books of theirs are worth looking at.

Self-check

To measure your understanding of the overview of an OD project, ask yourself the following questions:

▢ Are you aware of the various types of organization structures that you could consider? The structure you currently operate with may or may not be the best one for your purposes. What you need to recognize is that making structural decisions at too early a stage in the design process may compromise the design possibilities. Those of you who draw up a new organization chart before you have done any preliminary work are setting yourselves up for failure. Any structural changes need to be thought through carefully – how many of you have had to go to B & Q in the middle of a do it yourself (DIY) project because you have not given enough thought to what you are trying to achieve and the best method of doing so? In organizations, botch jobs are very costly.

▢ Could you describe to someone else the bones of the method? The fact that it is five phases, that manager and HR practitioner take different roles in the process, that a high-level and a detailed-level team is convened from the workplace to work collaboratively and in an iterative way on generating the design, and that the philosophy of the method is one of participation and involvement.

▢ Do you feel comfortable with the approach? Be honest with yourself in assessing how far you are comfortable with an approach like this. If your style is naturally directive and controlling or you work in a highly bureaucratic and/or hierarchical organization, it might be too much of a stretch to start a process which is essentially organic and rather free-flowing. It is not a highly engineered or blue-printed approach. If you have a high need (or your organization does) for clarity, known deliverables and rigidly defined outcomes then this method may not be for you. Essentially you are working with an emerging shape that crystallizes rather than a pre-defined shape.

Do you know what to do next? Having got to this stage in the book you should already be starting to think about what to do next in relation to your project. The types of things you should have in mind are questions around team membership skills and attributes, roles of the various stakeholders, time and resource that will be required, documentation and process controls that would work for you, risk assessments and quality assurance, and most importantly the communication and involvement planning.

Have you talked to other people about organization design? Organization design takes many forms and it is good to talk with other people about their experiences of what works and how they have approached it. The more you can exchange knowledge on the topic, the more confident you will feel about your own skills and readiness to undertake the change. The Chartered Institute for Personnel and Development in the UK is a useful source of advice for HR practitioners as is the Society for HR Management in the US.

Are you feeling ready to start? If you are not feeling curious, excited and ready to learn more about the OD project at this stage then you need to consider whether it is something that you will be able to work on intensively for a significant period of time. Organization design requires focus and attention, not least because you have to keep the business operating as you re-design the organization around you. Organization re-design is a similar process as having your bathroom or kitchen remodelled. Many of you will know the difficulties of keeping your household going effectively and smoothly as you have this done – it is often a hard enough task without the builders being in situ.

Do's and Don'ts

- Do at least skim read the whole book so you have a broad understanding of the process
- Do think about the good and bad change management programmes you have been involved in and get ready to apply your learning from these
- Do start the communication and involvement process right now
- Don't think that collaboration and participation don't pay
- Don't try to make the process linear. It is iterative (but presented in a linear format here for the sake of clarity)
- Don't neglect to develop any technical skills you will need going forward

Summary – The Bare Bones

- Organizations will perform the way they are designed to perform
- Organization design is more than organization structure
- Design choices begin by knowing the business strategy and what it aims to deliver
- To improve productivity, performance and profit you need to get a good fit between people, work, the informal organization and the formal organization
- The organization design approach described in this book is participative and collaborative
- You need good change management skills
- Communication heralds your first actions

References/Useful Reading

Galbraith, J. (1995). *Designing Organizations*. Jossey-Bass.

Kondrasuk, J and Lewison, J. (1997). *Organization Structures: A Primer.* Society for Human Resource Management.

Nadler, D. A. et al. (1992). *Organizational Architecture: Designs for Changing Organizations*. Jossey-Bass.

2

You and Organization Design

'Leaders who take the same risks they ask of others – changing their own behavior and giving up a measure of comfort and control – truly inspire and energize others.'

Hesselbein, F. and Cohen, P. M. (1999).
Leader to Leader. Jossey-Bass.

Overview

Both of you (HR practitioner and line manager) are, in your different ways, leaders of the OD project. This chapter starts by asking you to think about the particular skills that an OD project requires you to have. In the collaborative approach, that this methodology is based on each participant plays a different role. Presented are some ways of working out your own role in relation to other people's roles in the design process. Following this is an explanation of what to do in each phase, with a short discussion on the importance of being clear about your own and the other participants' capabilities.

This discussion is followed by a tool that will help you assess your skills and then the self-check, do's and don'ts and bare bones summary.

Think about Your Organization Design Skills

For those currently in operational HR, you need to be aware that you will need to take on a very different role from that of a conventional HR practitioner. Organization design work (indeed any change management work) requires you to move well beyond the traditional boundaries of managing transactions to mobilizing a number of strategies to improve human performance and organizational effectiveness.

Equally those of you in line management roles who are initiating and implementing the change need to be confident that you have the chutzpah to carry it through. It is you who are setting the course and you who must visibly lead the way. You will be asking your staff to take a risk by doing things differently and you can inspire and energize them in this if you are willing and able to change your own behaviour and to give up some measure of comfort and control. If you do not demonstrate that you are completely committed to the new agenda you will not get it off the ground.

As you read through this book draw on your experiences of change programmes. Try to recall how you have felt about them either as an instigator of the programme or as a recipient of one. From these various perspectives think about what leadership attributes you have seen in operation which have worked, which have not worked, where you would do things differently, and so on. This reflection will help you match your skill and experience with what is presented here (it will also enable you to make comparisons, consider what similarities and differences there are between this approach and others you are familiar with and integrate anything new with your existing knowledge base).

Think about your own change management skills. How might you apply these in each of the five phases? You will see that the OD project involves you in initiating activities that invite or require people to do things differently. Identify where you may need to become more skilled or to adapt your current skills. To work effectively on an OD project you need to have between you the attributes shown in Figure 2.1.

Must have	Nice to have
Organization analysis skills	Highly developed conceptual skills
Problem-solving skills	Constant creativity
Ability to build commitment	Ability to think originally
Ability to build involvement	An optimistic outlook
Knowledge of power and political realities	Empathy
Positive 'can do' attitude	Ability to advise in a non-directive manner
Line management experience	Influencing skills
Listening skills	Networking skills
Strong tolerance of ambiguity	Persuasion in selling ideas

Figure 2.1 Organization design skills

Additionally you should have demonstrated technical skills in change management and facilitation.

Assuming that you have the attributes listed you then need to think about your style and behaviour in deploying them. It is not an exaggeration to say that your behaviour and that of other managers at the various levels of the organization can make or break a change programme.

Work Out Your Respective Roles

This organization design method assumes a partnership role between the HR practitioner and the line manager. Further, it assumes that both will have presence in the project from inception until the second review. This means that you must be ready, willing, and able to work together on the OD project for as long as it takes.

For your partnership to endure through the ups and downs of the coming months you will both need to either have or develop a keen sense of self. You need to be fully aware of your own strengths and weaknesses and in what situations you deploy these for good or ill. You also need to know what you want from each other in the partnership.

This is necessary because what you are jointly aiming to achieve is to turn the vision of a new organization design into a value add for the organization. You both need to believe in the vision and have a joint understanding of its objectives. With this common ground you need to be able to see how and where you can jointly deploy your skills to get the vision and objectives operationalized.

If you can forge a strong working relationship with this common purpose it will start off powerfully. However, as with any relationship you need to take certain continuing actions to sustain it and also to keep on renewing your commitment to it. What you will find as the OD project goes forward is that your roles, responsibilities, and activities change but the commitment to its success must remain constant.

Starting up the partnering relationship requires you to like and respect each other enough to be open and tell the truth. To get to this stage take some time to establish rapport and learn what each other's needs and expectations are from the project. Develop enough confidence in each other to know that if you say you are going to do something then you will do it. At a basic level, you have to be able to trust each other. As in any relationship, you may not always get your way, but you should each be able to have your say.

One of the tensions inherent in this kind of partnering process is that as well as the role you have in the OD project are the roles that you have elsewhere in the organization. Some of these may bang up against the role you are playing here. For example, line managers leading OD projects may recognize the need to employ an outside facilitator to run a workshop, but they have a managerial role to work within a strictly defined budget for the department and know people are under a lot of work pressure so attending a workshop may not be in the best short-term interest. As an HR practitioner you may feel that some of the organization design proposals are going to mean lay-offs and you know that your HR colleagues are already suffering from the fall-out and flack of previous reduction in force programmes.

For both of you success in this sort of multiple role working requires you to be able to balance the various demands of each without becoming stressed and demoralized yourself. You need to be able to maintain your optimistic outlook and 'can do' attitude for the duration of the OD project. If at this stage you can see the inherent role tensions being too great you would be wise to question whether you are the right person to lead or work on this project (in spite of what it may feel like you always have a choice).

You need to work out the roles you will play in the project for all the reasons presented below. There are probably further reasons that relate to your specific situation and you should consider them as well.

First, in order to give each other clarity on what a partnership means to you. If you think of the HR practitioner as being the consultant to the OD project and the line manager as the leader of it then the likelihood is that the line manager will take one or more of the project leadership roles along the continuum summarized in Figure 2.2 and the HR person will adopt one or more of the multiple consultancy roles summarized along the continuum summarized in Figure 2.3.

Clarity and understanding around where each of you naturally falls on the continuum will help you work through how this can be used in your partnership role to deliver a value added project.

Second, you need to know what your own level of change readiness is because a large measure of your success in your organization design role will depend on your readiness to change your own behaviours. If you are going to be asking other people to take risks, think laterally, give up what

Strategic management	$\rightarrow$ Tactical management	$\rightarrow$ Operational management
Give direction: Why do we want to do this?	Plan oriented: How do we achieve the goals	Action oriented: What, when, where, and who
Thinking long term, beyond the immediate problem	Thinking three to six months ahead	Thinking days or a few weeks ahead
Challenging the organization	Solution oriented	Listing jobs to be done, quick fixes
Redefining the problem to be tackled	Organizing, planning, and co-ordinating	Spotting opportunities for immediate action
Giving an innovative perspective	Planning within an appropriate and flexible framework	Mitigating risks
At whichever point on the continuum defining the task, planning, briefing staff, controlling, evaluating, motivating, organizing and setting an example		

Figure 2.2 The role of the line manager

Facilitator role	$\rightarrow$		$\rightarrow$		$\rightarrow$		$\rightarrow$	Expert role
Objective	Process counsellor	Fact finder	Alternative identifier and linker	Joint problem solver	Trainer educator	Informational expert	Advocate

Non-directive style	$\rightarrow$		$\rightarrow$		$\rightarrow$		$\rightarrow$	Directive style
Questions to encourage reflection	Observes problem solving process and gives feedback	Gathers data and stimulates thinking	Identifies alternatives for the client and helps assess consequences	Proposes alternatives and participates in decisions	Trains the line manager	Determines policy or practice	Represents the line manager argues the case on his/her behalf

Figure 2.3 The role of the HR practitioner

they know and embrace uncertainty, you must be prepared to do the same yourself and show that you are doing so. If one of you is less willing to demonstrate changing behaviours than the other then part of the partnering relationship will involve coaching and encouraging the less willing partner.

Remember that when you initiate an OD project you will automatically be impacting (and changing) the culture of the organization. Behavioural changes in the people will have to happen if you are to get the best from the new design.

As you think about the organization design work, you are planning, think about your readiness to change in other aspects of your life. When you have changed, was it a staged process? Generally, people move from not thinking about changing behaviour (precontemplation), to thinking about it (contemplation), to planning to change (preparation), and then testing out ways to do it before actually starting (action).

Where people find themselves in circumstances which they have not chosen they have a much harder time changing. To move forward, people need strategies to make the 'pros' of changing outweigh the 'cons'. Your roles are critical in providing the 'pros' of change and encouraging people to change. Thus you need to demonstrate your own capacity to change.

Third, you need to figure out your roles so that together you can be more than the sum of your parts. You need to be able to work together effectively to resolve conflicts and dilemmas and you need to present a joint and consistent front as the project ramps up and is implemented. There are many useful tools for assessing your strengths and from these you can assess how yours will mesh with other people's strengths. You will each have different strengths to play to and the project needs a balance of strengths to get it off the ground. You may find as you assess your own strengths that they are not sufficient for the project to go forward with. At this point, you have some choices – among them developing yourself or recruiting other people to get what you think you need.

Know What You Each Need to Do in Each Phase

Each one of the five phases requires the line manager and the HR practitioner to be working together but on different aspects of the project as Figure 2.4 shows.

This difference in your activities dictates the role that you each play. As a rule of thumb each phase requires a slightly different role emphasis from each of you as Figure 2.5 outlines.

Be Open with Each Other about Your Capability

If you have not worked with each other before, you need to be open with each other on your capabilities and attributes, to maintain a dialogue on the progress of the project and to identify issues and concerns as they arise. This sounds easier than it is but a good starting point is to schedule time to discuss what attributes each of you brings to the project. Also on

Design phase	Manager activity	HR practitioner activity
Preparing for change	▪ Deciding that change is necessary to achieve business outcomes (including assessing the drivers for change) ▪ Assessing various options for making the change ▪ Evaluating the chosen route (organization design or not) in order to feel confident about the way forward ▪ Ensuring the sponsor is supportive of the way forward	▪ Coaching the manager to decide (or not) to change ▪ Providing information and support to the manager to help him/her make the right choices ▪ Probing and challenging to ensure the manager is on solid ground in his/her decision
Choosing to re-design	▪ Determining the scope and boundaries of the project ▪ Getting sponsors and stakeholders on board ▪ Identifying potential project team leaders and members for the high-level and detailed-level teams	▪ Drafting the high-level scoping document ▪ Following up with sponsors and stakeholders ▪ Guiding and suggesting on potential project team leaders and members

Creating the high-level design and the detailed design	▪ Initiating the design process
	▪ Keeping a firm grip on its progress via the high-level and detailed-level teams
	▪ Intervening and stepping back appropriately
	▪ Keeping the day-to-day business running
		▪ Helping manager and project team define and agree
		  – Core business purpose
		  – Unique selling point
		  – Vision, mission, objectives
		  – Principles
		  – Boundary statements
		  – Critical success factors
		  – Measures of success
		  – Target areas – processes, systems, technologies, facilities, skills, culture, people
		▪ Working with the project manager to manage the assignment including creating the project structure and plan, process mapping, identifying issues, and opportunities for improvement

Handling the transition	▪ Leading the transition process ▪ Motivating people to work with the changes	▪ Surveying responses to change and relaying to manager

Figure 2.4 Manager and HR practitioner activity

Design phase	Manager activity	HR practitioner activity
	• Projecting confidence and optimism • Adjusting plan appropriately	• Recommending actions as needed to maintain progress • Supporting and guiding people into new state
Reviewing the design	• Commissioning a post-implementation review about eight weeks after project closure • Assessing the findings against the intended project outcomes • Taking action to address issues and concerns to ensure benefits of change are delivered • Transferring knowledge, skills, and learning gained in the OD project	• Ensuring post-implementation review is thorough and reliable • Guiding and supporting manager to understanding, communicating, and acting on the findings • Following through on the agreed actions and recommending a second review about six months after project closure

Figure 2.4 Continued

	Line manager role	HR practitioner role
Phase one – Preparing for change: the diagnosis	Strategic management	Fact finder Objective Process counsellor
Phase two – Choosing to re-design: the scoping phase	Strategic management moving towards tactical management	Fact finder
Phase three – Creating the high-level design and the detailed design	Tactical management moving towards operational management	Alternative identifier Joint problem solver
Phase four – Handling the transition	Strategic management moving towards tactical management	Facilitator to expert (the full continuum)
Phase five – Reviewing the design	Strategic management	Advocate Facilitator Objective Process counsellor

Figure 2.5 Roles as OD project progresses

the agenda for this meeting will be defining and agreeing your respective roles as you prepare for phase one. As the project proceeds your roles will adapt and change. It is as well to think at this point how you will recognize the need to revisit your roles and perhaps readjust them.

Having scheduled time to discuss your attributes, roles, and partnership in the project you need to assess the attributes you are bringing. It is better if you both take the same assessment so that you are talking from common ground. The next section presents one tool for assessing your current profile in relation to leading a change project. There are many others and it may be that you find you already have one that you have both taken. However, if you decide to try out the one presented here and you find that between you there is a balance of the four desirable attributes you are good enough in shape. If between you there is a shortfall on any of them you need to work out how you can get them – you need the balance to optimize your chances of success.

Useful Tools

Tool 1: Self-assessment

To manage change effectively you need to be skilled at collaboration, innovation, delivery, and integration. Assess yourself against the following inventory (adapted from: Fritts, P. J. (1998). *The New Managerial Mentor*. Davies-Black Publishing).

For each of the following items assign four points to your top choice, three points to your second choice, two points to your third choice, and one point to your least preferred choice.

	Points		*Points*
1. The most important factor in the success of a business is:		2. When things get chaotic in my department, I:	
(a) Efficient operations	......	(a) Look for creative solutions	......
(b) Committed people	......	(b) Provide encouragement and support	......
(c) A clear vision of the future	......	(c) Take prompt and decisive actions	......
(d) Challenging goals	......	(d) Analyse the cause of the problem	......

	Points		Points
3. I prefer organizational change that is: (a) Planned and incremental (b) Innovative and wide ranging (c) Targeted and results oriented (d) Focused on learning and personal growth	....	4. I particularly enjoy: (a) Building collaborative teams (b) Promoting new ideas up the line (c) Achieving impressive results (d) Developing improved systems	....
5. My typical approach to decision-making is to: (a) Explore innovative solutions (b) Take the most practical course of action (c) Collaborate with team members (d) Systematically evaluate alternatives	....	6. The best way to prepare for an unpredictable future is to: (a) Re-engineer (b) Help people learn how to cope with change (c) Create a tangible vision (d) Achieve current objectives	....
7. My most important job should be: (a) Improve operating efficiency (b) Meet performance goals (c) Build effective teams (d) Find new ways to satisfy customers	....	8. I try to optimize individual performance by: (a) Coaching and developing people (b) Using personal motivation techniques (c) Creating more interesting job designs (d) Championing change as a career opportunity	....
9. It is most important for people to have: (a) The tools to get the job done (b) High motivation to achieve	....	10. My preferred stage in project work is: (a) Generating new ideas (b) Team building (c) Designing work flow (d) Goal setting	....

	Points		Points
(c) Co-operative and friendly co-workers	......		......
(d) The ability to cope with change	......		......
11. The main purpose of networking is to:		12. In problem-solving sessions, I like to:	
(a) Build new relationships	......	(a) Brainstorm new ideas	......
(b) Use influence to get results	......	(b) Encourage group dialogue	......
(c) Solve co-ordination problems between units	......	(c) Promote expedient solutions	......
(d) Broker support for new initiatives	......	(d) Map out the problem	......
13. The most critical element in team development is:		14. I tend to think of myself as a:	
(a) Conflict management	......	(a) Conceptualizer	......
(b) Defined roles and responsibilities	......	(b) Relater	......
(c) Breakthrough thinking	......	(c) Analyser	......
(d) Performance focus	......	(d) Doer	......
15. I prefer to motivate people with		16. I get great satisfaction from:	
(a) An exciting vision of the future	......	(a) Helping people to learn	......
(b) Opportunities for personal development	......	(b) Exploring new marketplace needs	......
(c) Special rewards and recognition	......	(c) Implementing quality initiatives	......
(d) Stretch goals	......	(d) Achieving performance expectations	......
17. People tend to see me as:		18. My typical interpersonal style is:	
(a) Driven	......	(a) Analytic	......
(b) Efficient	......	(b) Direct	......

	Points		Points
(c) Creative	......	(c) Empathic	......
(d) Supportive	......	(d) Charismatic	......
19. Businesses should place the greatest importance on: (a) Human learning potential (b) Breakthrough technology (c) Strong leadership (d) Quality systems		20. The people I work best with are: (a) Technically oriented (b) Innovative (c) Action driven (d) Collaborative	 ....

On the scoring sheet which follows record your points assignment for each item and add up your totals for each of the four columns.

Question	Collaboration	Innovation	Delivery	Integration
1	b	c	d	a ......
2	b	a	c	d ......
3	d	b	c	a ......
4	a	b	c	d ......
5	c	a	d	b ......
6	b	c	d	a ......
7	c	d	b	a ......
8	a	d	b	c ......
9	c	d	b	a ......
10	c	a	d	b ......
11	a	d	b	c ......
12	b	a	c	d ......
13	a	c	d	b ......

Question	Collaboration	Innovation	Delivery	Integration
14	b	a	d	c ......
15	c	a	d	b ......
16	a	b	d	c ......
17	d	c	a	b ......
18	c	d	b	a ......
19	a	b	c	d ......
20	d	b	c	a ......
Total				

If you have to manage change effectively you need to have roughly the same score in each of the four columns. If one or more of the columns has a significantly lower score than the others, you need to think where you can get the skills (either by working with another person who has them, developing them in yourself, or using some of your team to support you where you are weaker).

This tool is useful to help you recognize each other's strengths in the planned re-design and discussing how and when you can challenge and support each other best.

There are many assessment tools of this nature available on the market and it may be that your organization already has one that is in common use. Be encouraged to assess in some way your ability to manage change even if you feel the tool presented here is not for you.

Tool 2: Books
Buckingham, M. and Clifton, D. O. (2001). *Now, Discover Your Strengths.* Free Press.
Buckingham, M. and Coffman, C. (1999). *First, Break All the Rules: What the World's Greatest Managers Do Differently.* Simon & Schuster.
Dent, S. M. (1999). *Partnering Intelligence.* Davies-Black Publishing.

Self-check

This section has been concerned with developing a partnership between HR practitioner and line manager. To check whether you are on track for doing this successfully, ask yourselves the following questions:

- Have you established rapport? One measure of this is feeling comfortable in each other's presence so that even if there is a hierarchical difference between you this does not interfere with the authenticity you can show and the trust you can place in each other to achieve a common goal in the face of setbacks, obstacles, and competing demands.

- Have you determined your partnership approach and roles? What you are looking to confirm here is that the roles you take enable you to maintain a balance of power and interest over time. You each need each other if the work is to get done and the relationship is to last to the end of the project's final review. You should aim for a reciprocal relationship where you are both giving and receiving. Only you will be able to judge equity in this relationship and take steps to redress the balance if necessary.

- Are you confident you have sufficient complementary skills and attributes to work as a successful team? As has been stated you both need to be able to take a step back and assess your own strengths and discuss these with each other. Identifying any shortfall requires you to take some form of action to plug in the missing attributes to make your project leadership strong.

- Are you sure you can role model change behaviours? Your reflection on your attitudes to change and how easy or difficult you have found it in the past to change your behaviour will give you clues on your ability to role model change behaviours. As facilitators you must not only understand the nature of change processes and how they affect you, but also how people in your organization may be experiencing particular changes, and how this will impact the success of the venture.

- Have you got the change management technical skills? It is not enough to have the personal qualities necessary to make success in the project a likelihood you also need to have some knowledge and understanding of the technicalities of organization design and change management. If you do not have this it may be worth taking a short course in these or at least doing some of the reading recommended in this book.

- Have you got a go-forward plan? During your first meetings you need to agree when and how you are going to do the phase one data gathering and how you are going to communicate on this. Additionally you need to have thought through which of you is going to approach those you have identified as prime stakeholders in this project (there is more on stakeholders in Chapter 7).
- Are you agreed on the focus and approach? The organization design method advocated here is based on collaboration, participation, and involvement. If your styles of operation are at odds with this it will be difficult, and probably impossible, for you to work with what is described. However, if this is the case it may be worth reflecting on whether you can change your style of operation. There is ample evidence to suggest that successful change projects recognize and use the fact that employees want to be a part of a process, not apart from it.

Do's and Don'ts

- Do spend some time agreeing your roles up front so that you are presenting consistent messages
- Do be honest with yourselves about your capabilities
- Do make sound judgements about the time and commitment you can devote to this project
- Don't proceed unaided if you identify that you don't have the necessary skillset between you
- Don't fight shy of giving each other the necessary challenge and support in formulating your preliminary plan
- Don't agree to work with each other if you do not have the right level of rapport and understanding (this will feel like a long-haul even if it is of relatively short duration)

Summary – The Bare Bones

- It is you who are setting the course and you who must visibly lead the way by demonstrating you are prepared and able to change your own behaviours
- You need to be self-aware and know clearly what skills and attributes you individually and jointly bring to the project
- You will be taking on different roles and leading different activities in each phase
- To lead and manage the change you need to have an open and trusting relationship with each other

3

Finding the Right Sponsor

'In excellent companies, the role of the sponsor is not to supervise the project manager but to make sure that the best interests of both the customer and the company are recognized.'

Kerzner, H. (1998). *In Search of Excellence in Project Management.* John Wiley & Sons, Inc.

Overview

As you start, the first activity is to get your project off the ground and simultaneously identify a sponsor for it. This latter is something that is frequently paid scant attention to but it is critical in a large and complex organization where people are jockeying for resources, credibility, and visibility and no less critical in smaller organizations. Whatever the size of your organization you need to have someone on your side who is outside the piece of the organization you are working with, and who is capable of seeing where, how, and what you are planning fits into the overall scheme. The role of the sponsor is to actively champion the change you are proposing and to do this throughout the life cycle of the project.

The Role of the Sponsor

Numerous OD projects are less successful than they might be because they do not have an effective sponsor from the start. Frequently this is because the role of the sponsor is either not adequately spelled out when you are asking someone to take on this role or you have not thought through exactly what you are looking for in your sponsor. Different projects need different types of sponsor. Choosing the wrong person has the potential to turn what could have been a successful organization design into a local, and perhaps enterprise-wide, disaster with consequent financial and political ramifications. To avoid this you need to be confident that the chosen person knows what he/she is taking on, has the time, interest and energy to do a good job and agrees to do it until the end of the second review of the project.

What you are looking for is someone to help guide your people through a difficult period of change and a sponsor who is committed, skilled, and collaborative is an ideal choice. A good sponsor becomes part of the project leadership team – albeit not usually in a hands-on operational way. But to find a person who can take on this role effectively requires some upfront thought and the rest of this section explains the steps to take to find him/her.

Why You Need a Sponsor

The main reason to find a good and appropriate sponsor for your project is to assure the power, lobbying, and working for the change at higher levels than yours in the organization. This is critically important if what you are attempting is of medium or high risk and is 'different' or innovative in any way. Usually the sponsor is a couple of levels higher than the line manager leading the change on a day-to-day basis in the organization. The sponsorship role varies and changes as the life cycle of the project proceeds, but in essence your sponsor needs to be an active and visible figurehead for the whole initiative and should provide leadership in terms of:

- Establishing and communicating the reasons for the change.
- Demonstrating and building commitment with the higher echelons of the organization.
- Agreeing with the approach and signing off the resource requirements.
- Supporting the change with obvious actions including removing obstacles, advocating and 'selling in' at the highest levels.
- Acting as a role model for the new behaviours.

- Monitoring progress to ensure that the project meets its overall objectives and delivers the agreed benefits.
- Holding accountability to stop or re-align the project if the original objectives and benefits are unlikely to be realized.

A second reason for identifying a good sponsor is because he/she can help you set the style and tone of the project. The sponsor's own orientation to change and the way he/she can role model the behaviours you are looking for as you design your organization can help send powerful messages to your community. If the sponsor can demonstrate that he/she too is learning on the project and gaining skills and experience working with you and your team it will help contribute positively to the way the project is perceived by the people it most impacts.

A third reason for getting the right sponsor relates to the full skill set you need at the leadership level. As you know, effective business change programmes and projects require clear, active and visible leadership from the top. If the assessments you make of your own skills do not amount to the full complement you think you need for success then choosing a sponsor who has the skills to contribute or bridge the shortfall would be a sensible tactic. One of the things you may not have time for (even if you do have the skills) is doing what needs to be done to achieve buy in from the organization. The common denominator of successful change projects is having a champion who is intent on doing this.

A fourth reason for getting good sponsorship is to do with ensuring that your project is contributing to the overall welfare of the organization. Someone who is in the right position in the organization, with an overview of what is going on, will help you be more conscious of what you could or should be contributing to the overall good as you begin to think through your design. From this start-point the right sponsor will support you both realizing your contribution through the new organization design and getting this contribution recognized and properly rewarded (by whatever are appropriate organizational rewards). This form of support will be of great value to you as it is all too easy to get stuck into local thinking in a project of this nature.

Finally, the right sponsor – someone who is close enough to your customers and competitors, products and services, to have good knowledge and insight of what you are aiming to achieve – will help you formulate and assess your design plan with this in mind and in all likelihood, with a different perspective from yours. Seeing the problems and issues from a range of perspectives will help you refine your approaches to them and perhaps open your eyes to opportunities and possibilities that you had not thought of yourself.

How to Find Your Sponsor

Identifying the right sponsor for your OD project involves you in doing five things, pretty much in the order presented here.

1. **Plan for sponsorship** – work out how strong a support you need and from where (not who at this stage). Your first task is to discuss the type of sponsorship you need. You are likely to have some insight into the presenting problems and issues at this stage and need to pick a sponsor who is sensitive to these. For example, if you think your design will have a major impact on the culture of the organization (formal/informal organization pairing as described above) do you want a sponsor who is the epitome of the current cultural mindset and values or do you want someone who is a bit of a maverick and will give you some interesting viewpoints? These are presented as two extremes but it will pay you to think carefully about the type of person you are looking for.

   If the presenting problem or issue is in the formal organization/ work pairing it would pay you to find a sponsor who is interested and skilled in the processes and systems of getting the work done.

   Whoever you go for, you need someone who has organizational credibility (and who is likely to be able to maintain this for the duration of the project) who is interested in the presenting aspects of your problems/issues and who has organizational overview.

2. **Write a clear description of the sponsor role and activity**. In the next section the roles that the sponsor takes on at various stages in the project are spelled out. Suffice it to say here that you need to have what almost amounts to a job description for the sponsor. The personal attributes that *you* need to have in order to manage change are also needed by the sponsor. You also need to consider what other governance aspects of the project will be brought into play. For example, if you are anticipating a steering group, would one of the roles of the sponsor be

to chair the meetings? If your project is not of the size to require a steering group are you expecting the sponsor to veer towards being a coach and mentor for you rather than being a more hands-on leader of the project? Spelling out what your needs and expectations are of a sponsor might seem a waste of time when you have in your mind that Mr or Ms X would be the perfect candidate. However, it does give you the chance to reconsider this from a more reflective viewpoint.

3. **Approach more than one person who you think would be a suitable candidate** (beware of the usual suspects). Often in large organizations there are a number of organization design and change projects going on simultaneously. Interestingly the pool of people considered suitable project sponsors is much smaller than the number of initiatives which seek sponsors. A kind of classic demand outstripping supply situation ensues. What then happens is that 'the usual suspects' get over-committed in their sponsor role (remember that the sponsors are also trying to do their 'day-jobs' too) and are unable to add much value to the project. There is very little point in selecting a sponsor simply because it is de rigueur or an organizational requirement to have one – you have to pick someone who is going to positively contribute to your project.

   If you are in the situation of not knowing whom to pick because you feel all the usual suspects are over-committed, it will pay you to be a bit creative. There may be excellent sponsors waiting in the wings for their opportunity to shine in the organization. One source of supply is people in the organization who have done MBAs and are seeking development opportunities. If there is a succession plan process you can identify others who have organizational credibility, who need wider experience and who would be only too happy to take on something meaty to prove their value to the organization.

   Discussing your sponsor needs and expectations with more than one person will enable you to select the best fit for your project and you may also learn a lot in the process that will help you as you plan for it.

4. **Specify the accountabilities to the potential sponsor**. The person you select as a sponsor for your project is agreeing to take responsibility for ensuring that it meets its overall objectives and delivers the intended and expected benefits. If you can influence it you should get the sponsor to agree to have this responsibility included in his/her

Role of sponsor	Accountabilities
Gatekeeper	▪ Ensure the project adds value to the overall business purpose ▪ Ensure the project has a business case and terms of reference (if needed) ▪ Sign off the terms of reference and business case ▪ Ensure key milestones through the life of the project are satisfied ▪ At the closure of the project, see that the benefits are realized and post-implementation reviews are carried out
Monitor	▪ Validate the plan ▪ Hold regular reviews of progress against plan at a high level (at an operational level, this is the responsibility of a project manager) ▪ Review the business case regularly and check any proposed changes of scope, cost or time for their possible effects on the business case ▪ Ensure risks have been identified, and are being tracked and mitigated as far as possible ▪ Give overall guidance on policy, direction, and scope ▪ Ensure the project delivers the benefits specified in the business case
Supporter and coach	▪ Set the line manager/HR practitioner up for success ▪ Give support to the line manager/HR practitioner as required (Support may be in the form of direction, guidance, lobbying for additional resource and resolving serious problems)
Decision-maker	▪ Make decisions that are outside the scope of the project or the line manager's accountability ▪ Decide, define and maintain a clear outcome for the project, with clear measurements of success
Champion	▪ Champion the project within the business at a senior level ▪ Chair steering group meetings (if appropriate) ▪ Maintain an ongoing, senior level relationship with key suppliers and other stakeholders to ensure they give full support to the project
Problem solver	▪ Resolve the more difficult or serious problems that the project team does not have the skills or experience to resolve
Resource negotiator	▪ Ensure that adequate and appropriate resources are available to ensure the delivery of project benefits on time

Figure 3.1 Role and accountabilities of sponsor

performance objectives so that his/her success in the role can be measured in some way. During the lifetime of the project the sponsor will be adopting a number of different roles each with different accountabilities. Figure 3.1 summarizes these.

5. **Ensure the person you select understands the role and is committed to it**. Ideally the sponsor should be the individual who has the most interest, and the most to gain from the successful implementation of the project. A sponsor who only steps in when things have gone wrong (or right!) is not someone who is going to give you the support you need as the project proceeds. Part of the sponsor selection process involves the art of managing upwards. You want to find a sponsor who gets noticed (favourably) by people higher up the organization or if the chosen person is already at the top, you want him/her to be in political favour. The task of the sponsor is then to get the 'buy in' mentioned earlier at the higher level in the organization. This can be done either directly or indirectly. Direct methods include getting on an agenda to give a presentation, giving regular progress reports on what is being accomplished and so on. Indirect methods include writing pieces for the newsletters which are on general organizational circulation, being quoted in the trade press, etc. One caveat – it is likely to be you not the sponsor who pulls together all the materials for the presentations and newsletters.

Useful Tools

Tool 1: Sponsor Question Prompt Sheet

The following questions can be used as prompts in your discussions with potential sponsors to enable you to identify issues and areas of strength and weakness together. You can also refer to these questions when you are assessing in your own mind where your sponsors' strengths and weaknesses lie.

1. Is your sponsor dissatisfied with the current situation? The sponsor needs to be dissatisfied with things as they are now – otherwise the motivation to support the changes you are proposing will not be great. If your sponsor is satisfied with the current situation, or feels it is 'tolerable', then you need to explore this.
2. Is your sponsor clear about what needs to be changed? Does your sponsor understand fully what the change will be, both in terms of 'hard' changes to structures, processes and systems, as well as the softer behavioural and cultural changes? If they have only a vague or

incomplete idea of what the change will encompass, you cannot expect their support or that they will promote it effectively.

3. Does your sponsor truly believe in the business case for change? If the sponsor is not convinced that the change is necessary they will not be effective in convincing others. You need to make sure that your sponsor fully understands and buys in to the business case on an ongoing basis.

4. Does your sponsor understand the impact of the change? Is the sponsor fully aware of the impact, both positive and negative, on people, organization and other initiatives? There should be no surprises along the way.

5. Is the sponsor willing and able to commit the necessary resource to the project? Does your sponsor fully appreciate the resource input needed to make the change a success? Is he/she willing and able to commit the necessary people, time, money, training and access needed?

6. Does your sponsor demonstrate public support for the change? Does he/she actively seek out opportunities to communicate strong commitment to the change and will he/she give it full public support?

7. Is your sponsor willing to take tough decisions to make sure the change happens? Will your sponsor face up to difficult issues? Will he/she, for example, ensure that the people who uphold the new way of doing things will be rewarded and recognized and take actions to correct anyone who undermines the changes?

8. Does your sponsor play an active role in monitoring progress? Will your sponsor ensure that monitoring procedures are quickly established and proactively track progress so that he/she can identify and resolve issues? Or do they plan to play a more passive, and less effective, role in ensuring that the project progresses?

9. Does your sponsor provide sustained support for the change on an ongoing basis? Does your sponsor demonstrate consistent, sustained support for the change and reject any course of action which would be inconsistent with the goals of the project? Do they make sure that the conditions are right for the project to succeed, or do they only give it their full support when there are no other demands on their time and resource?

10. Will your sponsor give support to everyone involved in the project? It is important that the sponsor is not simply working at the high level of the project but is also visible and involved at the detail level. Everyone who will be affected by the change should feel supported by the sponsor in some way.

Tool 2: Books

Kerzner, H. (1998). *In Search of Excellence in Project Management.* John Wiley & Sons, Inc.

Taylor, J. (1998). *A Survival Guide for Project Managers.* Amacom.

Self-check

To assess your progress in finding the right sponsor, ask yourselves the following questions:

- Have we planned for sponsorship? By this point you should be clear that having an effective sponsor is one of the critical success factors in an OD project. To get the right sponsor you need to have thought through what you would like the person to do and how you would like him/her to do it. You should also have given some consideration to the style and approach of the ideal sponsor to ensure they fit with your project.
- Have we been creative in our thinking of who to approach? Remember that simply opting for one of 'the usual suspects' may not give you the skills, expertise and involvement that will make your project successful. If the sponsor sees the role as having something in it for him/her in terms of development opportunity, career enhancement, or positive organizational visibility you will get someone who is more interested than a person who sees taking on the role as an added burden or a somewhat unwelcome extra.
- Have we approached more than one person? Viewing the selection of a sponsor almost as a normal recruitment exercise will give you a range of people to make a choice from. You not only need to select on clearly identified criteria, but also feel that the chemistry

is right between you and the person you choose – after all the project will have ups and downs and may last longer than intended. You want the sponsor to be with you all the way.

■ Have we got a complete description of the part the sponsor will play? Clearly it is difficult at the beginning of your project to predict with any real accuracy how the role will pan out. Nevertheless the information given in this section will have given you a good oversight of the role. Choosing a person who can flex and adapt as the project proceeds should be one of the criteria for selection.

■ Are we confident that the person will be right for the duration of the project? One of the issues in choosing a sponsor is that usually the role is an add-on to the person's day-to-day job. You may find that their initial enthusiasm for sponsoring your project wanes as other priorities hit the top of their agenda. It is very demotivating for your team if the project sponsor dips out of scheduled meetings or becomes unavailable at critical decision points. Again it is difficult to predict whether this may happen to you but it is worth considering having a conversation with your sponsor on what the contingency plan might be if he/she cannot commit to the level you expect and need as the project continues.

Do's and Don'ts

■ Do chose a sponsor who will work actively in the best interests of the project

■ Do work out exactly what your project needs in terms of sponsor style and approach

■ Do keep the sponsor in the loop at all times

■ Don't underestimate the power and influence of the sponsor

■ Don't think that the project will run successfully without an active sponsor

■ Don't ignore the need to get buy in from the rest of the organization for your design project – your sponsor can be of huge help on this

Summary – The Bare Bones

- Project sponsors provide guidance, support and championing, for managers leading OD projects and their project teams
- The role of the project sponsor changes over the life cycle of a project
- You need to invest time and effort in choosing the right sponsor for your project (not necessarily one of 'the usual suspects')
- Sponsoring a project can be an excellent development opportunity for the right person
- The sponsor should be clear what part you are expecting him/her to play in your project's success

4

Phase One – Preparing for Change

'Changing the formal organization is sometimes the most effective way to influence the informal operating environment.'

David A. Nadler and Michael L. Tushman (1997).
Competing by Design. Oxford University Press.

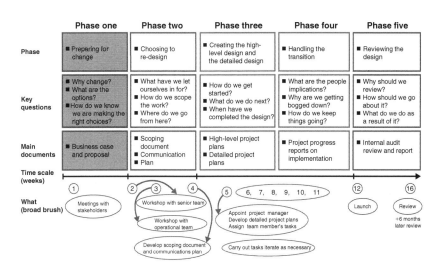

Figure 4.1 Phase one – preparing for change

Overview

The first phase of the OD project is highlighted in Figure 4.1. In this phase you are aiming to answer three questions.

First, 'Why change?' Without a satisfactory answer to this question you will not be able to build the necessary business case or get the sponsorship and resources to make your OD project deliver successful results.

Second, 'What are the options?' You may know that something has to change to improve your business performance, but without some groundwork and research you will not know that it is something to do with organization design. Your diagnosis may suggest that organization design is one of a number of options available to deliver the change you want.

Third, 'How do we know we are making the right choice?' In a sense you can never be certain that you are making the right choice. However, there is a great deal you can do to ensure that the choice you make has an excellent chance of delivering the results you want. This is dependent on several factors including your own skills, the support you have from other stakeholders, your understanding of what is going on both in the organization as a whole and in your part of it.

This first phase can be done rapidly if you have the resources to do it and you will see that the timeline suggests it can be done in a week. One way that works well is through meeting with stakeholders in focus groups to get the information you need. The documentary output from this phase of the project is a business case and/or proposal.

How you present this is a matter of what is acceptable in your organization. Organizations differ in the way they approach and document OD projects. Find out what the protocol is in your organization.

Taking each of the questions in turn let us examine them in a bit more detail.

Why change? Your start-point is the recognition that either something is about to change or something is currently not working well, and you need to take some actions to protect and develop productivity, performance, and profit. Usually this recognition comes at a particular point when it is necessary to do something to solve the presenting issues immediately. Your task at this point is to try to identify what is the particular presenting problem, issue, or concern that has caused you to think that things need to be different. Common areas are customers, competition, emerging technologies, asset management, business strategy, employment market, supplier demands, outsourcing decisions, attitudes, and behaviours.

On the topic of problems or issues, it is worth noting that they are not necessarily bad things. A problem is often framed as something negative, for example, 'our customer feedback is not good'. If you reframe the problem or issue, then it becomes more positive and actionable and you will find it easier to engage and motivate people to work with you. In this example 'our customer feedback is not good' the problem reframed becomes 'What can we do to make our customers happier?' or 'How can we improve our customers' feedback?' Framing an issue or problem with a 'what' or 'how' question will help you start from a positive mindset, which you can then follow through with action and avoidance of blame.

However, being able to state at a high level, an issue that you have to address is not enough to generate the actions which will address it. To do this effectively you need:

- To specify the particular presenting problems or issues needed to be addressed
- To define your purpose in wanting to re-design.

Take this example of Parkland Memorial Hospital's presenting problems.

> *Practically overwhelmed by the increasing number of babies, critically short of nurses, and operating in a building designed for 3,000 fewer births a year, Parkland's Labour & Delivery (L&D) department had to re-engineer how it delivers babies.* (Note that in 2001, Parkland delivered 16,597 babies in the same building.)
> Charles Fishman (2002).
> *Fast Company*, 63, October, 106.

Now read how the issues were specified and the purpose for wanting to re-design was identified.

When births at Parkland Memorial Hospital first started to rise dramatically, the hospital and the	*Specify the issue(s)* *Issue 1: a need to respond to demographic trends*

medical staff cast about for a way to take care of all of the women. *As reported, 'The conversations weren't just about how to solve the problem. They were about how to solve the problem and keep the same level of quality. It's important to be said: We weren't just resolving the crisis of the moment. We decided to try using certified nurse-midwives – to put them on staff and reorganize not just the medical staff, but also the patient flow and the geography of L&D, around them. It was a whole new role. Designed to free up doctors' time to handle more complicated deliveries'.*	*Issue 2: taking care of all the women* *Issue 3: maintaining the same level of quality* *Issue 4: resolving the crisis of the moment* *Purpose: To free up doctors' time to handle more complicated deliveries.*

Reading this small case makes it seem as if specifying the presenting problem or issue is an easy task but that is not necessarily the case. In the example above there are four issues but having identified these, a number of questions arise. Here are a few examples:

- Which is the presenting issue – the one in front of the others?
- Are we looking for one solution that will resolve all four issues?
- Are we looking for a short-term solution or a longer-term one?
- Is there one issue that would give a greater return on investment if we resolve it than the others?

Equally in the example, the response to introduce a new role sounds straightforward but it was in fact very complex with wide ranging implications. It achieved its purpose –

> *... by careful design. One that embraced a strategy for performance, innovation, and customer care based on a set of contradictory – even counterintuitive – ideas.*

There are several reasons why you need to specify the problem or issue in order to answer the question 'why change?' First, it is very easy to think that something is the problem when, in fact, it is the result or outcome of the problem. For example, you have to change the way you hold data on personnel in order to comply with legislation. Compliance is the outcome you want it is not the problem. There may be numerous problems or issues related to this – your technology will not enable compliance, your staff skills are insufficient, the time scales are very short and so on.

Second, you need to specify the issues in order to design your project to achieve your outcome. Without having a good perspective on the range of issues you risk designing something which addresses only some of them.

Third you need to specify the issues, to be able to validate these with other stakeholders. To successfully initiate an OD project, as many stakeholders as possible should be working in concert. In order to get the outcome you want (e.g. legal compliance) you have to get to a good degree of consensus on what is getting in the way of this, and what is working in its favour.

What you will find, however, if you start to ask members of your management team (or any of the stakeholders in your part of the business) individually what they think the issues are, you will get a range of responses depending on their individual perspectives. You need to get stakeholders working together, specifying the issues in a collaborative way or else risk alienating stakeholders who think you are going about this in the wrong way (more on this later).

Fourth (and most crucial) you need to identify the issues and problems in order to help you to define your purpose in re-designing. If you are not crystal-clear about your organizational purpose, your design will not deliver it. Remember that an organization will perform the way that it is designed to perform. Clarifying the purpose is again something that sounds easier to do than it is in practice. A section in Chapter 5 guides you through the process.

What are the options? The brief answer is that until you have done a data gathering exercise and analysed your information, you will not know what the options are and if your heart is now sinking as you think of doing one (in terms of time, resource, analysis, and so on), aim not to feel daunted. It can be done in a quick and relatively painless way – as described in the data gathering exercise section.

In order to generate options for re-design you need to have enough good information at your disposal to work on. Thus you must gather data, validate and analyse it. Some suggestions for doing this are presented in the 'Useful Tools' section. However, there are a variety of approaches you could take and all that matters, whether you use the tools given here or not, is that you go through an information gathering activity and analysis. If you do not do this you jeopardize the success of your OD project.

The focus of the data gathering you do should be around the four elements of an organization described in the Figures 1.2 and 1.4. Just to recap on this: systems theory describes four major elements of an organization – the work, the people, the formal organization, and the informal organization. The way these four elements relate, combine, and interact affects your business performance. The elements can combine to make six pairs and the more pairs that work together well, the more effective your organization will be.

You can see this in the Parkland Hospital example where the purpose for re-design was '*To free up doctors' time to handle more complicated deliveries'*. What happened here was a design focused on the formal (organizational) structure, but which impacted the informal organization, the work, and the people:

> *The professional staff in Parkland's L&D areas is divided into an elaborate hierarchy. At any given moment, there are 14 distinct levels of medical staff. … The hierarchy involves a precise definition of duties and authority at every level. There are three different kinds of nurses, for instance, each allowed to do different things.*

But although the Parkland Memorial Hospital has an extremely hierarchical organizational structure it works (counter intuitively) to deliver great customer service.

> *And yet in practice, the L&D floors could not be less hierarchical. L&D has an egalitarian, all-hands-on-deck spirit.*
>
> *The L&D areas, for instance, operate within rigid, carefully codified rules about medical practice, a method that is unusual even for an academic medical center. But those rules play out in a workplace culture of notable informality and flexibility.*
>
> *'This is not a building,' says Dr. Kenneth Leveno, head of the obstetrical service at Parkland and a professor at the affiliated medical school, University of Texas Southwestern Medical Center at Dallas. 'It's an* idea. *It's an organized system with expectations, a team approach. The staff believes in Parkland obstetrics. It believes in taking care of people well.'*

There are three reasons for answering the question 'What are the options?' with a data gathering exercise:

First, you need to get sufficient information to know which parts of the system are working well and which are working less well. You may think you know what parts are working and where the rubs and issues are, but it is possible that you have a partial view and it is worth testing this out. Who has not identified with the points made in Scott Adams' Dilbert cartoons, 'The Office' and 'Back to the Floor'? These are popular and touch a nerve because they point out in far too many familiar ways that managers and leaders often have very little idea what is going on at the day-to-day operational level or how the currents are flowing in the various parts of their organization. Information that you collect and assess before you leap into the decision to design or re-design (from now these words will be used inter-changeably) will give you a firm foundation for going ahead, if that is what is shown to be necessary. Given the upheaval and the heartache that goes with many design projects it pays to get good information up front. You may be surprised at some of the results of your survey and analysis.

Second, you need to start involving people in thinking about and preparing for the change process. From the very start of the OD project, you need to involve those who will feel the direct or indirect impact of it. They need to understand and participate in the design 'journey' if they are going to give active support and co-operation and accept the changes the new design brings.

No doubt, from your own experience you know well that people do not like to feel that they have no control in a change process – the least they like to feel is that they have a say in it. If you actively seek views, give people the chance to express them, and more importantly have them appreciated, listened to, and acted on, then you minimize the chances of resistance, subversion, dropping morale, wasted effort, and loss of direction that so often goes hand in hand with change.

Third, you need to have a sound basis for making some decisions about whether organization design or re-design is going to deliver the results you are looking for. This information gathering exercise clarifies which of the pairs in your system are working and which are not. It is important at this stage to know that only the pairs that include 'formal organization' signal organization design in this methodology. This means that only if your survey and analysis reveal that one, two, or three of the pairs,

- People/formal organization
- Work/formal organization
- Informal/formal organization,

are *not* working well, then you should consider an OD project. If results show these formal organization pairs are working well then organization design is not the right way to handle the change that you are proposing.

How do we know we are making the right choice? By going through the data gathering exercise, using the tool given in the 'Useful Tools' section and then discussing the results with your management team and your sponsor, you should get a good idea of where you want to focus your change efforts. It may be that the analysis suggests that you can achieve your purpose without changing the formal structures – it is worth considering various possible routes in the light of further information. In the last analysis you will not know you are making the 'right' choice whatever you choose. You will be making the best choice you can based on the evidence available at that time.

You can gather more evidence by working through the checklist 'twenty characteristics of success and failure, in organization design' given in the 'Useful Tools' section. This checklist helps you to assess whether your organization has more of the characteristics for success than for failure if you take the re-design route.

If the result of working through this checklist shows that you do not currently have enough of the characteristics for success, you must address this before going any further. Think of yourself as an expedition leader – you would not want to set off into the unknown with faulty or missing equipment, similarly you must have the right conditions to deliver a successful OD project.

Your Roles in Phase One

Below (Figure 4.2) you will see an extract from the table presented in Chapter 2 (Figure 2.4) . It summarizes your activity in this phase. This activity centers around two interventions: first, the data gathering exercise and second the assessment of whether your organization is ready to initiate an OD project. Discussion of these two interventions follows.

But before you start the project running (with the data gathering exercise) you need to agree what levels of involvement you are able to have in this first phase of the project.

As you start to plan things out, you will see that an OD project is quite demanding in terms of time and you will have to carefully balance these time demands with the time demands of keeping your 'day job' running effectively. You must be realistic in identifying how much time

Organization design phase	Manager activity	HR practitioner activity
Preparing for change	• Deciding that change is necessary to achieve business outcomes (including assessing the drivers for change) • Assessing various options for making the change • Evaluating the chosen route (organization design or not) in order to feel confident about the way forward • Ensuring the sponsor is supportive of the way forward	• Coaching the manager to decide (or not) to change • Providing information and support to the manager to help him/her make the right choices • Probing and challenging to ensure the manager is on solid ground in his/her decision

Figure 4.2 Phase one – preparing for change, manager and HR practitioner activity

you can devote to the project. If you can see that your time working on it is going to be limited, consider how to draft in extra resource to act as a project manager. Think creatively on this; some projects have used people returning from leave of absence or from international assignments, others have used recent MBA graduates, people returning from parental leave or staff on the re-deployment scheme – it does not have to be someone from your part of the organization.

Your next step (with your sponsor's input) is to agree on a preliminary plan. This should include: how and when you are going to do the preliminary data gathering, how and when you will initiate phase one, what communications you need to put out and when. It should also provide an estimate of time scales and resources required for at least the first phase (usually it is difficult to estimate beyond this at the first meeting because you do not have enough information to go on). Additionally you must agree which of you is going to have some early discussions with key stakeholders.

The Data Gathering Exercise

This involves you in taking the following steps:

1. Making the case for doing the case for data gathering. The data is gathered using Tool 1 presented in the 'Useful Tools' section. You will not always need to make a formal case. In fact it is more likely to be a suggestion that needs to be agreed to. You need to be clear why you think data gathering is a good thing to do as you are likely to counter opposition from those who have determined that they just want you to get on and design the organization.
2. Considering the various ways that you could get the information you need. You need to involve a diagonal slice of the organization and have a representative sample of people from each layer of the slice. However, you do not need to have large numbers involved as you are aiming for a sense of the situation rather than the detail of it. Some possibilities for getting involvement are:
   - Small focus groups
   - Larger workshops
   - Face-to-face interviews

- Telephone interviews
- On-line survey completion with a selected sample
- A combination of these.

Part of your decision on what is the best method will depend on how much time you have available to do this piece of work. It can be done very quickly – for example you could hold a focus group a few days after making the decision to go ahead.

3. Involving people who are going to be indirectly impacted – other departments, suppliers, or customers. They all have a view of your organization and it may be very different from yours. Having a number of perspectives is very useful and often gives otherwise hidden insights.

4. Assessing the risks of doing the data gathering. Any intervention of this nature sets hares running. You need to know how you are going to handle the informal side of the organization and work with the inevitability that people are curious about what is going on and what the implications are for them.

5. Knowing how you are going to communicate the fact that this exercise is taking place. This is a crucial part of this stage of the process, as it will help to mitigate some of the risks of doing it and it sets the tone for the communication work you need to do as the OD project gathers pace.

6. Going for the 80/20 rule. You do not need to make an industry out of this stage. Your purpose is to get some baseline information to make a decision on whether formal re-design should be the focus of the change process or whether there should be some other start-point.

7. Analysing the results – again not in a heavy duty way. For example, if you have run a focus group, you will have a good grasp of the presenting issues and the interplay of the four elements which make up the six pairs described above. You simply need to be confident that this focus group is reliable and that their conclusions are valid and representative.

Is Your Organization Ready for an OD Project?

By doing the preliminary data gathering you have given yourself a snapshot of what is not working well and what is working well to achieve your business objectives in the current organization. Also you have ascertained that by making the formal organization the focus of your change project, you are likely to achieve your purpose in improving your business performance.

You have spent a bit of time assessing your own capabilities in relation to change management, discussed these with each other, and agreed the roles you will start to play in the change project. Additionally you have thought through what you require in terms of sponsorship and have identified a potential sponsor. By this stage you will have a good overview of the presenting problem or issue that you need to address. Usually this will relate either to issues or problems with the demands being made by customers or to environmental demands; that is, the inputs to the organization described shown in the Figure 1.2 or a combination of both.

To clarify your thinking and to start the involvement and buy in process you need to hold a workshop involving no more than three to seven people: you (line manager and HR practitioner) plus some direct reports of the line manager and one or two stakeholders, perhaps from interface departments, who are interested in helping you assess your readiness to initiate an OD project. All these people need not necessarily be part of any continuing high-level team (which you will need if the project goes ahead) but it will be helpful if they are invited with this in mind. If some of them have participated in the data gathering exercise that too would be helpful.

Before the meeting you should already be clear that you want to effect your change around an OD project and have a communicable view of where you are trying to get to and why. Note that this is not the same as your purpose statement which comes later. What you need to present here is a direction. Read the illustration below and you will be able to see what is meant about direction rather than purpose.

Procter & Gamble had decided to choose a blue-chip tech company to run its worldwide computer systems and data centers.It was a $3 billion race that Hewlett-Packard simply couldn't afford to lose.

In the harsh light of day, HP was clearly out of its league. Just consider the likely competition: IBM is a $81 billion behemoth in the services industry, with dozens of billion-dollar deals in its portfolio. EDS, which invented IT outsourcing when Ross Perot founded it in 1962, boasts $21 billion in annual sales. Despite its

> *merger with Compaq, HP had yet to make its first multibillion-*
> *dollar score. At best, HP was the dark horse, and everyone in that*
> *Atlanta conference room knew it.*
>
> Bill Breen (2003).
Fast Company, 74, September, 65.

The direction HP wanted to go in is something on the lines of 'winning the Procter & Gamble contract'. At that stage in the HP project participants did not know the detail of how they were going to do this or their specific purpose in going in this direction. The first meeting in the 'Atlanta conference room' was held to get consensus on the direction.

The workshop you are having in this phase has the following objectives:

- To validate the findings of the data gathering with key stakeholders.
- To position your assessment that the way forward is an OD project and get support for this.
- To discuss and agree the main issues or problems which are preventing you getting to where you want to be.
- To discuss and agree key factors which could help you get to where you want to be.
- To review, assess and agree whether you are in good shape to go forward with an OD project.
- To provide the baseline information to make your business case.

Your meeting should be scheduled to take about three hours and should be led by a skilled facilitator. Figure 4.3 shows a suggested outline for the session.

Once you have reached this point write your business case. A template for this is given in Appendix 1.

Useful Tools

The purpose of Tool 1 is to help you identify whether it is the formal organization which should be the focus of your change process – the results coming from its use, will point you in the direction of organization design or not. As it stands, it is a basic, simple but effective way of

Time	What	Why	How
09:00 (15 min)	Introduction to session and purpose. Including: ■ Your ball-park of where you are trying to get to, for example improved customer service or full compliance with a new piece of legislation ■ Your case that this is a design project related to the formal elements of the organization and not another type of change project	Attendees know why they are here and the intended outcomes	Line manager to open
09:15 (15 min)	Brief presentation of key findings of data gathering – sticking to the areas which are relevant to your intended project that is the aspects of formal organization	Participants get a feel for the current state of play	Presentation from HR practitioner or line manager
09:30 (30 min discussion 15 min summarizing and confirming agreement)	Open discussion: ■ What's striking about the analysis? (The working well and the working less well) ■ What's surprising and not surprising? What's important to think about in relation to where you are trying to get to	To start to move the group towards some common ground on what it will be important to factor into the high-level plan for re-design	Skilfully facilitated discussion to keep people on track. Logging key points. Summarizing what is important to think about divided into 'working well' and 'working less well' buckets. Confirming agreement with the group that this is the list to work with in the next timeslot
10:15 (30 min discussion 15 min summarizing and confirming agreement)	Paired discussion taking the 'what it is important to think about' some pairs taking the 'working well bucket' others the 'working less well bucket'	To identify the basics of what is preventing or driving you towards your goal	Using the five whys (see Tool 3 in the 'Useful Tools' section) or similar inquiry tool to get to some root causes Capturing the key 'aha's' Confirming agreement that these are the critical elements

11:00 (10 min)	Individual completion of the checklist *twenty characteristics of success/failure in organization design*. (See Tool 4 in the 'Useful Tools' section.)	To encourage people to reflect on the conditions for success of an OD project and match these to what they know from the analysis and the critical elements to consider which they have just identified	Completing the checklist
11:10 (20 min)	Comparison and discussion of individual's responses to ascertain common ground and take comments on what aspects caused people to stop and think	To invite people to identify common ground and to get some feel for where there is a significant disparity of views	Facilitated discussion of the response to the checklist
11:30 (10 min)	Are we in shape to go-ahead, knowing what we know now?	To get agreement on whether you are in a good position to proceed or whether you need to do some groundwork first	Facilitated discussion using the information you have collected through the session. Checking against the checklist 'twenty characteristics for success and failure in organization design'. (See Tool 4 in the 'Useful Tools' section.)
11:40 (20 min)	Summary and next steps	To inform and direct people on the next steps	Line manager picks up from what's emerged from the session and summarizes what he/she feels are the next steps, including who, what and by when
12:00	Close		

Figure 4.3 Outline for a manager workshop

assessing at a 'gut feel' level where things are working well and where they are not working as well as they might be.

You'll see that it has four parts under the headings 'work, people, formal organization, and informal organization'. As explained earlier each part forms a pair with each of the other parts and it is only where it is obvious that 'formal organization' is part of a 'not working well' pair that you should consider opting for an organization design focus for your planned change.

You can adapt these tools to use in a variety of ways, both quantitative and qualitative. For example, adding a ranking scale, and asking people to complete them on-line would give you a quantitative assessment. Using each question as a basis for discussion (without the tick-box judgement on whether the component is working well or not well) would give a qualitative response. You could use a combination of quantitative and qualitative methods. You could add in your own questions making sure that you add them to the appropriate section of the survey, perhaps taking them from your employee opinion questionnaire or similar.

Tool 1: What Elements of Our Organization Work Well?

Part 1 – What works well?	Well	Not well
Work – the basic tasks and their parts to be done		
Does everybody know what is expected of them at work?		
Do people know how the work they do fits into the bigger picture?		
Is each job designed to deliver effectively to organizational performance?		
Are decisions about the work production made at an appropriate level in a timely way?		
Is there overlap or duplication in the work done?		
Are there an unacceptable number of errors or reworks?		
Is the work-flow process transparent from start to finish?		
Does everybody have the materials and equipment to do their work effectively?		

People – the characteristics of individuals		
Does each person have the right skills and abilities to do the job?		
Is each person motivated by his/her manager in the way that is right for him/her?		
Are people's needs and preferences acknowledged appropriately?		
Are people encouraged to develop their talents?		
Does everybody have the opportunity to do what he/she does best every day?		
Does everybody receive regular praise and recognition for good work?		
Do people enjoy what they do and show that enjoyment?		
Are a range of viewpoints and opinions respected, valued and used?		
Formal organization – structures, processes, and methods that are formally created to get individuals to perform tasks		
Are functions grouped together in a way that delivers best?		
Do co-ordination and control mechanisms support what you're trying to achieve?		
Are jobs divided up in the right way to get the work done?		
Are working conditions good?		
Are people management systems working effectively?		
Are cross-functional teams able to function effectively as part of the larger performing system?		
Is each level organized effectively to achieve its respective goals?		
Do the reward systems support what you're trying to achieve?		

Informal organization – 'the way we do things round here'		
Do people understand the way things get done?		
Do team members get on well with each other?		
Do different teams work well together?		
Are you open to informal/flexible working arrangements?		
Do people know whom to contact if they need to know something?		
Do you know which are the critical jobs in your department?		
Do things get done more by 'who you know' than through formal systems?		
Do things get stuck in organizational politics?		

Tool 2: What Paired Elements Work Well?

Component pairs – Think about paired components – which work and which don't work as well?	Work	Don't work
Individual/formal organization		
Are individual needs met by formal organizational arrangements? For example, working hours, rostering patterns.		
Do individuals know where they are in the organizational structure? For example, Who their manager is, who reports to whom?		
Does the mission and purpose of the department make individuals feel their work is important?		
People/work		
Are individual motivated by the work they do?		
Do individuals have the skills and abilities to do their work?		

People/informal organization		
Do people feel included and part of the department?		
Do you have informal and social events to help build rapport amongst people in your department?		
Work/formal organization		
Is the department structured in a way which delivers the best business results?		
Does the way that work is organized encourage people to give their best efforts to it?		
Work/informal organization		
Does the informal and social aspect of the department help people do their work better?		
Do people take on work on their own initiative or are they assigned it in a formal way?		
Formal organization/informal organization		
Is the way you say you do things (e.g. performance management) the same as the way you actually do things?		

If the pairs which include 'formal organization' are not working as well as others then you need to think about re-structuring. If the pairs that work less well do not include 'formal organization' you can improve things without re-structuring. (Being aware that making changes in one pair will also impact other pairs.)

Tool 3: The Five Whys
This is a questioning technique for getting beyond symptoms and uncovering not causes. It increases the liklihood that you will look past the presenting problem to the real issue.

The table below gives an example of the technique in action.

Question	*Answer*
1. Why did the machine stop?	It blew a fuse.
2. Why did the fuse blow?	The fuse was the wrong size.

3. Why was the wrong size in the fuse box?	The engineer put it there.
4. Why did the engineer do that?	The supply room issued the wrong size fuse.
5. Why?	The stock bin was mislabelled.

(From www.maaw.info taken from Deluzio, M.C. (1993). The Tools of Just in Time. *Journal of Cost Management* (Summer) 13–20.)

Tool 4: Twenty Characteristics of Success and Failure in Organization Design

Use this as a survey or checklist in discussion with stakeholders.

	Yes	*No*
1. There is pressure from the environment internal or external for change		
2. People at the top are de-motivated, or disruptive		
3. Leadership is provided by a key line executive with a clear goal for change		
4. There is a collaborative identification of problems		
5. There is a willingness to take risks in new organizational forms		
6. There is a realistic long-term perspective		
7. There is a willingness to face the situation and work on changing it		
8. The system rewards people for the effort of changing and improvement, not just for short-term results		
9. Changes made show tangible results and quick wins at all levels in the organization		
10. There is time and resource available to manage the change as well as do the job		
11. There is discrepancy between what managers say and what they do		
12. The organization has a large number of initiatives going simultaneously		

13. There is confusion between ends and means		
14. There is conflict between what line people need and want and what staff people think they need and want		
15. There is a lack of co-ordination among a number of different activities aimed at increasing organizational effectiveness		
16. There is an over-dependence on experts and specialists (internal or external)		
17. A large gap exists between commitment to change at the top of the organization and the transfer of this interest to the rest of the organization		
18. The organization tries to fit a major organizational change into an old organizational structure		
19. There is a desire for a 'cook book' solution (e.g. If we adopt The Balanced Business Scorecard all our problems will be solved.)		
20. The organization applies an intervention or strategy inappropriately		

If you have answered 'yes' to most of the first ten questions you are in a good position to consider organization re-design. If you have answered 'yes' to most of the question from 11 to 20 you need to do some preparation work in your department before contemplating a re-design.

Self-check

Collecting data on the way the four elements of your organization currently work and analysing the information should help clarify your thinking about whether to opt for an organization design focus for your planned change. To find out whether you are making progress in data collecting, ask yourself the following questions:

- Is the information collectable? That is, first you are able to adapt the tool appropriately for your situation and use it as a foundation for gathering qualitative and/or quantitative data. Second, you are able to get a representative sample of people to give you valid and reliable responses.

- Are people interested in participating in the process? If you find that attendance at your workshop or focus group is towards the bottom of people's agenda because they do not see the value of it you need to do a bit more groundwork to sell the need for their input.
- Are people whom you have not selected to participate in this first exercise still feeling some inclusion in the process? This is where the way you position and communicate the activity is crucial. You need to communicate to those not directly involved in this stage of the information collection process as well as with those directly involved.
- Is the information collected revealing some patterns to work on? A good outcome is if there is clarity that some pairs are working well and some working less well – as stated to go for an organization design intervention you are looking for pairs with 'formal organization' working less well. If the information you have collected reveals no patterns this is more difficult to work with as it suggests that organization design is not necessarily a better start point than any other (e.g. a skills development programme, or a business process re-engineering). However, no pattern is still good information. It simply means you have to be clear in your own mind that organization design is the right start point and that your design plan will address the issues revealed in the survey.

After the workshop with key stakeholders, you will know if you are on the right track in specifying the problems and issues, getting to agreement on elements to consider, and heading in the right direction with an OD project by asking yourself the following questions:

- Does where we plan to go feel right; that is, are the issues specified? What you are looking for is some consistent information that will help you move forward in the right direction. If the information is inconsistent this is not necessarily a show-stopper but you should stop and think what is going on if that is the case.
- Are those you are talking to and who are involved with the work so far in sufficient accord with the aim of the OD project to make you

feel you have good enough level of support for you to proceed? Already you should have invited participation from a number of different people and, generally speaking, the more involvement you have the better the end product will be both in terms of plans produced and motivational benefit.

- Having got some early 'design sketches' for the project are you willing and able to tackle it yourselves? Remember that you have to keep the day-to-day work of the department going. Are you convinced of the effort to reward ratio in determining to go ahead with what is often a disruptive and time-consuming process.
- As you complete the various levels of analysis and discussion, are you getting to some root causes? What you are aiming for here is not finger-pointing and blame about why things are not working well. You are aiming to identify what is already working well that you can build on and where things are not working well what you can take accountability for and take action to redress in your new design.
- Are your people contemplating change? Because the actions you have already taken will have been noticed by people (not only those directly involved) you should be hearing some corridor talk about things changing. Generally people go through a five-step process in order to change: 'No way' (pre-contemplation), 'I may start' (contemplation), 'I will make attempts' (preparation), 'I am successful' (action), 'I am still successful' (maintenance). This is discussed in more detail in Chapter 7 … what you need to know at this point is that people should be contemplating change in a positive way.
- Are you getting buy-in to the purpose of the organization design outcomes? Unless it demonstrates a clear benefit to the business strategy in terms of profit, performance, and productivity, you will not get sufficient on-going support even if you have it at this stage. Be completely certain that, you could answer hard-nosed questions about what you are aiming to achieve with this and why it is the best route forward.
- Is your sponsor a willing, able, and active champion? Again, without vigorous sponsorship you may well find yourself out on a limb further down the road (one of the good reasons to keep the project moving swiftly and on track).

Do's and Don'ts

For the data collection:

- Do think carefully about how you are going to communicate the intent to do the analysis
- Do select a range of participants for a workshop or survey response (job role, level, age) – a diagonal slice of the organization works best
- Do remember to feed back the results of the analysis to the participants and others
- Don't think that this analysis is a waste of time
- Don't ignore what the analysis tells you
- Don't feel bound to use the analysis in the way described here. You need to do an analysis but choose a method that works for your situation

For the key stakeholder workshop:

- Do look for good evidence that patterns and themes are emerging
- Do present a clear direction to go towards
- Do look for current factors which might help or hinder you going in that direction
- Don't spend time debating the detail in your workshop – keep things moving
- Don't get into any form of blame or recrimination – things are as they are
- Don't go forward until you feel you have a good level of agreement and support

Summary – The Bare Bones

- Identify the particular present problem you need to solve or resolve
- Find out how the four elements of your organization (work, people, informal organization, formal organization) are performing individual and in pairs

- Decide whether an organization design focus is the right way for you to proceed with your change project
- Agree your roles in this phase
- Make sure that you have sufficient agreement and support from key stakeholders (management and sponsor) to go ahead in the direction you propose
- Confirm that your organization has the characteristics for success before you go down the organization design route

5

Phase Two – Choosing to Re-design

'People have to be grouped so that they can have the power, information, knowledge, and rewards that allow them to co-ordinate their efforts and cause them to feel collectively responsible for their performance.'

Lawler, E. (1996). *From the Ground Up.* Jossey-Bass.

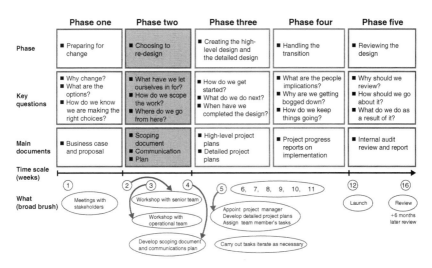

Figure 5.1 Overview of phase two

Overview

Phase two starts when you have decided that you are ready to go ahead and that you have a reasonable idea of what you are 'putting your hand up for'. In this phase, highlighted in Figure 5.1, you start from knowing where your organization is now (current state) to clarifying where you want your organization to be (future state). Phase two is about determining the size and shape of the transformation project that will get you from current to future state.

Determining the scope of the project (size and shape) is no mean task. Be realistic about the process. It can take several iterations to get stakeholders agreed on the way forward. The outcome of the phase is a scoping document and a communications plan. This chapter focuses on the scoping activities that result in the plan. Chapter 6 guides you through the communications plan.

At the end of this chapter you will know what you have let yourselves in for, how you scope the work, and where you go from here. The following section considers each of these three aspects in more detail.

What have we let ourselves in for? At the end of the scoping phase you produce a tightly constructed document that builds on the business case or proposal coming out of phase one. It has a different slant from the business case as it outlines the work that is likely to be required as you migrate from your current state.

Scoping documents usually include the following (adapted from Hallows 1998):

- A thumbnail sketch of the past history of the organization, the current performance, and the future it is facing. (Some of this is repeated from the business case.)
- The vision/purpose. (The next section gives you more information on writing vision and purpose statements.)
- Detailed description of future business capability.
- Details of operational measures for future costs, performance and service levels to be achieved.
- The boundaries of the project and principles for implementing it. (The next section gives you more information on boundary statements.)

- A first cut definition of structure and composition of changed organization in terms of:
  - Market proposition and customers
  - Structure
  - Workflow and business processes
  - Systems and technology (tools and equipment)
  - Operating policies and procedures
  - Communications
  - Stakeholders (including any unions represented)
  - Risk
  - Leadership
  - Culture and working practices
  - People (including skills, knowledge, behaviour, development needs, career paths, job design, and responsibilities, performance management, reward, recognition, incentives, motivation)
  - Models of new functions
  - Facilities
  - Data required for future operations
  - Costs

Depending on the requirements of your organization you may need to include various financial analyses; for example, cost benefit analysis, return on investment analysis, internal rate of return estimates, and break-even analysis.

A timeline, which shows the milestones and the critical success factors for the project.

Thus in phase two you have let yourself in for doing the work to get to the point of being able to write the document. Accomplishing this is a significant workload. To avoid failure along the way do five things:

1. Establish a sense of urgency (Kotter 1995). Creating urgency is essential to get your project off the ground. In British Airways the first question when initiating a change or OD project was 'What is the burning platform?' In Marks & Spencer, it was 'What is the compelling story?' Without something that is going to capture people's imagination, stir them into action and get them to follow a metaphorical flag you will quickly revert to business as usual. You have to present something that will convince people that staying in the

current state is going to be less comfortable than venturing into the unknown. Kotter suggests that it is only when 75% of the organization's management is convinced that business as usual is unacceptable that you can successfully initiate an OD project.

The Levi Strauss case below illustrates one method of creating this sense of urgency. As the case is a little dated, and given the recent history of Levi Strauss you may want to argue that this is not the best method to create a sense of urgency. Please resist this urge as the method is good, it went askew in the latter stages of the transformation with errors in consolidating improvements and institutionalizing new approaches.

How do you convince people in a company that this successful change is worth the risk?

You create a compelling picture of the risks of not changing. We let our people hear directly from customers. We videotaped interviews with customers and played excerpts. One big customer said, 'We trust many of your competitors implicitly. We sample their deliveries. We open all Levi's deliveries.' Another said, 'Your lead times are the worst. If you weren't Levi's, you'd be gone.' It was powerful. I wish we had done more of it.

We also collected magazine covers about great companies that were going through turmoil because they had failed to change. They weren't hard to find: GM, IBM, DEC. We blew up those covers, put them on posterboards, and carried them around the organization. It sent a powerful message: Do you want us to join this list?

> Sheff, D. (1996). Levi's changes everything.
> *Fast Company*, June/July.

---

2. Create a powerful guiding coalition (Kotter 1995). No matter what your skills are or how charismatic your personality is you cannot undertake an OD project without a united group who are all intent on actively helping the organization get to where it needs to be. The coalition usually comprises the senior team within the organization where the OD project is happening, the sponsor and a handful of other powerful supporters. A useful way of checking whether you have a

powerful enough coalition is to check the power bases you have within it. There are five power bases from which a leader can operate (Weiss 1999): positional, expert, resource, coercive, and referent (referent leaders are those to whom others may look because they believe in them that they can be at any level in the organization) you want all of these represented in your guiding coalition. *Power Bases*

3. Paint a vision and purpose of the future. This becomes the 'flag' for you to wave and which people will follow. It has to be clear and easy to communicate. Without a vision, your OD project will founder. Gordon Bethune (1998) tells a great story of how as CEO he transformed Continental Airlines using the 'flag' statement **Fly to Win** and building an organization design and transformation plan under that banner. Kotter's (1995) rule of thumb is 'if you can't communicate the vision to someone in five minutes or less and get a reaction that signifies both understanding and interest, you are not yet done with this phase of the transformation process.'

4. Accept that design and re-design take time. As mentioned earlier, moving through each of the phases is essential. One of the most consistent comments from people working through this process is their underestimation of the amount of real time and elapsed time it takes. It is impossible to generalize on the time any one project will take, as all kinds of variables will intervene. This methodology plans for it to take no longer than three months which from experience has proved a reasonable time estimate in organizations, or parts of organizations with up to 300 people.

   The reason why it takes a great deal of up-front time is because the early stages of the process require involvement and participation from your people. Although this may feel like a waste of time, it does have the pay-off that people who are involved in designing the new organization are more committed to making it work than people who have the new organization thrust upon them. The well-known aphorism holds – people do not resist change; people resist being changed.

5. Manage the challenges you will face in initiating the change and then leading people through it. Peter Senge (1999) brilliantly identifies and discusses the ten key challenges you will be facing from your staff as you lead them into the scoping and design and implementation phases of your project (or indeed any change project). No OD project is immune from facing the majority of these.

> *'We don't have time for this stuff'*
> *'We have no help'*
> *'This stuff isn't relevant'*
> *'You're not walking the talk'*
> *'This stuff is ****'*
> *'This stuff isn't working'*
> *'You don't understand what we do'*
> *'Who's in charge of doing this?'*
> *'We keep re-inventing the wheel'*
> *'Where's all this taking us?'*

You need to thoroughly plan for meeting these challenges and think through ways of dealing with them. They are interdependent. Success in one challenge may make it easier (or harder) to deal with the others. Confront them at the outset by preparing for them before they have appeared.

How do we scope the work? The quickest and easiest way to start off the scoping phase is for you to prepare a 'strawman' that should have, at least in outline, all the elements that you expect to see in your final scoping document.

Present your strawman at a one-day workshop with your senior management team, and following their further work, input, feedback, and amendments take the revised version to the next level of management team and/or those you have in mind to do the detailed design and planning work. At both workshops be willing to listen to participants and rethink things as necessary.

It is through iteration that this process works. People feel involved in the decisions and discussions and become interested in making them work (or not). Involving your team enables you to identify who is working with you and who is not. It also enables them to buy in to the process (or not).

A typical senior manager scoping workshop has as its purpose 'To assess and evaluate xxxx's proposal to re-design our department/ organization.' A template used successfully on several British Airways' OD projects is shown in Figure 5.2.

A week after this workshop you should hold a second workshop this time with your next level of management team and/or those you expect to be working on the detailed design plans. During the week between

Time	What	Why	How
08:30	Introduction to day and purpose		Xxxx to open
08:45	Presentation	To introduce senior management team to the why and what of xxxx proposals	Xxxx to present
09:00	Discuss and refine the purpose of the organization (*see section on vision statements*)	To ensure that participants have a common view of why the organization is in business, what it seeks to deliver and how it operates to do this	Facilitated discussion
09:20	Discuss and refine goals/objectives for next year or two	To ensure that participants have a common view of the goals/objectives of the department	Facilitated discussion
09:45	Discuss the strengths and weaknesses of xxxx's proposal in achieving the purpose and goals	To ascertain levels of support for the proposal To go over the ground again to confirm that people know what is intended	Facilitated discussion/ SWOT and STEEP analysis (*see Useful Tools section*)
10:15	Overview stakeholder analysis (*discussed in Chapter 7*)	To identify and categorize people involved in or affected by proposals (in order to later develop an involvement and communications plan)	Group exercise
10:45	Overview risk analysis (*discussed in Chapter 9*)	To identify the risks involved in changing the organization structure in order to develop a risk mitigation plan	Group exercise
11:15	Break		
11:30	Decide what are the key barriers and enablers to address in moving from now to new organization	To get understanding of full implications of changing the organization structure	Force-field analysis and Group discussion (*see Useful Tools section*)

Figure 5.2 Senior manager scoping workshop

12:15	Agree the boundaries and principles on which to make the transition	To bound the transition in a communicable way. To frame the way the transition takes place	Group discussion
12:45	Recap on morning		Xxxx
13:00	Break		
14:00	Look more in detail at what needs addressing and where the priorities lie	To start more detailed consideration of specific areas and/or change levels	Group work to identify and agree obvious areas that will need to be worked on
15:45	Pool thoughts on more detailed areas – get input from rest of group	To share thinking and output To start building very high-level project plan	Plenary session/ report back
16:15	Break		
16:30	Agree method and assign responsibility for next steps	To move into next stage of process	Xxxx

Figure 5.2 Continued

workshops, the senior managers should have developed their thinking in relation to the areas of responsibility they have been assigned and have fed it to you for incorporation into a revised strawman. You can decide to have the senior managers present or not depending on your situation. Either way works although experience suggests that managers will be more vocal if senior managers are absent.

The format for the workshop with this group mirrors and extends the one you held with the senior management team. Having run these two workshops, you now have to review the consolidated output from them both and rewrite your scoping document for presentation to your stakeholder groups.

The participative nature of this approach means you will have secured a high level of support from your total management team for the next, detailed design, phase of the project. A word of warning here – if you have any doubts at all about the strength of support from your team do not proceed. This is not the moment for going it alone, or deciding to go ahead in the face of opposition.

Assuming you have the level of support you need, together with a clear scoping document, you now need to appropriately communicate what is going on to the rest of your department. Chapter 6 looks in more detail at communication and your communication plan. This chapter continues first by discussing vision and purpose statements, second by considering the roles you play in this scoping phase and third by giving you some more about the techniques of scoping. Finally, it presents the self-check, do's and don'ts, and the bare bones summary.

The Vision, Purpose, Boundaries, and Principles

The first workshop in phase two (with your senior managers) opens with a discussion on the vision or purpose of your organization. In the author's experience, people tie themselves up in the semantics and 'wordsmithing' of vision or purpose statements. Additionally they spend time agonizing over whether a phrase or sentence is a 'vision' or a 'purpose'.

The methodology outlined in this book uses the two words inter-changeably. This is because some people baulk at the 'touchy-feely' connotations of 'visions', and can spend unnecessary time debating the value of these, and this is often before they start to consider what the 'purpose' of their organization is – a topic on which each person at any meeting has a different and valid perspective.

Remember that your aim in having the vision/purpose debate is to agree in the briefest possible and communicable way an aspirational statement (the vision) of what your organization is there to do, and how it is going to do it (the purpose). Continental Airways statement 'Fly to win' is a good example of both a vision and purpose statement. Flying is what the organization is there to do. Winning over other airlines is how they are going to do it. Along with the 'what' and 'how' of this phrase is the implied aspiration – 'and we are going to keep on doing this.'

What you are not usually trying to do in coming up with your vision and purpose is to design the marketer's dream phrase that will stand in media history books as one of the landmarks. What you are trying to do is convey to your people the sense of why they should follow you into a different type of organization, with a memorable and workable 'flag'.

Creating your statement can take as long as either you want it to or you allow your team members to get lost in the debate. The suggestion here is that you go for the 80/20 rule, time-bind it and have ruthless facilitation to keep you on track. If you cannot get it perfect in the time allocated abandon the debate and work with the feelings and intent you have evoked in the discussion. You can always take time outside the meeting to develop a more elegant phrasing.

You will have seen that the second session in the senior management workshop is a discussion of the goal or objectives of your organization. (Again, these words are interchangeable in this methodology.) This is because the purpose statement must be able to cascade into strategic elements and then measurable objectives. If it remains at the aspiration level, you will not be able to design a workable organization and you will have no method of tracking the success of your implementation and ongoing delivery.

Crawford (1995) says that a good purpose statement has a number of characteristics. It must be:

- Short, so that it is memorable. It should be limited to thirty words or fewer.
- Value based, so that it clearly expresses the values for which you stand.
- Declarative, because you should be prepared to declare your purpose, not just publish it.
- Future oriented, not a statement of what you are or what you do now.

It would be even more effective as a statement if within it you were able to reflect the unique characteristics of your organization or department in a way that distinguishes you from others in your domain.

Do not think that this is a once and for all statement. It should have a shelf life of between one and two years at which point you should review its relevance and currency.

Here is an example of the Marks & Spencer (2003) vision and purpose statement that has the characteristics, Crawford (1995) suggests:

- We will be the (retail) standard against which all others are measured (the vision).
- We will make aspirational quality available to all (purpose).

Once you have the vision and purpose statement you then need to identify the strategic elements and the more detailed goals and objectives, which support this. Let us illustrate with the Marks & Spencer statement.

It has some key elements. For each of these you need first to identify what each 'looks like' and second to define a SMART (stretching, measurable, attainable, realistic/relevant, time related or trackable) objective related to it. Figure 5.3 illustrates the process as applied to the first two elements of the Marks & Spencer vision.

Bradford and Cohen (1998) give some excellent guidelines for testing the vision. The activity they outline is one to try out in the senior managers' workshop. It involves alternating between high level and detail level, at each level evaluating your vision statements, strategic elements and objectives against particular situations, actions related to these, and interface activities. Some questions for managers, to answer that will test your proposed vision (and/or their amended one) are against the past, present and

Element	What it looks like: these form the strategic elements	Objective (note that these are not the actual Marks & Spencer 2003 objectives)
The retail standard	■ Being profitable, innovative, respected by customers and suppliers	■ Achieve revenues of xxx million by 1 January 2004 ■ Win industry recognition for innovative products in food and textile products ■ Expand existing customer use of additional products and services by 15% per year for each of the next two years ■ Develop our supply chain process to achieve ... by ...
Aspirational quality	■ Being passionate about product (e.g. the traceability of ingredients in food) to be the best by miles at special foods ■ Having a preoccupation with innovative fabric technology to offer an unrivalled choice of irresistible clothing ■ Having excellent products reasonably priced with a clear pricing structure	■ Introduce xxx new food product lines ahead of competitors gaining xxx% market share as a result of this ■ Develop xxx technology and apply it to our garments ahead of competitors gaining xxx% market share as a result of this ■ Leverage our 100% own brand to ensure customers get higher quality products at a lower price than those offered by competitors

Figure 5.3 Marks & Spencer vision

future aspects of the work of your department, examples follow:

- Look at key past decisions and ask team members what they would have done differently if they were using the vision as a guide. Is it sufficiently tangible? Taking a Marks & Spencer (hypothetical) example, how would a recent decision to have cut research and development funding in food technology have looked if you had all been committed to the proposed statement about 'innovative food products'.
- Ask each manager to indicate how his or her area would now change in the light of the proposed vision.
- Look at critical decisions, which are in the pipeline, and ask how what effect the proposed purpose has on them.
- How does the proposed vision impact present practices and potentially new products and services?
- What aspects of these would need to be re-aligned?

The boundaries of the OD project are the 'givens' which form the framework within which you create your design. Shown, as an example in Figure 5.4, is a set of boundary statements that formed part of the scope for a re-design in a business unit of British Airways.

The boundaries for re-organization

- The re-organization should not require recruitment of more staff
- There should be look alike between head office organization and area office organization
- Alliance implications should form part of the thinking about the design
- The re-organization should not incur bottom line expenditure
- There should be clear communication channels
- Customer contact must form the focus
- Specialized roles should be identified
- Priorities should be established and negotiated
- The structure is bounded by current or planned IT systems
- Any decision made must make business sense (it must be justifiable and quantifiable)

Figure 5.4 Boundaries for a British Airways re-design project

The principles for achieving the objectives are again something that you, the leader of the department or organization, have to outline. Effectively the boundary statements are the 'what' and the principles are the 'how'. Figure 5.5 is an example of principles from a different British Airways business unit which was implementing a human resource information technology (HR IT) system.

Principles

- Ensuring visibility and transparency of British Airways people processes
- Having seamless processes both internally and externally
- Using one process for all
- Enabling individuals to take responsibility for their own data and career
- Ensuring appropriate accessibility to everyone – anytime and anywhere (flexible access)
- Being user friendly – simple and flexible supported by a multi-functional service centre
- Developing new technical skills and change of mindset
- Demonstrating self-service behaviours

Figure 5.5 Principles for an organization design project

Having a clear vision, strong boundaries, and agreed operating principles provides the foundation from which to develop your detailed design.

Your Roles in Phase Two

In this phase, your key role is to get on board the primary stakeholders – your management team members. Chapter 7 has details on other stakeholders you need to think about and how to do a stakeholder analysis.

Your activities in phase two are summarized in Figure 5.6.

In taking on these activities the line manager is moving between strategic management (e.g. when determining the boundaries of the project) and tactical management (e.g. when identifying team members). The HR practitioner supports this activity by fact finding (e.g. pulling out data related to the performance reviews of potential team members).

Before you leap into action trying to get stakeholders on your side, think carefully about how to do this. It will pay you to spend time to reflect consciously about your management and consultancy style. Remember, you must role model the behaviours that you want your management team and the project team members to use. Therefore, for example, if you are dictatorial in the selection of team members and you want them to work collaboratively you will be setting up a disconnect which will come back and bite you.

You also need to think carefully about the people you invite to the workshops. The suggestion made earlier is to have a first workshop comprising your senior managers and a second comprising the senior managers and their direct reports. However, this suggestion may not

Organization design phase	Line manager activity	HR practitioner activity
Choosing to re-design	▪ Determining the scope and boundaries of the project ▪ Getting sponsors and stakeholders on board ▪ Identifying potential project team leaders and members for the high-level and detailed-level teams	▪ Drafting the high-level scoping document ▪ Following up with sponsors and stakeholders ▪ Guiding and suggesting on potential project team leaders and members

Figure 5.6 Manager and HR practitioner activity

work for you in your situation. Your role is to find a body of influential people who may be working on the project and who it will affect and to get them on your side. Who is involved in the project and their way of working with you in planning and implementing it will have a marked effect on its success or failure. Note that the people in these early workshops may not be those who are subsequently involved in the day-to-day running of the project but they will be people who have a voice in who is involved and how it runs.

As you think about positioning the OD project, think too about the vehicles, strategies, and tactics you will use. This book suggests running workshops but be flexible in your thinking. There is no right or perfect way to set the OD project scene. Any forum that allows rigorous debate on the strawman with sufficient time allowed so all participants will feel you have heard and acknowledged their voice is likely to be effective. Your role is to determine the right positioning methods for your situation.

Remember there is all sorts of 'noise' in the system. Your role is to take into account the way people in your organization are thinking, feeling, and acting as they see the project gathering speed. Choose a forum for debate that works for you, that results in pragmatic and realistic 'go-forward' decisions. Consider what the 'sacred cows' are in your organization and decide what the result of slaying any of these might be. (Projects have sunk quickly when someone has slain a cow without due consideration of the repercussions of the action.)

As you work through the phase, notice how the people you work with respond to what is going on. This will help you in your role of selecting the right people for the right roles to work on it.

More about Scope

Hallows (1998) notes that in his view the scoping phase of a project is one that is traditionally given the least amount of attention. But you have learned that working through the phase and producing a scoping document are not things to gloss over. The production of your document protects your future best interests.

What may cause a project to overrun are changes in the scope. If you have not documented the scope at the outset you will not know what is changing. When people started to talk about 'scope creep' in British Airways it caused a certain shiver of dread in sponsors and stakeholders. Scope creep is dangerous to your project and can happen without you noticing if you are not vigilant. It is something you need to stringently guard against. However, by taking the precautions outlined by Hallows (1998) you can mitigate some of the risks. Summarized below are his recommendations:

- Ensure that you have an agreed statement of the scope of the project (which is the objective of the workshops in this phase).
- Communicate the scope to everyone in your organization through a range of media.
- If you have new people joining the project or your organization make sure they familiarize themselves with the scope of the project (particularly if they are going to be in a role which could change it).
- Aim to have regular meetings that consider any requests or considerations for change in scope. (However, do not go into too much bureaucracy on this.)
- When you are at critical decision points in the project refer back to the scoping document to ensure that your decisions are consistent with the scope.
- At any review points in the project, make sure you include the scoping document in the process.
- Before you approve a scoping change, reflect on it carefully. Think through the repercussions that a change might have. Pay particular attention to how a change will affect the budget and schedule.
- If you do decide a scope change is in order, ensure you have the support of your management team and your sponsor in approving it.

Turning to the information you need to develop the scoping document – the workshops outlined have proved to work well but in some cases, they may not yield enough information or agreement to enable immediate go-ahead. If you feel uncomfortable with the output ask some more questions either of yourself (so you can present answers as part of your proposal) or of your management team. Some more examples of useful scoping questions include:

- **Business performance**
  - When did you last review your organization and the way it works?
  - What are the principal activities and processes that it performs?
  - How is work organized to ensure these are performed?
  - How are you currently measuring business and individual performance: financial, operational, employee, and customer?

- **Customers**
  - To what extent is your organization meeting your key customer's expectations in terms of: what is provided, when it is provided, how it is provided, the price at which it is provided?

- **Capabilities**
  - What organization design and change capabilities do you have in your organization?
  - What capabilities do you have that must be retained in order for you to continue to deliver?
  - What capabilities might you need to recruit or develop to continue to deliver?

- **Culture**
  - What is it like to work in your organization?
  - What are people admired for?
  - How do people in your organization currently feel about:
    - Strategic direction
    - Customer satisfaction
    - Training, development and reward
    - Work organization and co-operation
    - Management effectiveness
    - Business efficiency
    - Respect and fairness
    - Employee satisfaction and commitment and how would they like to see this change?

■ **OD project**
  – What would success look like to you: time scales, budgets, deliverables, milestones, impact, and value?

Useful Tools

This phase of the project demands that you assess your current state against your 'to be' or future state and do a gap analysis that informs you of where you need to focus your organization design activity. Three tools that can help you do this are force-field analysis, SWOT (strengths, weaknesses, opportunities, and threats) analysis and STEEP (social, technological, economic, environmental, and political) analysis.

Tool 1: Force-Field Analysis
Developed by the organizational researcher Kurt Lewin, force-field analysis identifies those forces that both help and hinder you from closing the gap between where you are now and where you want to be (Figure 5.7).

How to use force-field analysis
■ Use the diagram shown writing in your own 'to be' purpose or vision. Under the horizontal line list all the forces which are currently stopping you from getting from where you are now to the future state.
■ Above the horizontal line list all the forces which are driving you towards your 'to be' purpose or vision.

These 'forces' are often shown as arrows: the driving forces are those pushing you towards the 'to be' state, and the restraining forces are those pushing away from it.

Figure 5.7 Force-field analysis

It is often helpful to assess the relative strengths of both helping and hindering forces. Some groups use a scale (e.g. 5 = very strong, 4 = strong, 3 = medium, 2 = low, 1 = weak) to evaluate the relative impact of the forces. For graphic representation, proportionately sized arrows show relative strengths graphically.

Once the analysis is complete, your group can use this information to generate potential solutions. Some ideas that the group can explore:

- How to increase the number or strength of the helping forces.
- How to decrease the number or strength of the hindering forces.

Tool 2: SWOT Analysis

The SWOT model provides a framework for the analysis of major internal factors affecting the way the organization currently functions and anticipating future operations. The model is an unattributed strategic planning tool.

Strengths:	Weaknesses:
Opportunities:	Threats:
Maximize	Minimize

What to use it for

Use SWOT during this phase of your project to determine the future and current state and the gap between them.

By first focusing on the future state you can avoid a detailed and unhelpful review of current operations.

How to use it

- Stage 1: Brainstorm the future internal state of the organization. In particular, address opportunities and threats.

- Stage 2: Brainstorm the current internal state of the organization. In particular, focus on strengths and weaknesses. Note that some strengths may also appear as opportunities and some weaknesses as threats.
- Stage 3: Rank each item according to its impact on the organization's future purpose, using a high/medium/low weighting.
- Stage 4: Brainstorm activities to take advantage of opportunities and maximize strengths.
- Stage 5: Brainstorm activities to address threats and minimize weaknesses.
- Stage 6: Add the activities to your change action plan, showing time scales, milestones, resourcing, and budgets. Ensure that these new actions link with and inform your communications and involvement.

Tool 3: External Environment Analysis – STEEP

The STEEP model provides a framework for the analysis of major external factors affecting the future of the organization. The model is an unattributed planning tool.

Factor	Examples	Impact on organization (e.g.)
Social	Demographic change Diversity Work-life balance	New labour markets New working practices Different types of contract
Political	Change of government World trade policies War	Regulatory change Redefinition of competitors Government support
Economic	Economic cycles Currency values Trading relationships	Outsourcing/sub-contracting Price and tariff changes Distribution channel changes
Environmental	Hydrocarbon use Rain forest destruction Ocean degradation	Compliance requirements Sourcing decisions Lobby group influence
Technological	Next generation products Wireless technology Internet impact	Keeping systems current Making best use of investment Knowledge management

STEEP can be used to identify significant external change drivers that must be taken into account as you scope the project and move into the more detailed design phase. The analysis should focus on the future and forecast the impact of each change driver on the targeted organization.

How to use it

STEEP analysis is produced in a variety of ways, e.g. desk analysis using internal or external expert sources of information in the factor areas, brainstorming during a workshop; you can ask individual members of your management team to research particular factors and bring their findings back to the group who can then jointly produce the final analysis. How you decide to do it depends on your circumstances.

Your management team (and/or the high-level team you constitute in phase three) will need to determine the impact of each factor on your organization.

Self-check

Scoping the organization design sets the boundaries for your work. Having an effective scoping process resulting in an agreed project scope sets your project off on the right foot. Ask yourself these questions to assess how you are doing in this phase of the project.

■ Are you reflecting leading standards of behaviour? This requires you to think through the behaviour that you want people to use and then demonstrate using it yourself. However, this in itself is not enough. You need to align relevant processes to reinforce the desired behaviours. One way of doing this is to make the behaviours explicit and then to adjust performance management systems to reward the required behaviour and penalize the 'old' behaviour. Marks & Spencer took this approach. The company stated high-level behaviours:
  - think customer
  - own your part in delivering results

- be honest, confident, listen, and learn
- be passionate about product
- be one team

and lower-level competences by broad job role and designed HR systems to reinforce these; if your OD project requires behaviour change and you have not included a method of reinforcing it in your scoping document you need to go back and do this.

- Are you building up a compelling story for the change? If you are not convinced of the need for change you will not be able to convince your team of it. In some circumstances corporate offices decree that something is going to happen which forces change on people. An example of this occurred in British Airways when a new corporate and centralized accounting system came into play. For field offices, this meant a loss of accounting autonomy and a complete new way of operating. Many field office managers opposed the change but had to go along with it. The corporate change team had a hard battle on their hands re-designing the finance organization.

- Do you have 75% of your management team on your side? Even if you are yourself convinced of the need for change you still may have to convince many other people. However, you may be in the fortunate position where almost everyone recognizes the need for change. External events often force this realization – a take-over bid is an example, or in the case of British Airways, the circumstances arising following 9/11 forced organization design changes on the organization.

- Do you have a vision and purpose statement that you can work with even though it is not perfect? Rest assured that trying to get to the perfect vision statement is on par with trying to create gold from iron. All you need is a good and communicable sense of where you want to get to with an agreement on it. You need to be able to describe it in a few words and conjure up the right images in people's minds. Given the pace of organizational life, be certain that your vision statement is not going to endure through centuries. Be content with 'good enough' in this particular instance.

- Do you know which of the ten common challenges you are most likely to face? All OD projects face challenges and you must have a good idea which of these you are most likely to face as you initiate your project in order to be ready for them. Sometimes they come as a curved ball. An example of this is an OD project in Xerox that called for re-organization of the project management function. In the space of six months five of the most expert project managers moved out of the department leaving a huge gap in knowledge. The OD project was somewhat derailed as it struggled with the challenge of sudden loss of expertise.

- Are you clear about the need for and role of a project manager? An OD project is a project that you must run in a disciplined and organized way. This becomes an even more essential demand when you are trying to keep the 'day job' going at the same time. If you are serious about re-designing your organization you cannot leave it to your idle or spare time moments. It requires professional project management support. The thing to bear in mind on this is that project management bureaucracy can have the opposite of the intended effect. Instead of oiling the wheels, the process sometimes succeeds in stalling the project. Choose a pragmatic project manager who will keep the end in mind.

- Do you have a strawman to present to your management team? You need to have sketched the OD project in sufficient detail that you can present it to your management team. You then need to work with them to shape it in a way that makes sense. This might be a hard call for you. It is your 'baby' and you want people to accept it the way it is. Be gracious in allowing that other people have other perspectives and be open to these. The main purpose of your strawman is to present a start-point not an end point. Its secondary purpose is to circumvent the difficulties you will have if you start this phase of the OD project with a question like. 'Well here's all the information. Where do we go from here?'

- Do you know what tools and approaches you are going to use to scope the work? Your situation is unique and you have to judge what will work to get you to where you are going. There is no one blueprint for getting you from your current state to your future state. Reflect on what you have read in this book and on your own experiences of change projects. Take this learning and develop approaches to getting support and buy in that will work in your situation.

Do's and Don'ts

- Do get a well-bounded and agreed definition of your scope
- Do have a compelling 'flag' for people to muster behind
- Do model the behaviours and approaches you want in your re-designed organization
- Don't spend time on wordsmithing
- Don't proceed until you have a high level of support
- Don't neglect project management disciplines but do use them wisely

Summary – The Bare Bones

- Recognize what you have let yourself in for as you initiate this project
- Identify and use carefully good tools and approaches to scope the project
- Formulate an agreed 'to be' state and measure the gap between it and your current state
- Enlist the support of your management team and only proceed when you have this
- Plan how you will meet the key challenges that are likely to arise as you go forward
- Recruit a pragmatic project manager

References/Useful Reading

Bethune, G. (1998). *From Worst to First*. John Wiley & Sons, Inc.

Bradford, D. L. and Cohen, A. R. (1998). *PowerUp*. John Wiley & Sons, Inc.

Crawford, G. J. (1995). A vision to follow. *Ways* 6(June/July).

Hallows, J. (1998). *Information Systems Project Management*. Amacom.

Kotter, J. (1995). Leading change: why transformation efforts fail. *Harvard Business Review*, March/April.

Senge, P. (1999). *The Dance of Change*. Nicholas Brearley Publishing.

Weiss, A. (1999). *Good Enough Isn't Enough* .... Amacom.

6

The Communications Plan

'Inadequate description of change often results in implementation breaking down at lower levels and employees questioning management's knowledge of the details.'

Timothy J. Galpin (1996). *The Human Side of Change.* Jossey-Bass.

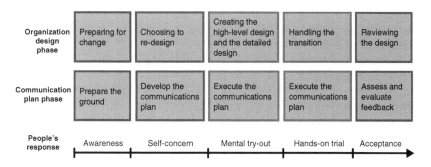

Figure 6.1 Phases of the communications plan

Overview

Good communication is fundamental throughout any project and although most people know how significant it is, very few tackle communication with the importance it deserves. As soon as you start thinking about your OD project you need to start thinking about how you will communicate, what you are doing, your methods of communication, why you are communicating, and when people will connect the communication

Stage	Question
Awareness	What is all this organization design and change about?
Self-concern	What's in it for me?
Mental try-out	What will it be like after the new design is in place?
Hands on trial	What can I do to make the new design work effectively?
Accceptance	How can I make sure the whole organization benefits from this?

Figure 6.2 Stages of change

with the progress of the change. Figure 6.1 illustrates the phases of your communication plan and how they fit into the phases of the OD project.

The communication process deserves significant attention because as soon as you start to mention changing things or start any change in activity you will have an effect on people. They will respond to what they see and hear, what is going on or to what they guess might be going on in various ways. Some will be wary, sceptical, or anxious. Others will be fearful. Communicating effectively goes some way towards helping people to understand and participate in the OD project rather than feeling it is being 'done to' them by outside forces.

Without good communication (and sometimes even with it) people are likely to misunderstand, resist, and perhaps sabotage or subvert the project. The result of this is likely to be time and effort lost in regenerating morale and motivation.

Your role is to help people, through the way you orchestrate your communication, to work their way through the process of accepting change. Briefly, this means you have to be successful in informing them about what is going on, and then generating an understanding and inviting participation through what you tell them. Doing this successfully results in people moving through the stages illustrated in Figure 6.2 and finding satisfactory answers to the question posed at each stage.

The communications role is likely to be taken on by both the line manager and the HR practitioner in the first instance. As the project progresses, you may find that you need a communication team or a specialist. Whoever takes on the role needs to demonstrate some specific capabilities. First, you need to be an effective and communicative champion of the changes that the new design brings. Second, you need to make sure that you do not surprise your managers and staff with anything you communicate – they should be involved from the start. Third, you need to use a wide range of communication channels and methods of keeping people in touch with what is going on. Fourth, you need to make sure that the messages that people get are consistent and coherent, and do not leave room for doubt or creative fiction.

Your communication plan has to unfold in tandem with the OD project and typically, it will comprise four stages: preparing the ground, developing the detailed plan, executing the plan, and then assessing and evaluating its success. Although this sounds like a linear and rigid process, in practice you must apply intuition, empathy, and creativity to get the process right. Thinking about communications, as you work with the phases of the OD project provides a useful structure and helps to ensure that you do not overlook important issues.

Additionally thinking through the communications strategy and plan assists in avoiding the many mistakes that come from a lack of planning. You can avoid common errors if you develop and implement a good plan. The types of thing you want to steer clear of are:

- Resorting to tactical communications made at the last minute.
- Believing that telling the message once is enough.
- Not ensuring that messages are consistent and co-ordinated.
- Not briefing managers to deliver the message.
- Relying too heavily on written communication.
- Failing to use existing communication channels to full advantage.
- Disregarding key levels of influence (junior and support staff can have very high levels of influence).
- Failing to segment the audience into stakeholder groups with different interests, concerns and needs.
- Communicating too late or too early.
- Treating communication as an afterthought and not integrating it fully as part of the OD project.

The following sections guide you through the development of a plan that will mitigate most of the risks of poor communication. A word of warning here – you are unlikely to avoid at least a few accusations of poor communication no matter how much you put into it. It is a well-worn truism that there is never enough communication. However, a well-implemented plan will mean many fewer brickbats thrown at you than no plan or a half-hearted plan.

The Elements of a Communication Plan

When you start to think about your communication plan, consider six key elements that underpin it.

First, you need to identify and segment the various stakeholder individuals, and groups. (Stakeholders are those whom the OD project or its outcomes will affect.) Analysing the stakeholder interests enables you to target your communications for each group – essential to do because stakeholders have different needs. You can design appropriate stakeholder communication based on their:

- knowledge of the OD project
- skills required for working with and in the new design
- level of information required
- previous experience of organization design and change
- influence in the organization and particularly on the success of the OD project
- current attitudes towards organization design and change.

Second, consider what your objectives in communicating are. These will change as the project proceeds but initially your objectives will focus on aspects of awareness – capturing attention, developing understanding of the project, and the case for change, and achieving buy-in. Down the line, in phase two, your objectives will be around issues of self-concern – assuaging anxieties, seeking views, managing resistance, and building commitment. Within phase three, your objectives will focus on aspects of the mental try-out – reinforcing the case for change, and linking the goals of the OD project to the well being of individuals and the organization. Phase four objectives centre on the hands-on trial that is identifying and mitigating risks, applying new ways of doing things, and demonstrating the accruing benefits. Finally, phase five objectives focus on reporting the lessons learned during the first phases, celebrating successes, and providing evidence that the change is sustainable.

The third element to think about in relation to your communication plan is your key message at each stage. For each phase stakeholders need to know what will change, how, and why. You need to think of ways of crafting your messages appropriately for each stakeholder group as well as identifying the best communication channels for what you say to each. The message can be defined as 'what you want the recipient to go away thinking or doing'. For example, the purpose of the message may be to:

- convey information (no action required)
- stimulate action
- promote changing behaviour
- convey caring and reassurance
- motivate towards a goal
- promote feelings of unity
- provide the 'big picture'
- show that you are listening and capturing concerns
- provide feedback.

The fourth element to think about is which communication channel to use. Broadly, there are two options: informal channels and formal channels. Informal channels include one to one meetings, 'water cooler' gatherings, and chatting with colleagues. Formal channels include video, orchestrated presentations, and written communications. Successful communication plans use both types of methods mixed and matched to the needs of the stakeholders. Whichever method you choose you must make sure you find out how stakeholders receive the communication, and you need to make sure that the medium matches what you are trying to achieve. For example, if you are aiming for participation and involvement, a formal presentation that does not allow people to have their say is going to give a mixed message. The selection of the appropriate medium depends on a number of 'whom' and 'why' questions related to the size of the audience, the likely reaction of the audience, the response you seek from the audience.

Timing is the fifth element to be aware of. If you time your communication wrongly it can give rise to all sorts of issues and concerns. If you decide to communicate to different stakeholder groups at different times, you need to take great care to manage these effectively. If you do not do this there are likely to be leaks, misrepresentations, and chatter on the rumour mill. The type of message will determine the timing of communication and vice versa. If you communicate carefully before an event, it may pre-empt many questions about details and implications and will alleviate concerns and confusion, and minimize resistance to change. Sometimes, however, communication occurs in response to an event, for example, crisis management. In this situation, communication needs to be very fast to minimize disruption.

The sixth and final element is accountability. Decide who has accountability for drafting, developing, and implementing the communication plan and assign this power to that person. You also need to make sure that the person accountable understands, supports, and has the capability and motivation to communicate your messages. You should select someone to be accountable based on their:

- Knowledge of, and support for, the OD project.
- Knowledge of the audience, position, and credibility within the organization.
- Interpersonal skills and ability to listen and gain confidence of the audience.
- Role in the OD project, for example one of change agent or sponsor.

The Detail of a Communication Plan

A communication plan is a document that describes clear and specific objectives and activities for communication, in relation to your specific OD project. Your communication plan should detail, for each phase of the project, the target audience who will receive the communication, the vehicle or channel of the communication, the person who will deliver the message, the timing of the event, the location of the event and delivery of the message, the actual message you want to communicate. Your sponsor and your management team(s), if they have not developed it, must agree to the plan and endorse it.

In phase one of the communication plan (preparing the ground) your goal is to build a communication strategy and to create interest, curiosity,

What	How
Determining the project organization	■ Confirm the scope and approach, the team and the work programme
Gaining support for communicating	■ Obtain agreement within your management team for communication objectives and success factors ■ Establish informal networks and communication champions who will support the development and implementation of the communication plan
Analysing the current communication patterns in your organization	■ Assess the current communication climate ■ Evaluate its effectiveness ■ Determine local versus corporate communication accountability
Developing the communications strategy	■ Define the target audiences ■ Define the communication objectives (e.g. overcoming resistance to change) ■ Define the measures of success ■ Define the style and tone of the communications

Figure 6.3 Communication work plan activities

and enthusiasm for the OD project. You will still be defining the project itself. However, it is likely that many people will have heard about it and be concerned.

Your work plan during this phase should include the activities shown in Figure 6.3.

The main output of this phase is the strategy document that meets the objectives of:

■ Stating the scope of the communication plan, for example what it will facilitate and why.
■ Explaining the purpose of the communication plan, for example to inform, motivate, defuse, reassure or seek feedback.
■ Addressing problems based on the strengths and weaknesses of the current communications.

During the second phase of the OD project, you need to develop your day-to-day communication plan. It should document in detail, all of the communication events you will conduct during the OD project. It should

AUDIENCE 1: General Managers					
Audience	Objectives	Key messages	Channel	Timing	Accountable
General Managers	Obtain their buy-in and support Ensure General Managers understand their personal role and undertake appropriate action	Rationale for change We need your support and action to make this happen Efficient delivery of business plan and budgets Focus on commercial awareness Efficient use of resources Branches able to focus on delivery Effectiveness in process, systems and infrastructure Issues/project for first year Organizational structure and rationale Time scales for roll-out	*Face-to-face* Strategy away day Monthly update Project update presentations one to one	March Each month To be confirmed April	

Figure 6.4 Example of one element of a communications plan

include a detailed communication calendar/schedule, by audience group, which identifies proposed products, vehicles, messages and timing. Figure 6.4 illustrates this for one stakeholder group.

In phases three and four, you are executing the communications plan. As you do this, you need to be constantly reviewing and evaluating how successful it is in the light of various success factors. There are several of these and they usually include:

■ The timing of the communication.
■ Whether it is perceived and accepted as accurate by the relevant stakeholders.
■ How far you achieve two-way communication.

- The type of feedback and evaluation you solicit.
- Whether you are demonstrating co-ordination and consistency of communication materials.
- How you are identifying the key communicators/influencers and getting their commitment to your project.

During these two phases, you should be regularly soliciting feedback at two levels to check whether you are hitting the mark:

- On each communication event/item to test its effectiveness in communicating the message and raising awareness.
- On the effectiveness of the communication plan in generating commitment to and generating ownership for the planned business change. (Feedback at this level will be used to revise and improve the communication plan.)

Feedback can be gathered through questionnaires and feedback forms, focus groups, team briefings and communication 'champions' meetings with sponsors. You should then correlate the information gathered into either a communication effectiveness analysis or an employee feedback report.

In the final phase you need to measure the overall impact of the communication strategy and plan and assess whether they have achieved their overall objectives. During this phase you should:

- establish and co-ordinate feedback mechanisms and channels
- review the effectiveness of communication activities and events
- establish how much people's knowledge and perception of the OD project has changed since it was initiated.

The main output of this phase is a feedback report analysing the effectiveness of the implementation of the communications plan, providing stakeholders feedback on it, noting the learning points and celebrating the successes, recommending any revisions in the organization's communications strategy and planning for going forward.

Measuring Effective Communication

From the preceding paragraphs, you know that you need to measure the effectiveness of your communication at regular intervals throughout your project. If you do not do this, you lose the opportunity to adjust your plan and risk your communications missing the mark.

This section gives you more detail on what aspects to pay attention to in order to generate interest and commitment to the changes you are working towards in your OD project. There are five main aspects to question people on: the communicators, your communication channels, the communication process, the effectiveness of the communication, and the barriers to communication.

First, if the top management in your organization are not committed communicators (and seen not to be communicating a clear and shared message) you are at high risk of failing in your project. Communication must be regularly on your management agenda so that you will be giving consistent messages on aspects and progress of the changes that will or will not affect each stakeholder group.

If you are in the communications 'driving seat' you must make sure you know why you are communicating something and whether you are targeting the message appropriately. Knowing this is dependent on your having a fundamental understanding of the varying requirements of the individuals in your organization.

Questions, which ask for feedback on the sources of information (e.g. co-workers, top management, and immediate supervisor), its usefulness, relevance, timeliness, and accuracy, will help you here.

Second, the effectiveness of your communications channel depend on a number of factors including: the culture of your organization, whether the audience groups are homogenous or diverse, the relative cost of the different communication vehicles, and their relative benefits, the current frequency of use (or overuse) of different channels, and the speed of communication afforded by different mechanisms.

Again, you can ask people to rank or comment on each type of communication channel against its usefulness, accuracy, and timeliness and to rank the channels in order of their preference. This feedback will help you get consistency between the communication preferences of your organization and the channels used and help you avoid communicating via channels which could be missed or ignored.

Third, when you ask for feedback on the communication process you are looking for answers which will confirm (or disconfirm) statements like:

- Communication is the responsibility of everyone in the organization.
- Feedback is sought as part of the communication process.
- Feedback about communication is acted on.
- Communication comes from the management downwards.
- Communication is sent up from the organization to management.
- Communication is lateral, across all parts of the organization.
- People receive relevant and accurate information about the change in a timely way.
- Responsibility for communication is clear.

What you are trying to find out by asking about these process aspects is whether the prevailing pattern of communication is one-way or interactive, and how genuine the desire for involvement is. Additionally you are seeking information about gaps in the communication flow which you might need to address.

Fourth, effective communication is more likely to occur in a culture of openness and trust where there is willingness to obtain and share information and to listen and act on feedback. If one of your OD project's objectives is to develop or build on this type of culture, then you must ensure that your communication processes and messages are consistent with this.

People look for behaviour, signs, and symbols which work together to reinforce the communication messages. Without this consistency people are likely to become disillusioned or sceptical. A survey checking on the effectiveness of communication might look like that shown in Figure 6.5. (This is an extract only).

Fifth, you need to identify any barriers to communication and take action to overcome these. Common barriers to effective communication include:

- Poor communication skills of the senior communicators (this can be compounded if staff have a negative attitude towards senior management).
- A structure which favours top down communication rather than interactive (downwards, upwards, and lateral) communication.

Statement	Level of agreement
Communications are clear, concise and consistent	1 2 3 4 5 6
Communicators are effective	1 2 3 4 5 6
I benefit from the communications I receive	1 2 3 4 5 6
I feel involved in the decisions that are made by my organization	1 2 3 4 5 6
Top management is committed to good communication	1 2 3 4 5 6
Communication is an ongoing concern, not a series of special events	1 2 3 4 5 6
Communications mirror the vision/values/goals of my organization	1 2 3 4 5 6
Communication has a consistent image and brand which I can relate to	1 2 3 4 5 6

Figure 6.5 Survey on communications effectiveness (extract)

- The strength of internal politics working against the effective transmission and reception of the messages.
- Wrongly chosen channels (e.g. using a computer-based newsletter where staff have no access to computers).
- Not seeking feedback on communication effectiveness.

Do not be tempted to overlook regularly reviewing the effectiveness of your communications in these five aspects. It will give you an insight into any improvements or deteriorations during the course of the project and help you to take appropriate action. Many projects have foundered because of ineffective communication. Do not let yours be one of them.

Useful Tools

Tool 1: Communication and Involvement Map
This assesses how well one issue has been communicated to the different stakeholders. List the stakeholders down the vertical axis. For each

stakeholder group rate a low, medium, or high level of:

Awareness   How well informed is the stakeholder group about the issue?

Understanding   How well do people understand what the issue is and how it will affect them?

Buy-in   To what extent is the stakeholder group committed to and enthusiastic about the issue?

Ownership   How much real involvement and participation does the stakeholder group demonstrate?

Stakeholders	Awareness	Understanding	Buy-in	Ownership
Senior managers				
Middle managers				
Support staff				
Customers				

Complete the map by filling in each box using different colours according to the level of awareness, etc. When completed you will have an at-a-glance view of the organizational effectiveness of your communication.

You can obtain the information to fill it out in various ways: 1:1 discussions, at a workshop by observation, etc.

Tool 2: Communications Resourcing Wheel (Figure 6.6)
Once you have selected your communication channels for a particular part of your plan, for example a survey followed by a presentation of results with video and print material, this wheel helps you think through the presentation elements, the skills you will need to design and deliver the event, and who will be responsible for each element.

The bull's-eye is the strategic planning for the event. The three rings then outline stages one, two, and three of the planning. Each segment is colour coded to depict who will be accountable for which element. Figure 6.6 is not colour coded although you can see a colour code key.

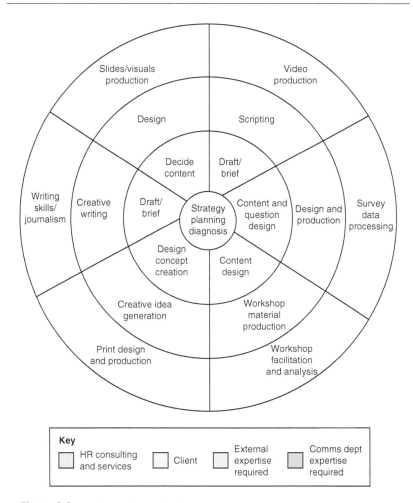

Figure 6.6 Bull's-eye for strategic planning

Self-check

Designing and developing a robust communications plan and delivering it effectively takes skill and commitment. Ask yourself these questions to assess whether you have done the groundwork well enough to be confident in your planning.

Have you specified your objectives? You need to know why, what, how, when, where, and to whom you are communicating at the high level; that is, as part of your communications strategy, and for each communication that you deliver. Without clear communication objectives you risk putting out mixed or inconsistent messages, or using inappropriate channels.

Have you created a demand for communication? People need to be interested and involved in your project (either positively or negatively). Unless they have this curiosity, they will not pay attention to what you are putting out. Compare the enthusiasm of people who are football fans and the way they follow the communication about their teams with people who are not football fans. How would you encourage someone who is very uninterested in the fortunes of a specific team to receive and pay attention to communications about that team? Your task is of this nature.

Are you thinking about communication all the time and not waiting for 'the right time'? You should manage communication at every stage of your project. You must skilfully integrate this activity into the day-to-day project work from inception to completion. There is no single 'right time' for keeping communication channels active and open, as these must be open all the time. There are 'right times' for communicating about specific events, or outcomes.

Is communication on the management agenda? You must ensure that all managers have effective communication at the front of their mind. It is not enough to have the topic as an agenda item at scheduled management meetings. Effective communication is something managers should weave into the fabric of their way of managing. Unfortunately, it often takes a lower priority in their thinking than operational issues. This is not good and in an OD project could be disastrous. In a change management situation, consistent communication is one of the keys to successful implementation. Do not allow your managers to duck their responsibility for this.

Have you defined audience/stakeholder groups? If you are putting out blanket communications without targeting specific stakeholder individuals and groups, you are missing an opportunity. Communication success comes from accurately delivered messages to distinct audiences using appropriate channels.

Are you leading by action and example (the most effective forms of communication)? If your communications state that you want people to behave or do things in a different way then you need to role model this in your own behaviours and actions. What you say and what you do must be congruent or people will notice the discordance (as any parent will know). Chris Arygris and Donald Schon (1974) wrote brilliantly on the effects of not aligning what you do with what you say if you want to look further into the topic.

Is your communication starting from the top? Harkins (1999) is eloquent on the 'distinct voice' that great leaders develop. His belief is that 'through tone and message, this voice embodies a leader's values and goals. It also projects his or her drive and personality. A strong voice of leadership is broadcast consistently and clearly in all communication, whether in speeches, memos, e-mails, board meetings, or interactions in the hallway. This voice influences and guides the organization, shaping its values, attitudes, and culture. When a high-impact leader has a strong voice of leadership, it reverberates among his or her peers and followers and throughout the organization.'

Is there real involvement at all levels? People at all levels in your organization need to be receiving and acting on your communications regarding the organization design. If your feedback suggests that involvement is lacking at some levels or within some stakeholder groups then you must do what is necessary to get the involvement. Passivity or pockets of resistance or both act against your chances of successful implementation.

Have you allowed for the power of informal networks? As Prusak (1997) points out 'much of the real work of companies happens despite the formal organization. Often what needs attention is the informal organization, the networks of relationships that employees form across functions and divisions to accomplish tasks fast. These informal networks can cut through formal reporting procedures to jump-start stalled initiatives and meet extraordinary deadlines. But informal networks can just as easily sabotage companies' best laid plans by blocking communication and fomenting opposition to change unless managers know how to identify and direct them.'

Are you using every possible opportunity and channel? (Too much of one thing has limited value.) It is easy to go with the channels of communication with which you are familiar but it is worth exploring channels that are less familiar. Using a new and different channel can be surprisingly powerful and worth an investment of resource on this basis. You may need to seek some outside or expert help if you are not sure of the range of communication options open to you.

Do's and Don'ts

- Do start to work on communicating from the very first time you meet to discuss a potential OD project.
- Do enroll expertise in helping you design and develop your communication plan.
- Do ensure your methods of communicating square with the style and tone of the change you are implementing.
- Don't underestimate the power of the informal organization's communication channels in helping or hindering your messages.
- Don't hide things – keep your communications open and transparent.
- Don't let the communications lag behind the OD project activities.

Summary – The Bare Bones

- Communication planning must start with your first meetings about a potential change or OD project.
- Leaders and managers must match their words and their actions to be credible change leaders.
- Targeting communications to specific stakeholder groups is critical to success.
- Using a range of communications channels to disseminate your messages is essential.
- People at all levels must be involved in the communications process.
- Feedback on your communications activity must be sought and then acted on.

References/Useful Reading

Argyris, M. and Schön, D. (1974). *Theory in Practice. Increasing Professional Effectiveness.* Jossey-Bass.

Harkins, P. J. (1999). *Powerful Conversations.* McGraw-Hill.

Prusak, L. (1997). *Knowledge in Organizations.* Butterworth-Heinemann.

7

Managing Stakeholders

'How companies define their stakeholders can make an enormous difference in how they implement their business idea.'

Schwartz, P. and Gibb, B. (1999). *When Good Companies Do Bad Things.* John Wiley & Sons, Inc.

Overview

Stakeholders in your project are those people who can influence it for good or bad, who have an interest in it in some way, and whom it affects. They can be people internal to your part of the organization, part of the wider organization, or external to the organization (e.g. customers and suppliers.) The way you design and implement your OD project is shaped in some part (often a large part) by stakeholder needs and responses.

It is essential that you begin thinking about the stakeholders as you start to work on your project. You have already learned that you need to target your communications to the needs of the various stakeholder groups but working with stakeholders is more than communicating with them. It is getting them on your side, and then getting them working on your behalf. You may think this is manipulation and you can view it this way. However, it will pay you to view working with stakeholders as critical to the success of your project because it allows them a say in how you can adapt what you are doing to meet their needs. If stakeholders see you involving them, listening to them, and being responsive to what they are saying then they will start working with you. Working with stakeholders from the start is in the best long-term interests of your project even if it may seem a heavy investment of resource to begin with.

OD projects bring a great deal of disruption to people, usually requiring new ways of working and skills development. A lot of the time, we forget that in order to change organizations we have to enable those individuals within the organizations to change personally. For you to implement your OD project successfully you have to remember to actively support people through their individual responses to the changes. With this in mind, a large part of your management of stakeholders should involve you preparing people for change and helping them view it positively. People directly impacted by the changes will benefit from your planning and delivering empathetic and ordered activities to support them through the transition.

The following sections guide you through two streams of work: first, managing stakeholders, and second, supporting personal change. This is followed by a discussion of trust and risk taking.

Managing Stakeholders

Your first task is to segment stakeholders. Assigning your stakeholders to a category helps you manage them effectively. This means first understanding their positions and perspectives, and second, developing, implementing, and evaluating plans to maximize their support for your project and minimize their resistance to it. It is important to recognize that each stakeholder category (or individual within the category) will have specific needs or issues that you must address. Different stakeholders can perceive the same changes in quite different ways depending on their:

- expectations of the organization
- vested interests
- previous experience of organization design and change
- existing pressures of work
- interests and affiliations
- particular characteristics and priorities.

You will not be successful in your project if you do not recognize these differences or if you decide to treat stakeholders as one amorphous group.

There are various ways you can classify or categorize stakeholders to help you manage them. The way you choose depends on the type of OD project you are planning and the type of organization you work in. One method is to think of stakeholders as falling into one of the seven categories:

1. *Sponsors*: As you have learned in Chapter 3 these are the people who approve the overall OD project and who act as champions for it within the organization.
2. *Advocates*: These strong supporters of the project lend their weight and influence to what you are planning to achieve.
3. *Impacted*: These people are indirectly affected by the OD project. Taking a retail example, customers may notice that you have changed your tilling layout but it does not fundamentally change the way they pay for their goods.
4. *Targets*: The people whom the project and process directly affect fall into this category. Continuing with the retail example, sales assistants may have to be re-trained to work with the new tilling layout. It has a direct impact on the way they do their jobs.
5. *Change agents*: This group of people includes those you have appointed to be instrumental in introducing the changes that are a part of your OD project as well as those who informally take on the role by virtue of their natural inclination or attributes.
6. *Blockers*: Unfortunately, a small minority of people will be bent on systematically attacking your project. These people are unlikely to change whatever you do. A good rule of thumb here is to work energetically to remove them from any sphere of influence and then spend time with those who are working in your favour. Betting on goodwill is more likely to succeed in the long term than betting on changing a blocker's mind.
7. *Casual*: Stakeholders who fall into this category are those who have a passing interest in what is going on but who are neither directly nor indirectly affected. Nevertheless, you must not neglect their level of influence. Observers and commentators often fall into this group and they can exert more power than you might think taking their role at face value.

A second method of classification is to identify stakeholders as falling broadly into three categories:

1. key individual players
2. key groups within the organization
3. key external players and influencers.

You can sub-categorize these groups:

Key individual players

Change sponsor: the director, senior manager or person who initiates and drives the change and who, in most cases, is willing to take overall accountability for the success of the change programme.

Promoter: the person(s) promoting a particular kind of solution to address given problems.

OD project manager: the person responsible for the performance outcomes from the OD project.

Change agents: staff assigned to specific roles to facilitate change and support line management in the process, based on their enthusiasm for the changes the OD project brings and their available skills.

Targets: users of the changed design, including those who expected to benefit from it in other business areas.

Champions: natural supporters or enthusiasts in the business who can become opinion leaders in generating support for the proposed changes coming out of the OD project.

Support players: those whose functional support is required for effective implementation of the project but who do not have direct accountability for it or a strong stake in it.

Key groups

These comprise mainstream employees whom the proposed change will directly impact and whose jobs and performance standards will be changed as a direct result of the change process. In most organizations, these include:

Senior management: This group is usually the board or an executive body, which is responsible for organizational performance. Members make key decisions. Their sustained and mutual commitment will be required to endorse the changes required and to maintain energy within the OD project.

Change owners: This is the management group which is 'buying' the change. It will have an operational impact on their business area – generating most performance improvement. You need to understand fully their needs, expectations, and preferred ways of doing things as you implement your OD project.

Line management: This is the intermediate management group between top management and employees. Ensure their wholehearted support for the project as it is critical to your success in the short, medium, and long term.

Employee representatives: This group represents the interests of the non-managers in your organization. It may be through Works Councils or through Trade Unions. Whichever representative body you have in your organization, you must involve it as a partner in your OD project. How far you involve it depends on the nature of your business and the interests of the representative body.

At a minimum, members of this group act as a useful focal point to give information about the task ahead, and help you avoid pitfalls. (This can be done either formally or informally or both.) Ideally, you should include members of your employee representative group as part of your project team.

Specialists: This includes those groups who may be responsible for policy, design, planning, technical specification or functional control of various aspects of the change, for example information technology (IT), finance, recruitment, training and development.

Support: This category of staff includes those who support the key operational groups, for example secretarial staff or facilities management. They often wield power in their role of gatekeepers for other stakeholder groups.

The two classification methods mentioned above work in most projects, but there are other types of categorization possible. For example, it may be preferable to identify key internal groups according to their business division, level of management, skill areas, location, or roles in the OD project.

Key external stakeholders

What constitutes an external stakeholder will vary according to the size and scope of the OD project. For some organizations, planning major organization design change without involving suppliers as stakeholders is inconceivable. For others, a broader view of the likely impact on third party groups is sufficient. If you work with outsourcing agencies or in a partnership or alliance with another organization, consider what role they play as stakeholders in your project. Such organizations could be either internal or external stakeholders. Which category you put them in depends on the nature of the changes your OD project brings about. However, the following comprise the usual list of key external stakeholders:

- Customers
- Owners
- Shareholders
- Suppliers
- Strategic partners
- Contractors
- Consultants and advisors
- Competitors
- Government agencies
- Local community.

Once you have categorized your stakeholders gather information about them in order to do an informed analysis. You can gather the information in various ways including desk research, workshops, interviews, and surveys.

One-to-one interviews are most effective with senior management and external stakeholder representatives. Workshops are often the best way to gather information on key internal stakeholder groups with a large number of people.

You will find that with major OD projects, the concerns, interests, and objectives of different stakeholder groups are frequently in conflict. Different levels of detail may be necessary for different kinds of stakeholder analysis, depending on the characteristics of the organization, the information readily available and the nature of the proposed changes. For example, an organization with hundreds of suppliers may require only a high-level review of them as a group, whereas one with a strong dependency on a number of key suppliers may need to treat them differently.

You must update the stakeholder information and classification periodically during the course of your project. This is because stakeholder positions usually change over time as the implications of a project become clearer. In addition, other stakeholders can emerge as the project proceeds.

For each stakeholder group decide what is going to be the best technique and approach to use to increase their level of commitment to your OD project and its outcomes. Commonly used techniques include:

- **Running change readiness workshops**: These are held before the OD project is up and running, to help identify the extent of your organization's capability for and willingness to change.
- **Revising performance measures**: This is a sensible way of ensuring that you align key performance indicators to what the OD project is trying to achieve. This technique is based on the principle that 'what gets measured gets done'. If you think through what people need to get done and implement measures of this effectively you can elicit the desired behaviours for the new environment.
- **Develop change agents**: This technique is one of identifying stakeholder groups and individuals who can play a key role in driving through change with their consistent commitment to and enthusiasm for the change. If you slowly build these up group by group to a critical mass, change agents can help others in the organization understand and accept the change.
- **Adopt a stakeholder**: Using this technique requires you to have each member of your organization design team 'adopt' an important stakeholder. The adopter then takes on the responsibility of communicating with 'their' stakeholder regularly about the project. This provides valuable feedback and warning of when stakeholders might be feeling particularly uncomfortable about the change.

- **Deliver quick wins**: This is a very popular technique for generating commitment to an OD project. People usually start to feel committed to the change when they see visible gains from the change early on.
- **Recognize those who are trying to jeopardize the change**: You need to keep your antennae tuned to use this technique. Often people become disaffected with OD projects if they are not part of an implementation team and thus feel excluded from what is going on. In other cases people may resent having to take on more of the workload from their colleagues who are working more directly on the project. Once you recognize the signs of resentment, tackle the issues and take appropriate actions.

Supporting Personal Change

The main barrier to employees and other stakeholders welcoming your OD project tends to be their fear of how the change will affect them personally. Resistance usually results from people feeling wary or scared about what the change will mean for them. For example, will their job change? Will they lose their job? Will they need to work harder in the changed environment? Most fears result from a loss of power and control over the job, uncertainty about what is going to happen next or indeed loss of the job itself. If you can identify and allay or confront these fears as early as possible into the project, and pay attention to new fears as the project proceeds, you will get people involved and improve your chances of making the change work.

Concentrating on the employee groups – at a simple, almost stereotypical level, you can categorize their fears as follows:

Senior managers: Members of this group are afraid the project will fail or that the promised outcomes of the change are not achievable. This would have a knock-on effect on their organization's credibility, particularly if they are in the sponsor role. The nature of their job means that sometimes they feel distanced from the work that is going on and wonder what is happening.

Middle managers: These stakeholders tend to be fearful that their jobs will go, reduce in scope, or get bigger and less manageable. Most change programmes have significant impact on middle management.

You may recall the 'de-layering' that took place in large organizations in the 1990s usually affected the middle management group the most.

Front-line employees: This group fears that they may lose their job because of the OD project or they fear that their role will become more complex or less enjoyable. Front-line staff tend to be the most overt resisters of change perhaps because they feel they have the least power to influence it.

The change curve (Figure 7.1) is a helpful way to describe the typical emotional cycle that people go through when faced with change. When you first moot the idea of changing something, there is often a numbed or shocked feeling as people block off what is happening. As the numbness wears off, people start going into denial, often refusing to believe that the change will happen or be implemented successfully. As you communicate more detail about the change, people tend to start worrying about what it means for them and what is going to happen to their jobs.

As the change gets underway, people generally start to feel more concerned. This is usually quite an unsettling period, where uncertainty is

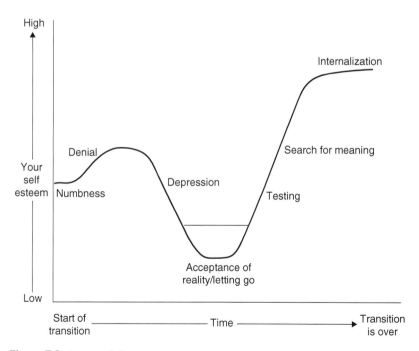

Figure 7.1 Stages of change

high and people are depressed about the future. Once in the thick of change, where the inevitability of change is accepted, people feel at their lowest. This is because change, even when positive, is not without its complications.

When people are ready to move on from this point, they start testing the change – how it will feel, and what it will mean for them. This tends to lead to some kind of association of personal meaning about the change and finally to internalization. That is when the change becomes a part of the 'norm'.

Although everyone knows that life is change (the only certainty is that life is uncertain) often people are fearful because they have not been reassured about what is going on and/or they feel their anxieties have not been taken into account. Your task is to help people to accept the inevitability of change without fearing it. As not all change will result in a positive outcome for all individuals, one way is to help people develop confidence that they can handle whatever comes along. To reduce fear help individuals come to terms with and mitigate whatever it is they feel they are losing. Do this as part of the OD project but recognise you may be able to draw on other resources to help people transition into the new environment. For example, if your organization has an Employee Assistance Programme or an Occupational Health Department you could approach these for help.

For you to be successful in your project you must get the majority of the stakeholder to the point where they have internalized the change. You may find that putting new business processes in place is a much simpler task than getting people to use them effectively. This is often the outcome of a poorly managed transition from the old to the new. The 'grey' time between doing things the old way and doing things the new way can be the most difficult part of any change experience.

Consider and agree your strategy and tactics for helping stakeholders initially understand the impact of change and then think about what has to happen to make this change acceptable to them. In many instances, it will be a case of listening to and talking with people. For example, on larger scale change projects 1:1 sessions, group review meetings, or informal discussions can all help progress the change.

Note that the process of undertaking stakeholder analysis is important in two ways. First, you can choose to involve several people in gathering information about the stakeholders and then analysing it, which will increase their involvement, and interest in the project.

Second, each contact with a stakeholder (either individual or group) is an opportunity to convey messages about what is going on. Take care to ensure consistent messages if a number of people are gathering information.

Trust and Risk Taking

As your project starts up and gets going your role is to enable the stake-holder individuals and groups to move from the current state to the future state trusting that what they are moving into will bring benefits. They must be willing to take the risks that will go with making the change.

Geoffrey Bellman (2002) discusses aspects of trust and risk related to change projects in his book *The Consultants Calling*. He notes that 'you cannot eliminate the real risk present in change work. Building trust can make risk more acceptable, but it will not make risk go away.'

You can do a lot to increase the stakeholders' ability to trust in the project and be willing to take the risks that go along with it and Bellman discusses these in some detail. The following two lists are adapted from his discussion.

To develop trust:

- Be open about the change project and about yourself.
- Encourage stakeholders in your project to talk to others who have been through similarly sized and shaped projects. People will learn from others' experience.
- Discuss other change projects that you have worked on or been involved with. Show that you are applying your learning from these into this project.
- Learn about the specifics of people's role and involvement in the project. The more you understand where they are coming from, the more you will be able to help them move forward.
- Show stakeholders that you are sympathetic to the way they think and feel about their role and the part they play in the organization.
- Find out what they think needs to carry forward into the future state and why.

125

- Demonstrate your belief that they can create a successful future state that they will be motivated to work in.
- Point out how you are trying to help stakeholders achieve a successful outcome to the project.
- Remind stakeholders that you are all working for the success of the organization.
- Encourage stakeholders and be supportive especially when they seem to be struggling.
- Offer input and feedback without criticism.

To make risk more acceptable:

- When you see risky situations point them out and help stakeholders deal with them.
- Be a model risk taker showing stakeholders that you are willing to take risks yourself.
- Voice your doubts and fears about the project as well as your hopes and dreams for it.
- Show that you are not fearless but that you are able to handle your fears – teach them how to do this if appropriate.
- Follow through on all the commitments you make to them.
- Model the behaviour you want to engender in the stakeholder groups and in the future organization. For example, if you want more openness, then be open.
- Share responsibility for getting work done.
- Help stakeholders recognize that changing is a process and progress will come one step at a time.
- Prepare stakeholders to mitigate risks by planning, taking planned actions, and staying focused and on track.

You may find yourself in more than one dilemma as you try to build trust and a risk-taking environment. Some examples of these (framed as questions) are:

- How do you work with stakeholders who may be rivals or have competing interests and different objectives?
- How do you re-design for profitability without sacrificing your interest and concern for your people?

■ How do you maintain your own sense of integrity if you have to work on aspects of the change that you do not agree with? (For example, redeploying people, or making them redundant.)

Handling dilemmas is another of the skills you have to deploy – particularly in relation to the stakeholders and their responses to the change. It is a good idea to do some work with your management team and key stakeholders on managing dilemmas. The exercise below is an example of one used successfully with stakeholder groups in helping them see each other's perspectives, build trust amongst them, and come up with a solution that they can work with. (It originated as a real dilemma faced by a department head.)

Instructions

1. You must all agree on the same solution.
2. You cannot add to or amend the solutions given.

Dilemma

Three months ago you joined a new department with the brief to make it more effective and reduce the overlap and duplication. You designed an approach that did this without loss of jobs but with a certain amount of re-skilling. You have just come back from an executive briefing where you have been told to reduce your department by 50% within the next 12 weeks. What do you do?

1. Vigorously build a business case demonstrating that the path you planned will deliver productivity gains sufficient to pay for all the staff without making any cuts.
2. Go along with the corporate injunction despite what it means for your people.
3. Involve your people in coming up with a plan to reduce by a certain amount but not by 50% and make the case for that.
4. Resign your position as you feel that working in that environment compromises your integrity.

Working through this sort of exercise with stakeholders helps prepare them for the real dilemmas they will inevitably face as the project proceeds.

It also helps them think through the risks that they are willing to take as they propose solutions or try to come to an agreement.

Useful Tools

Tool 1: Stakeholder Analysis, Version 1
Use this to map all those who are involved in or affected by the change as follows:

- Identify the individuals and groups
- Determine the commitment of each to the change
- Determine the level of influence of each in the change.
- Plot the position of the various stakeholders on the matrix (Figure 7.2).
- Identify and agree where you need to focus your communication and involvement effort. Where the level of commitment is high with people who have a high level of influence this is positive and you should

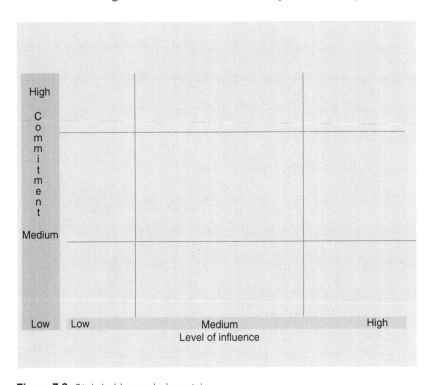

Figure 7.2 Stakeholder analysis matrix

maintain it. If there is low support from people who have very little influence over the success of the project this is not ideal but neither is it a cause for concern. Where a high level of support is needed but not evident you need to develop strategies to raise and maintain levels of support as a matter of urgency.

■ Plan the actions you will take to get the stakeholders you need most working with you.

Tool 2: Stakeholder Analysis, Version 2

Complete the form (Figure 7.3) as follows:

Stakeholder: indicate the stakeholder by name of individual or group.

Type: indicate the type of stakeholder (e.g. individual, group member, external player.)

Interest: describe the stakeholder's interest in the change.

Resources: indicate the resources the stakeholder can put into the change.

If you are meeting with the stakeholders to collect this information, structure the meeting along the lines of:

■ Establishing the stakeholders' mission or purpose and relating it to your design's key goals and performance indicators. This will 'hook-in' the stakeholder to what you are planning.

■ Extract from the stakeholders what their expectations and needs are from your organization.

■ Ascertain what impact the OD project outcomes will have on the stakeholders.

Stakeholder	Type	Interest	Resources

Figure 7.3 Stakeholder analysis form

- Elicit what reactions the stakeholders are likely to have in response to the change.
- Find out what power the stakeholders wield in relation to your design and implementation plan.
- Assess what would maximize stakeholder support for your project and formulate an action place that would achieve this.

Self-check

As you think about your stakeholders and plan the actions you will take to gain their support for your project, consider the questions below. If you have good answers to all of them, you are well on the way to working effectively with your stakeholders.

Have you planned to conduct a stakeholder analysis at the start of your project? To get your project off to a good start you need to know at the outset who is going to work with you and who is likely to work against you. It is not enough to have a 'gut-feel' about this. You need to work out systematically on how you are going to get the critical mass working in your favour.

Do you have a clear picture of your stakeholders? If you have done a good stakeholder analysis you will know who the primary stakeholder groups are, their level of influence of the success of the OD project, their levels of support for the change, and their areas of resistance.

Have you planned for periodic reviews of the analysis? As the project proceeds and the organizational environment changes your stakeholder group is likely to change also. If, for example, a key individual leaves the organization their successor may take quite a different view of your project and you will have to start from square one in gaining the new person's support.

Do you know what other projects are competing for your stakeholders' support? It is unlikely that your OD project is the only change project that affects your stakeholders. In most instances, they will be feeling the impact of other, perhaps significant, projects. Get the full picture of what is going on so that you can co-ordinate your efforts with others.

Have you created an involvement strategy? Create the strategy and mechanisms that will keep your stakeholders informed of the progress of the design work. Part of this should include ways of getting their feedback and reaction as the design emerges so that you can make adjustments or take action as necessary.

Have you accepted the importance of managing external stakeholders as well as internal stakeholders in your project? It is not enough to know that you need to include external stakeholders, for example customers and suppliers in your stakeholder analysis; you must also plan to take action in relation to these. At a minimum, they should know what is going on. It would be better if they had a more direct involvement in the project design and implementation.

Are you clear what stakeholders (individual and group) are expecting from the project and what it will take to get their support? Once you have done your stakeholder analysis develop a clear set of actions related to getting the co-operation and involvement of each group in an appropriate way. Not all stakeholders will want day-to-day involvement, for example.

Have you planned a communications strategy that keeps stakeholders informed on a continuous basis as to how the project is proceeding? Most projects change as they unroll so it is essential to keep a regular two-way communication flow between yourself and your stakeholders. As you know, the communication channels you choose must be appropriate to the stakeholder group you are targeting.

Are you willing and able to confront the reality that your integrity may be called into question if your proposed re-design cannot avoid the result of taking actions unpleasant to individual stakeholders? One of the things you have to face working on an OD project is that the design may have unfortunate consequences for individuals. It is important that you maintain a strong sense of perspective, and have the personal confidence to manage complex, perhaps distressing situations, and dilemmas.

Are you supporting people facing the changes your OD project brings in a way that prevents them feeling and acting as passive victims? Your task is to enable people to feel positive and optimistic in the face of change – willing to take accountability and risks in order to benefit from the changes. Even if job loss is a possibility, there is every reason to help people prepare for this and help them believe that they have a good future ahead of them.

Do's and Don'ts

- Do segment your stakeholder groups
- Do complete a thorough analysis of each group
- Do aim to understand each individual's response to the implications of your OD project
- Don't plough ahead until you have some key stakeholders working in your favour
- Don't ignore the power of blockers and resisters as you develop your organization design implementation plan
- Don't underestimate the necessity of recognizing and handling moral dilemmas as the project proceeds

Summary – The Bare Bones

- Conduct a thorough and complete stakeholder analysis at the start of your project
- Plan appropriate actions to involve your stakeholders in the OD project
- Communicate regularly with the stakeholders during each stage of the project
- Review your analysis as the project proceeds and/or as circumstances change
- Be understanding of individual's responses to change and help them handle it effectively
- Know your own strengths and limitations in managing change and handling dilemmas

References/Useful Reading

Bellman, G. (2002). *The Consultants Calling*. Jossey-Bass.
D'Herbemont, O. et al. (1998). *Managing Sensitive Projects*. Routledge.
Jeffers, S. (2003). *Embracing Uncertainty*. St Martin's Press.
Shaw, R. B. (1997). *Trust In the Balance*. Jossey-Bass.

8

Phase Three – Creating the High-level Design and the Detailed Design

'The roles design team members play during an event alternate between thinking and acting as participants and thinking and acting as a design team.'
Jacobs, R. W. (1997). *Real Time Strategic Change.*
Berrett-Koehler Publishers.

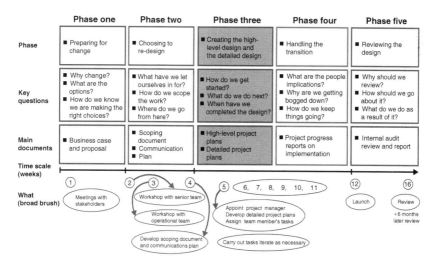

Figure 8.1 Phase three – creating the high-level design and the detailed design

Overview

During phases one and two of the OD project, you have done the preparation and scoping work you need to do. The output of these phases is a well-constructed business case for the change together with a scoping document. Phase three (Figure 8.1) starts when your sponsor has signed off your scoping document and when you have a communication plan that you have already started to implement.

Now your task is to develop the work that these documents represent into first an outline design and then a series of detailed design plans. The documentary output of this phase is the high level and detailed plans that will ensure safe passage from current to future state.

Putting it another way, in this phase you flesh out all the actions you will take that move you from the current state to your future state. In effect, you will be doing a detailed gap analysis between the two states and listing out everything necessary to do to bridge the gap. You also consider the structure of the re-designed organization.

This phase can take a long time and there is the inherent danger of sacrificing your current operation and profitability while you concentrate on the OD project. Think how to handle the balance between getting the new design ready to go whilst keeping the business running effectively.

To work through phase three effectively you need to be able to answer three questions. First, how do we get started? Second, what do we do next? Third, when have we completed the design? The remainder of this section guides you through answering these questions.

How do we get started? First, constitute the design teams. Second, instruct those you select to work on the project about their roles and responsibilities. Third, set up the project management structure. Fourth, develop a high-level plan (if you have not already done this as part of your scoping exercise).

1. Set up two levels of design team: the first team comprises senior staff and key stakeholders who have a good overview of what is going on in the organization, and can judge how the overall design you shape will affect business performance. Members of this team are likely to be your management team (but not necessarily all of them) plus one or two others. Keep the membership to no more than seven people but select those who have the influence and interest to be proactive in

Work streams: Project 1	Work streams: Project 2
Market proposition Management structure Stakeholder work People matters Culture Communications Practicalities	Infrastructure Teamworking Performance measurement Manpower planning Communications and negotiations Equipment requirements

Figure 8.2 British Airways OD projects work streams

your project. This team works at the high level setting and monitoring the direction of the project and keeping it on target.

The second level of team works on the detail of the design. It is not usually one team but several small teams each working on a different aspect of the organization. What these aspects are depends on the nature and purpose of your design. You are likely to have identified these from the work you have done in the scoping phase. Figure 8.2 shows the work streams for two different British Airways projects illustrating how different end games required different design focus.

Include someone from each level of your organization in each team but aim to keep the teams small, four to six people are enough. With a diagonal slice, you are working on the tested principle that those who do the work should re-design it. Without this, you will not be able to understand and influence or change work patterns at a day-to-day level. Usually one member of the high-level team leads each work stream.

Individuals you select for these teams must be capable of influencing colleagues, acting as change agents, and being proactive in doing the required work. Give them time to work on the OD project. If you cannot do this provide incentives to participate in some other way (e.g. accruing time to take at the end of the project).

2. Train all your team members to do their organization design roles effectively. This includes explaining the methods and approaches you will be using, building awareness on handling change, and clarifying the way the two levels of team will work together. Remember, this last is an iterative process with the high-level team creating the big picture design and the detailed-level teams working to make it operational.

If your project is a large one you may want to recruit additional change agents or change champions. They should be included in your training programme.

3. Set up the project management structure. You may have already appointed a project manager. If not, think about doing so. Chapter 10 gives more information on project management. Whatever its size and scope your project requires skilled use of project management disciplines to keep it moving and on track.

4. Develop a high-level plan with an outline timeline. Figure 8.3 is an example of such a plan from a Xerox business unit. Note that this

	Target completion	
	Status	Date
Step 1 – Framework for action Communicate statement from Director including: ▪ vision, unique purpose, objective, measures ▪ boundary statements Appoint half-time project manager	Completed	
Step 2 – Map current state People/skills/culture Customers Interfaces Conduct stakeholder analysis	Completed	by 05/02/.. by 05/02/.. on 27/01/..
Step 3 – Overview organization Develop high-level organization chart Conduct risk analysis Present high-level plan to stakeholders		on 27/01/.. in w/c 01/02/.. in w/c 01/02/..
Step 4 – Detail organization Compare current state maps with future org Identify gaps, and recommend how to meet Prepare detailed specification of BAx including: ▪ New ways of working ▪ Resource requirements – people, skills ▪ Reward and recognition frameworks ▪ Service level agreements Agree migration plan Test against worked examples		Start w/c 01/02/.. Start w/c 01/02/.. Start w/c 08/02/.. on 18/02/.. on 18/02/..
Step 5 – Deliver Job specifications People specifications Reward and recognition packages Performance management process Performance indicators/key performance indicators (KPIs) Test against worked examples		Start w/c 21/02/.. on 18/03/..
Throughout – communication		
Step 6 – Migrate		From 29/03/..

Figure 8.3 High-level plan

project, involving a department of 250 people, started on 10 January and completed on 1 April.

What do we do next? You and the high-level team develop the outline design bearing in mind the elements you have already assembled. Do this in four stages.

First, remind yourselves of the 'experience' your current organization brings to your customers and staff. Describe it in a hard or quantitative dimension, for example the external transactions between your organization and your customers or partners, the internal transactions between your part of the organization and other parts, the current purpose, the core competences, the work that is done and the outputs delivered. Then describe it in a soft or qualitative dimension – the 'touch' and 'tone' of your organization felt by those interacting with it. Acknowledge that through evolution or intent it is the design of your organization that brings this experience to your customers. (Your organization performs the way is it designed to perform.)

Now describe the 'experience' you want your future customers to feel. Make your description full and vivid. You can get to richness in your description by using creative thinking exercises that people find alarming at first and then enjoy! Metaphors are easy to work with. For example, in one workshop the question 'Why is your future organization like a ballet dancer?' evoked the answer 'Because it is flexible, moves quickly, and behaves gracefully.' In another workshop the question, 'What kind of fruit is your future organization like?' got the response, 'It's like a kumquat: small, and exotic.'

Second, map your current workflow from finish to start. This is not a misprint. Output to input maps identify bottlenecks, issues, interdependencies, overlaps, and duplication more quickly and efficiently than starting from the input end. (It is a bit like reading something aloud instead of to yourself. You are much more likely to spot errors of spelling, grammar, sentence construction as you concentrate on doing something less familiar.) Identify the elements that need to change and those that work well and can stay as they are. Relate these back to the diagnosis work you did in phase one – there should be congruence.

Third, compare the way your organization is performing now in terms of workflow and customer experience with the way you want it to perform in the future. This is the design gap.

Develop various structural options that are likely to deliver the work and the customer experience within the scope you have agreed and documented. For each option, consider:

- its viability in terms of the performance it will deliver to your customers,
- the scale of change it would require to get from where you are now to the future state,
- the key aspects you need to work on to bridge the gap (these will form the detailed design teams' work streams).

Even with all these considerations, you are likely to come up with more than one viable structure.

Fourth, present these together with your customer experience description to your sponsor and key stakeholders for input and feedback.

Get support for the description and one or more of the structural options together with a decision to proceed. At this stage, you are still at the high-level design. You will not know whether you can deliver the structure and experience exactly as you present it until your teams have done the detailed design work. Once you have sponsor and stakeholder support you move to the next stage.

Each of these stages is a sizable chunk of work. There are various ways you can tackle them, for example in focus groups, in a larger workshop, detailing specific people to work on each aspect. The method you choose depends largely on the time and resource you have available. Do not skip over any of these steps.

What do we do next? Assemble the work stream members. Their initial task is to analyse your structural design options. Do this in one workshop where members of all the teams are present. Remind them of the process so far and then encourage them to 'test' the design for workability. Is it likely to deliver the future state? Ensure you log amendments, new ideas, issues, and concerns and if necessary go through another round with stakeholders. When you are satisfied that you have a preferred design that will deliver the future state it is time to move on to the detailed design.

Each work stream then does the detailed design for their aspect of the whole design, working independently but in concert. To get this started schedule design meetings, and give teams the agreed design, together with the scoping document and a high-level plan outlining the types of actions and outputs you envisage by work stream. Figure 8.4 is an

Transformation issue/obstacle	Programme milestone	Responsibility	Supported by	Date by which resolution required	Main tasks	Main tools or methods	Issue/s requiring further clarification
Culture: poor communication and 'my patch' thinking; poor consistency of processes				Ongoing effort and progress	Devise clear communication in relation to, for example, common processes, one organization, one approach to implementation, etc. for inclusion in broad messages Communicate to all stakeholders on an ongoing basis	Attendance at relevant forums Continuous prompted feedback from stakeholders	
Culture: reluctance to change				Communication for each stakeholder group by – xxx Non-technical skills issues defined by – to be agreed, approach to dealing with them agreed by xxx	Devise clear communications in relation to new roles/ responsibilities/culture, in order to manage expectations of users; communication of this nature also to be included in training material	Competency profiles at user level Competency profiles for new roles	Need to decide timing/phasing of transition to new roles

Figure 8.4 Work stream project plan

Transformation issue/obstacle	Programme milestone	Responsibility	Supported by	Date by which resolution required	Main tasks	Main tools or methods	Issue/s requiring further clarification
					Profile competencies required in new roles		
					Identify non-technical skills issues in conjunction with HR		
Organization design/structure				Broad implications at enterprise and organizational level determined by xxx	Assign clear process owners who take responsibility for policy, process and delivery and understand day-to-day operations	Organization design templates	As above
				More detailed implications of the above by xxx	Establish new organizational structure at an enterprise, process, and tactical level	Organization structure charts and job evaluations	
				Implications for tactical design determined by xxx	Determine phasing/ timing of transition to new structure/s	Job descriptions and competency profiles	

Figure 8.4 Continued

example from a project that did this. Each team's objective is to design, for their part of the whole system, the conditions for peak performance workflow in your organization together with an implementation plan that will get you there. Their work must align with each other team's work to deliver a sum that is greater than the individual parts.

Depending on the scale of your project, it takes between four and eight weeks for the teams to deliver their implementation plans. Each team reports weekly to the senior management team usually via the project manager who co-ordinates and monitors them.

The project manager's focus is on each work stream delivering to target. Weekly status reporting helps him or her see what is going on across the portfolio of work and with the high-level team make the adjustments necessary to keep all work streams aligned, focused in the same direction, and on track. Presented in Figure 8.5 is a typical status report form.

As teams complete the work, pass it to the high-level team for analysis, feedback, input and testing of alignment. This iterative process continues until you think you have a fully designed future state organization together with an implementation plan to get you to it.

When have we completed the design? You have completed the design when you are confident that you have successfully done five things:

- firmed up your implementation plan
- met the 10 principles of good design
- 'walked through' your new design
- done an alignment diagnosis
- communicated with the organization and with stakeholders.

1. Firm up your implementation plan by confirming that you have all the resources necessary to deliver it and that it is deliverable within the time scale. (Have contingency plans ready as a precaution.) Ensure your sponsor has signed off the plan and is fully aware of its implications and impact on the rest of the organization. Sometimes projects go under at this stage because the plan raises questions about the viability of the project as a whole. Good project management disciplines usually include 'quality gates' or 'go/no go' decision points that ensure the plan is workable. Strike a balance between a plan that is too sketchy and a plan that frightens people in its depth. Look again at Figure 8.4. This was developed into a more detailed plan with timelines.

Work stream:

Key work stream achievements and highlights:

Key questions (Tasks in progress):

1. Has scope of the tasks changed?	Yes/No
2. Will target dates be hit?	Yes/No
3. Any technical problems?	Yes/No
4. Any review and approval problems?	Yes/No
5. Any alignment and integration concerns?	Yes/No

Last week's work stream tasks and activities:

Task	*Activity*	*Progress*

Work stream tasks and activities for this week:

Task	*Activity*

Summary from resource schedule:

Previous week (31)	*Organization*	*Consultants*	*Current week (32)*	*Organization*	*Consultants*
Planned			Planned		
Actual			Actual		

Milestone status:

Milestone	*Agreed date*	*Delivered date*	*Reason for revision (as per scope change request)*	*Revised date*

Figure 8.5 Project status report form

2. The ten principles of good design provide a thought-provoking check for your plan. They are discussed in more detail later in this chapter. Review the principles with the teams and your sponsor. If this raises issues and concerns, work on addressing these before you start the implementation process.

   You are likely to have a good design if you have followed the participative, collaborative, iterative, and integrative approaches this methodology advocates. You will not have a good design if you have imposed your thoughts without consultation, rushed into the re-design without reflection, or skipped some stages.

3. Walk through the design by taking some typical pieces of work or work processes (ones you will be doing when you have implemented your design) and map them to the new state. This will enable you to identify obstacles or bottlenecks. You will also be able to see if the new design achieves your objectives and remains within the boundaries you have set.

4. Do an alignment diagnosis (see Tool 1). This is to make sure that you think logically about each element of your re-design in relation to each other element. Look for consistency and coherence. Check that all the elements combine to generate the outcomes you have determined are critical to your success. Often this exercise uncovers misalignments (sometimes substantial ones) which you must address before proceeding. An unaligned system is not robust. Do the exercise with all your team members present.

5. Communicate with the organization and with stakeholders. This aspect is covered in Chapters 6 and 7.

Your Roles in Phase Three

In phase three the line manager switches between strategic management, tactical management, and operational management as appropriate. The HR practitioner takes the role of alternative identifier, joint problem solver, and trainer/educator. Figure 8.6 illustrates this.

Let us discuss the manager first. Start with the strategic role. You may find it difficult to take this on if you stay preoccupied with solving current problems and operational details. Lift yourself out of current state and into future state. This focuses your energy on what could be rather than what is. Future thinking begins with the customer demands. From this perspective, adopt strategic big picture 'outside-in' thinking. This

Organization design phase	Manager activity	HR practitioner activity

Creating the high-level design and the detailed design	▪ Initiating the design process
	▪ Keeping a firm grip on the progress of the design via the high-level and detailed-level teams
	▪ Intervening and stepping back appropriately Keeping the day-to-day business running
		▪ Helping manager and project teams define and agree
		  – Core business purpose
		  – Unique selling point
		  – Vision, mission, and objectives
		  – Principles
		  – Boundary statements
		  – Critical success factors
		  – Measures of success
		  – Target areas – processes, systems, technologies, facilities skills, culture, and people
		▪ Working with the project manager to manage the assignment including creating the project structure and plan, process mapping, identifying issues and opportunities for improvement

Figure 8.6 Phase three – Manager and HR practitioner activity

frames your design and the detail fits within. Tactical and operational perspectives will not build a sustainable design.

Interviewed, Robert Hanson, President of Levi's US brand makes this point:

> ***Think about the view from 2050.*** *When reenergizing Levi's staff, Hanson steers clear of 3-year plans. Instead, he talks about what Levi's will be remembered for in the year 2050. He wants his staffers to think about the legacies that they want to leave – not about tomorrow's sales numbers. Having a legacy will help them know what to do today, 5 years, and 10 years from now, 'I want the jeans that we create today to be in the Smithsonian in 50 years,' Hanson says. 'That's our challenge inside this company: to have an impact on American culture.'*
>
> Warner, F. (2002). Levi's fashions a new strategy.
Fast Company, November.

Once you have the big picture, take on the tactical and operational roles to get the project moving. Do not immerse yourself in the design detail leave that to team members, but do ensure that meetings are happening that the pace is being maintained and that motivation and energy are high.

Work with the sponsor and stakeholders, influencing them, converting them, and ensuring you can count on their support.

Now let us discuss the HR practitioner's role. Facilitate the design teams in their sessions. Concentrate on keeping the pace of the project, parking issues and returning to them, holding people's attention, giving them time to reflect, and then refining their thinking. Stop people over-analysing the current state. Coach your line manager and high-level team in stakeholder lobbying and painting the big picture.

Assess how your organization has previously tackled change to identify potential derailers of your project. Teach people to learn from the past. The HR practitioner working at Levi Strauss answers a question on their assessment as follows:

So many efforts like this fail. What steps did you take early on to improve the odds of success?

We did a fascinating exercise, midway through the design phase. We took 70 veteran managers from across the company and reviewed every major change program in our history. We went off-site for 2 days. We wrote on easels, filled up flip charts, basically created storyboards of change. Then we analysed which programs had worked, which hadn't, and why.

We reached two conclusions. One, we're much better at starting change than finishing it. We get people excited, charge forward, then somehow the momentum evaporates.

The second conclusion – and this had a real impact on us – was that we haven't done a good job preparing people for change. That doesn't mean sloganeering. It means getting down to the level of real human beings. What do they worry about? What gets them excited? What new skills and behaviours do they need?

So we created a collection of resources to help people move forward: videos, seminars, workbooks, self-diagnostics. You can't expect people to change if you don't give them the tools. But we don't spoon-feed materials to anyone. We create opportunities for people to change, but we can't change them. They have to change themselves.

Sheff, D. (1996). Levi's changes everything.
Fast Company, June/July.

Together (line manager and HR practitioner) you have the role of ensuring that the overall design programme is consistent and integrated, that it is running effectively (taking into account other project interdependencies) and is on track to meet milestones. Work with the project manager to make sure all bases are covered and appropriate action taken if not. The items to pay careful attention to are:

- Project baseline
- Resource schedule and allocation
- Inter work stream dependencies and assumptions and communication on these
- Risks to the project and the deployment of appropriate strategies to avoid risks
- Co-ordination and focus of the project teams' efforts
- Impact assessments on risk and issues
- Reporting of work stream and project status
- Proactive management of dependencies
- Recording of project expenditure
- Highlighting of and accounting for project budget variances.

Not Enough Time

Senge (1999) writes with insight on the challenge of not enough time. He points out that a change project will fail if people do not commit time to it and that the time required to undertake a re-design initiative will not shrink. He makes a number of suggestions on how to think differently about time use in order to make it more flexible and available. Here are eight of the many strategies he presents that have proved effective on OD projects.

Integrate initiatives: Combine several different initiatives, even if they started with different champions and participants. The goal is to enable progress on key issues and arrive at a commonly shared future. Integrating initiatives also reduces the risk of issues with interfaces, overlap, and duplication (see Tool 2).

Block off time for focus and concentration: Organize working and design sessions in blocks of time. A one-day workshop is far more intense and productive than two half-days. Time blocks (particularly off-site with a ban on mobile phone and BlackBerry use) encourage people to reflect and concentrate.

Trust people to control their own use of time: Those you ask to work on the project have to manage the balance of keeping their 'day-job' going and doing the design work. Managing the competing demands is hard going and not helped if you try to manage their time for them. Allow people to schedule themselves and reward them on results. Let people schedule their own time, you will find it builds motivation and trust.

Recognize the value of unstructured time: People who work on design projects must keep the pace up. They have to meet deadlines and targets. Too tight a focus on this is counter-productive. People's productivity increases if they meet each other casually to compare notes, see how things are going, and discuss concerns or issues. Without the pressure to rush into a decision or produce immediate results they can sometimes solve problems and gain insights to the benefit of the project.

Build the capability to eliminate unnecessary tasks: Organizations now expect one person to do the same work that several people used to do. For example, managers now share secretarial support or have none. The Chief Information Officer of a large agency trying to initiate a significant OD project remarked that he was doing all the administrative work himself, including writing the business cases, designing the presentations, inputting them into Visio (a software package), doing the room scheduling for meetings and so on. Additionally he was doing his 'day-job'.

As you initiate the project, eliminate some work. For example, stop the generation of reports that no one reads. Cancel regularly scheduled meetings that have no specific purpose or decision-making role. Decide whether you have to attend all the meetings in your diary.

Say 'no' to political game playing: Check that what you do is not about giving bosses the design you think they want, but about delivering value to customers. Lobbying and influencing stakeholders to support your project might involve politics and game playing but keep your focus on the interests of the organization and the customer. Maintain your integrity and demonstrate openness and fairness in your dealings. Unfortunately, in some organizations, this approach may be a 'career limiter'. Only you can make decisions around this.

Say 'no' to non-essential demands: Check that what you do is best use of your time. If something non-essential is in your basket do you need to do it? Distinguish between urgent and important. Cut out the non-essentials to give yourself more unstructured time. Let people know your views on time and encourage them to use yours wisely.

Experiment with time: Ask questions about time use in your organization. Miller (2001) suggests that personal accountability begins with asking a 'what' or 'how' question, contains an 'I' and focuses on action. Try this with questions about time use. Answer the questions 'If our purpose is vital, how can I avoid wasting the time we have to achieve it?' Assess the problems with time flexibility – what controls the amount of time you have available. Take meetings, for example – answer these questions for yourself:

- How does this meeting absolutely require my attendance?
- What will I specifically contribute to it?
- What value will I add to my job if I attend?
- How else could I make any necessary contribution?
- What can I do to make this an effective meeting?
- How will I be able to exploit or develop any of my strengths and skills in this meeting?

Assess the value of the meeting before agreeing to attend. Take any actions your 'what' and 'how' questions suggest to you.

Ten Principles of Good Design

In *Images of Organization*, Morgan (1997) brings out the design and management implications of viewing organizational problems from different perspectives in a way that helps develop approaches to organization that can lead to substantial changes in social life. Viewing organizations as organisms leads him to imply that well-designed organizations have:

Customer focus: Enable sets of people working together to produce and deliver products and services that meet customer requirements in the context of changing environments. This means building flexibility and adaptability to changing customer needs into the design.

Empowered and autonomous units: Design units around whole pieces of work – complete products, services or processes. The goal is to maximize interdependence within the work unit and minimize interdependence among work units. Taking this approach supports team-based working that motivates staff and tends to minimize overlap and duplication. The danger here is that 'silo' thinking springs up and people lose sight of the whole picture.

Clear direction and goals: Describe for each unit a very clear purpose, defined output requirements, and agreed on performance measures. People must know where they are going, why they are going there, what they have to do, and how you will evaluate them.

Control of variance at source: Design work processes so you are able to detect and control variances (errors) at source. This is a basic quality requirement implying that you provide the work unit with the information and tools to detect and prevent error before it gets anywhere down the line.

Social and technical integration: Think of the whole system and not the individual parts. Design work must link the social and technical systems. Technical systems include workflow, movement of information, work processes. As you design within your part of the organization focus on discreet organizational sub-systems as well as pan-organizational processes. The whole organization has to be able to work in concert. With this in mind, find ways to influence change in the wider system.

Accessible information flow: Design the flows of information carefully. Work unit members must be able to create, receive, and transmit information as needed. Without good formal and informal flows of information up, down, and across the organization the potential for conflict and misunderstanding arises.

Enriched and shared jobs: Give people broad jobs. Parcel up the work in a way that allows increased autonomy, learning, and individual motivation. Narrow jobs stifle people's creativity and lead to boredom. Broader jobs develop people. Beware, however, of giving people large parcels without thinking carefully enough about the content. More must also be better.

Good people management practices: Foster good people management practices through your design. This means thinking through the performance appraisal processes, the reward and recognition systems, and the career development opportunities. Chapter 12 talks in more detail about the people implications of re-design.

Management structures, processes, and cultures that support high performance: Achieve high performance by designing open and flexible management systems where you are concerned with achieving alignment and 'good fit'. Typical high performance structures are matrix or team based.

Capacity to reconfigure: Design your organization to be flexible and adaptable. In an environment that is changing at an increasing pace there is an advantage for those who can anticipate and respond to market forces quickly. Marks & Spencer is an example of a company that has experienced trouble doing this:

Commenting on performance (January 2004), Roger Holmes, then Chief Executive said:

'Total sales were marginally down this quarter, with growth in Food sales offset by a disappointing clothing performance, down 3.3%, of which 2% was volume. Stock commitments were well controlled and gross margin gains will be delivered as planned.'

'The fall in clothing sales was driven by a weak performance in certain key Womenswear areas, notably knitwear, coats and suits, where our ranges were not strong enough and the warm weather had significant impact. Where the product was right, such as in per una and casualwear, we achieved strong sales growth.'

Useful Tools

Tool 1: Alignment Diagnosis (adapted from Pfeffer 1998)
This is a five-step process. Do it with your design teams when you think they have got the full design ready.

Step 1: Consider all the elements of your re-design, including:
- vision/purpose/mission
- objectives for the next year or two

- strategies for achieving the objectives
- boundaries
- principles
- skills and competencies needed
- reward and recognition systems
- new ways of working
- market proposition and customers
- processes
- communications
- culture
- technologies and systems.

Step 2: Plot these (together with any other critical elements) on the vertical and horizontal axis of a grid, to form a matrix (Figure 8.7).

Step 3: Assess the extent to which these are internally consistent (logically related to each other) and externally consistent in aiming to produce the performance necessary for the effective implementation of your strategy.

You can do this by answering the following question: 'Does each element of the organization fit with each other element to make all work in the best possible way? (And how do you know this?)'. You can use a simple rating scheme for this as there may not be clear-cut yes/no answers.

For example – a strategy based on fast cycle times and being first to market with new products or services requires from employees a sense of time, urgency, and ability to innovate. Your reward and recognition systems therefore must specifically reward people for demonstrating these competencies. Your new ways of working must encourage people to be able to use these competencies in the workplace, and so on.

	Purpose	**Objectives**	**Strategy**	**Etc.**
Purpose	x			
Objectives		X		
Strategy			x	
Etc.				

Figure 8.7 Alignment matrix

	Teamwork	Problem solving	Caring	Flexibility	Etc.
Reward and recognition					

Figure 8.8 Alignment specifics

Step 4: Where there are indicators of misalignment, break down the elements into more specific components and identify where the misalignment is. For example, you have noted that your reward and recognition systems do not square with your strategy of fast cycle times. You need to find out where the problem lies. Ask what skills and behaviours are needed to deliver fast cycle times. On a second matrix (Figure 8.8) list these out. Note where (and where not) the reward and recognition system supports those skills and behaviours you need.

Having identified, perhaps, that the reward and recognition system does not support teamwork (which you have identified is required to deliver a strategy of fast cycle times) you might then ask what other elements of the re-design do (or do not) support teamwork.

Step 5: Continue the diagnosis as far as you need to uncover the major elements of misalignment.

Tool 2: Inventory of Change

Follow this process to align the range of changes that are happening outside the scope of your OD project. Do this in order to gain additional leverage for your project and to ensure that changes are co-ordinated wherever possible.

Process to follow:
1. Identify other planned or happening changes where the implementation of these will impact your project and stakeholders.
2. List the purpose and objectives of each of the other projects looking for conflicts and overlaps with yours.
3. Run workshops or focus groups for the sponsors of existing initiatives encouraging them to align with each other's (and your) projects, remove conflicts, minimize duplication, and co-ordinate implementation.

4. Review implementation timetables for each initiative and produce a matrix that shows when they will affect particular groups or locations. Where the timetables are unknown make some assumptions and plan for best and worst case impacts.
5. Look for instances of potential overload or things being delivered in the wrong order. For example, national installation of new procedures preceding some locations having the equipment installed to make these work.
6. Recommend ways of aligning, channelling, or integrating activity in the interests of the whole organization.
7. Log and circulate the overall implementation timetable highlighting any assumptions of critical dates.
8. Review this timetable regularly.

Tool 3: Alternative Scenarios (From http://www.mycoted.com)
Scenarios are qualitatively different descriptions of plausible futures. They give you a deeper understanding of future environments that you may have to operate in. Scenario analysis helps you to identify what environmental factors to monitor over time, so that when the environment shifts, you can recognize where it is shifting to.

Thinking through several scenarios is a less risky, more conservative approach to planning than relying on single forecasts and trend analyses. It can thus free up management to take more innovative actions.

Develop scenarios for your particular re-design. To begin developing scenarios:

1. Paint the specific vision of the future state.
2. Identify the major internal and external environmental forces that impact your product, service, or customers in the future state. For example, suppose your service is investing R&D funds. You have decided to position your organization for opportunities that might emerge by the year 2010. The major external environmental forces might include social values, economic growth worldwide and international trade access (tariffs, etc.).
3. Build four scenarios based on the principal forces. To do this, use information available to you to identify four plausible and qualitatively different possibilities for each force. Assemble the alternatives for each force into internally consistent 'stories', with both a narrative and a table of forces and scenarios. Build your scenarios around

these forces. For instance, a mid-western bank used scenarios to stimulate new ideas for maintaining a strong consumer-lending business in upcoming deregulation. Scenario story lines emerged for 'As at present', 'Heated', 'Belt Tightening' and 'Isolation'.

4. With the scenarios in hand, identify business opportunities and design options within each scenario.

5. Examine the links and synergies of opportunities across the range of scenarios. This would help you to formulate a more realistic strategy for investment and an organization design that fits your purpose.

Self-check

By this stage, you should be feeling confident that you are at the end of the design phase and are ready to move into handling the transition. Read the questions below (adapted from Senge 1999). When you can say 'yes' to the majority of them you have completed the design phase.

Are you certain of the results you want the new design to produce? Have a clear vision of the changed organization and what you want it to deliver. Ensure your stakeholders and your sponsor share this vision. Check that it aligns with other initiatives current or planned.

Do you know how the new design will make your business performance more effective? Specify what it is you are planning to make more effective, for example turnaround time, ease of customer use, or innovative product.

> *At a time when many global companies are hunkering down and retrenching, BMW is moving forward, placing a big bet that it has a winning design for future growth. Companies typically take risks because there is no other option: Their backs are against the wall and there's no choice but to change. BMW is making bold moves at the very peak of its success. 'Carmakers are running up against a very tough choice,' observes brand analyst Will Rodgers, cofounder of SHR Perceptual Management. 'Either they protect their market share and play not to lose, like GM and Toyota, or they go all out, place some big bets, and play to win. BMW is playing to win.'*
>
> Breen, B. (2002). BMW: Driven by design.
> *Fast Company*, September.

Do you know how the new design will benefit your customers? Focus on your customers and their needs to get a design that works. There is a wonderful (perhaps apocryphal) story about London Transport who designed a system guaranteed to get the buses to operate on time. Managers implemented the new systems and were delighted at the way drivers got to the depots on time. Passengers were less delighted. Investigation proved that bus drivers no longer stopped to pick up the passengers as getting to the depot on time had become the objective.

Do you know what values and attitudes might have to change to make the new design work? Changing values and attitudes is a long and tricky process with no guarantees of success. Aim to keep value and attitude change to a minimum. Focus instead on behaviour change and hope that any needed values and attitude change follows.

Do you know what effect the new design will have on aspects of your current work and practices? If you recognize the impact, you will be able to handle it and communicate it effectively. British Airways appeared to mishandle a situation with check-in staff when it tried to introduce swipe cards.

> *The scenes of chaos at Heathrow have prompted pundits to complain about British Airways' poor response to the walk-out. Yet while airlines can plan for official strikes, a spontaneous action by a few hundred workers irritated at having to clock on and off with electronic swipe cards is hard to predict. British Airways is introducing the computerised swipe-card system so that it can switch staff more quickly to where they are needed, e.g., when queues lengthen in some parts of a terminal.*
>
> *The Economist* (31 July 2003). One strike and you're out.

Are you confident that people are expressing their doubts, concerns, and issues honestly and openly so that the new organization is not sabotaged? This may be difficult to judge (as British Airways managers found). Keep your ear to the ground and be alert to rumours and sudden 'noise' in the informal communications channels. Ensure communications channels are kept open and people feel you listen to them.

Do you know what capabilities you need to develop to make the new organization work? Analyse your current skill base against your future state skill base. This will give you the gap between the two. Ensuring you have the right supply of capability to match the demand of your business strategy is part of the people planning work that forms one of the work streams of most OD projects. It is a topic covered in more detail in Chapter 12.

Are you confident that people will change enough to make the new organization work? This depends on whether you have convinced people that staying the way they are is not an option for survival. The airline industry is a good example of people changing in line with circumstances.

> *The surprising development there has been that unions at United, US Airways and American Airlines – all faced with extinction – have begun to make previously unthinkable concessions. These have helped to bring high operating costs down by more than a third, to a point where they can compete with more successful low-cost American carriers, such as Southwest, AirTran and JetBlue.*
>
> *The Economist* (31 July 2003). One strike and you're out.

Do you know when you must show results from the new design (and what these should be)? You may have an externally imposed timetable, or it may be self-imposed. Once you declare your plans you will have to deliver against them. Make sure that you aim for achievable stretch. Keep stakeholders informed of progress so you can regroup if necessary without causing surprise.

Is your organization ready to embrace the new design? If you have done your job well to this point people will be ready (if not eager) to transition to the new organization. People ready to change have been involved, motivated, and heard. They feel there is something in it for them.

Do's and Don'ts

- Do allow enough time to work on the organization design
- Do work through an iterative process engaging people as you go
- Do clarify the interfaces with service partners and/or other departments
- Don't get derailed because of poor communication
- Don't impose your design ideas – work with others
- Don't neglect the 'day-job' in favour of the design work

Summary – The Bare Bones

- Set up two levels of design team: the high level and the detail level
- Develop several design options within the boundaries you have set
- Get sponsor and stakeholder support for the preferred option
- Establish teams to develop detailed design and implementation plans for each work stream key to your overall design
- Work on an iterative basis, until you have a full system design that you are confident, will deliver your future state vision
- Test your design for workability and alignment before going into the implementation phase

References/Useful Reading

Gleick, J. (1999). *Faster: The Acceleration of Just About Everything*. Pantheon.

Miller, J. G. (2001). *QBQ! The Question Behind the Question*. Denver Press.

Miller, W. C. (1990). *The Creative Edge: Fostering Innovation Where You Work*. Addison Wesley Publishing Company.

Mills, Albert (2001). *Gareth Morgan: Sociological Paradigms and Organizational Analysis*. Aurora Online.

Morgan, G. (1997). *Images of Organization*. Sage.

Pfeffer, J. (1998). *The Human Equation: Building Profits by Putting People First*. Harvard Business School Press.

Senge, P. (1999). *The Dance of Change*. Nicholas Brearley.

9

Risk

'It is not enough to identify and quantify risks. The idea is to manage them.'
Lewis, J. P. (1998). *Mastering Project Management.*
McGraw Hill Professional Book Group.

Overview

You have heard the statement that '95% of change projects fail'. Identifying and managing the risks associated with organization design and re-design goes some way towards keeping your project out of the 'failure' box – a situation to avoid if you are to keep your stakeholders happy and add organizational value from your work.

In any project, there is a level of uncertainty about achieving the project's objectives on a quality, cost, time, or other basis. This uncertainty is project risk – defined variously. For example, Shell Group's definition is 'those factors which could influence the achievement of business objectives, either positively or negatively.' Marks & Spencer's definition is 'events, actions, or missed opportunities which could impact on the project's ability to achieve its objectives.' Both definitions are clearly about something going wrong or right in relation to achievement of objectives and the creation or protection of value.

Risk management is particularly important to handle carefully in organization design and other change projects. People have emotional reactions to changes that affect them and emotional reactions are hard to predict. This increases the risk for change projects if the plan does not deliver the intended benefit, or if the project planning and transition to new state seriously disrupt normal business operation, or if relationships are fractured or broken because of the change.

Having measures of the impact risks on your project is essential. Monitor them throughout the project to help determine whether to continue with aspects, identify where you have to pay close attention, highlight project improvement opportunities, and manage risk mitigation.

This chapter guides you through the process of managing the business risks associated with your OD project. Presented are six steps: understanding the context, clarifying the objectives, identifying risks, assessing risks, responding to risks, and sustaining risk control – the action plan. For the most part risks are not objectively quantifiable; nevertheless, a systematic approach to managing them works well. Figure 9.1 (adapted from: Marks & Spencer 2002) illustrates the risk cycle.

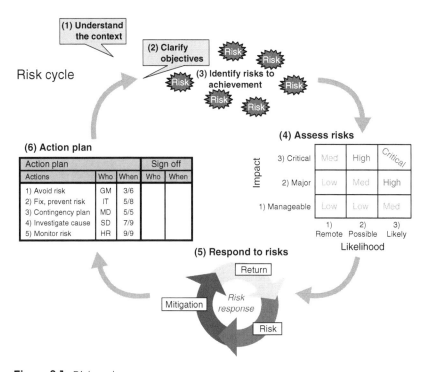

Figure 9.1 Risk cycle

Thinking about Risk: Understanding the Context, Clarifying the Objectives, Identifying Risks

The work you have already done in establishing your OD project has given you a good understanding of your business context. Aspects you have considered include:

- the nature of your part of the organization (products, services, customers, market position, and so on);
- the internal culture and operating style of your organization;
- the external forces that work for and against it;
- the boundaries and operating principles of the OD project.

You may already have completed a STEEP (social, technological, economic, environmental, and political) analysis. As you think about risk just check that you have considered the business context from enough angles. Two aspects that STEEP does not cover are:

1. the operational environment which includes the way your organization functions – aspects of cost management, capacity, efficiency, inventory management, HR, and so on;
2. the cognitive environment – which includes mindset, group interactions, trust, attitudes, judgement, corporate memory, etc.

Another way of understanding your business context is to look at it from the five types of risks that you are exposed to. Figure 9.2 presents these.

Consider your organizational context from more than one angle to give you a breadth of perspective and a diversity of view. Over the course of your project review the context you operate in. It is constantly changing. One way of doing this is to keep open dialogue and communication with a range of internal and external stakeholders.

You have already completed a good deal of work on clarifying and communicating the objectives of the OD project and the changes it will bring. You know what expectations you have set, and you know what you must deliver or what your key performance indicators are. Assuming design teams are working well together you will have milestones that

1. *Physical asset exposures* (e.g., motor vehicles, buildings, computers, inventories, brand equity, revenue, and expense flows)

2. *Financial asset exposures* (e.g., money, investment instruments, debt obligations, derivatives, and insurance)

3. *Human asset exposures* (e.g., employees, managers, board members, and key stakeholders)

4. *Legal liability exposures* (e.g., directors and officers liability, employment discrimination, product liability, and environmental impairment liability)

5. *Moral liability exposures* (e.g., ethical and value-based commitments and obligations)

Young, P. C. and Tippins, S. C. (2001). *Managing Business Risk.* Amacom.

Figure 9.2 Five types of risk

Specific: The 'fuzzier' an objective, the more likely it is to be misunderstood, or to be interpreted in different ways. Clarity, detail, and precise language will assist in consistency and focus.

Measurable: What is the end state, and how will you know when you have reached it? A scorecard, target or other means of measuring performance will make it possible to monitor what has been done, and what has yet to be done. What is not measured will probably not get done.

Aligned: Within and across entities, take care to ensure that the objectives of each of the 'parts' are designed to support the objectives of the 'whole'. For example, all Shell business objectives must be consistent with the Statement of General Business Principles (SGBP). This alignment is often accomplished via a cascading process, where high-level objectives are set first, followed by successive levels of detailed objectives. It is important to recognize where objectives are in conflict, so that they may either be revised or priorities established.

Realistic: Objectives are likely to drive desired action and behaviour when those who are responsible for their achievement see them as achievable. While a 'stretch target' may encourage people to test their limits and develop their capability, an 'impossible target' could lead to frustration and an 'easy target' could lead to under-performance.

Timely: Timeliness is important from two perspectives. First, the 'when' of an objective should be clear – what is the time horizon over which the results will be achieved? Second, conditions change, and no objective is likely to last forever; therefore objectives must be revisited regularly to ensure their continued validity and desirability. Shell International Limited (2000). *Risk Policy and Guidelines.*

Figure 9.3 Shell International's SMART objectives

measure your progress, towards achieving your targets. You will be communicating your objectives regularly to your stakeholders.

However, check again that you have clear objectives for your project – ones that are SMART. Figure 9.3 presents Shell International's description of SMART objectives.

Once you know your context and are clear on your objectives, you create a list of risks. Do this by holding a brainstorming session (see Tool 1). Remember risks are things that influence for good or ill the achievement of your objectives.

Getting Started – Analysing, Assessing, and Responding to Risks

Once you think you have your list of risks ask yourself some challenging questions:

- Does the list feel comprehensive enough?
- Does it reflect various areas of risk?
- Does it include internal and external risks?
- How does it compare with the risk lists of other similar and different projects in your organization?
- Does it reflect the input of a range of stakeholders?

Be aware that however long you spend on generating a list it will never be comprehensive and you will never be able to assess all the risks. As the context changes the risks change. Shell International compares the risk landscape to a bubbling pot – always in continuous movement with some risks coming to the top and others simmering just below the surface.

When you have satisfied yourself that the list is complete enough you start analysing and assessing the risks. At this point, you find that people's attitudes to risk vary enormously – some people are risk averse and others are risk takers. As you and your stakeholders discuss the risks on your list, you will see what different perspectives there are on the same listed item.

Help stakeholders acknowledge their different perspectives by encouraging them to do the risk attitude assessment (Tool 2). You will see that the diversity of view makes for heated debate. Aim to come to a mutual understanding on which risks are acceptable and which are unacceptable to your project. As you do this bear in mind that because the environment is dynamic what might be an acceptable risk today will be unacceptable tomorrow. Hence, ensure you re-assess regularly.

Likelihood weighting	Description
1	Remote
2	Possible
3	Likely

Figure 9.4 Likelihood weighting

Impact weighting	Description
0–3	Minimal impact – integration can continue even if this risk arises
4–6	Will cause a significant amount of extra work to keep the integration on course
7–9	Will directly affect the successful integration

Figure 9.5 Impact weighting

There are myriad tools available in the market to help you assess and monitor risk. Choose a tool that is fit for your purpose. You do not need to buy an expensive software package if a straightforward spreadsheet works. The assessment process starts by answering the question; 'which risks are the most significant?' Do this by working out which will have the most impact on your project and which are the most likely to occur.

Two methods are outlined below. First a two-factor risk assessment.

For each risk on your list, calculate a risk factor to determine whether actions are required to contain or mitigate it. Do this by first agreeing on the likelihood of the risk occurring and second agreeing the impact of the risk if it does occur.

The scale shown in Figure 9.4 quantifies the likelihood of the risk occurring.

The scale shown in Figure 9.5 quantifies the impact of the risk on the integration if the risk does occur.

The risk factor is the sum of the likelihood multiplied by the impact. The risks are then categorized according to their risk factors as green, amber, or red (Figure 9.6).

If the resultant sum places the risk in the green category, then no action is likely to be required. If the risk is in the amber category, then a discussion around whether or not to accept the risk needs to take

Risk factor	Risk category	Risk action
0–9	Green	Ignore
10–17	Amber	Discuss
18–27	Red	Manage

Figure 9.6 Risk factor

Raised by:	Project:	Date logged:
Summary of risk: enter a brief description of the risk such that it is immediately recognizable		
Description of risk and impact: enter a full description of the risk and the impact that it has on the project		
Issue/risk owner: enter the owner who is responsible for implementing the containment plan		Status: enter 'open', 'closed',or 'unresolved'. Enter initially as 'open'
Likelihood (0–3)	Impact (0–9)	Risk factor (likelihood × impact)
Containment plan: enter a detailed description of the plan to reduce the likelihood of the risk		
Action plan: enter the action to take if the risk arises		
Dependencies: enter any risk dependencies that you must manage		

Figure 9.7 Risk notification form

place. If the risk is in the red category, then risk mitigation actions are required and you must complete a risk notification form (Figure 9.7). Note that when you have discussed the risks in the amber category you may decide to manage some of these and you will then move them to the red category and complete a risk notification form for them too.

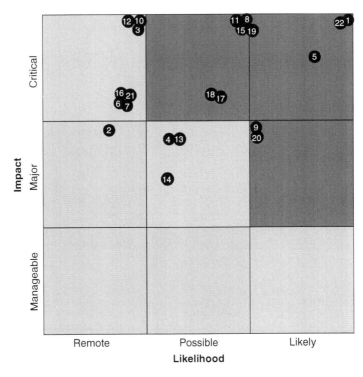

Figure 9.8 Risk matrix example

Completing the risk notification form (Figure 9.7) involves you planning what to do to reduce the probability of the risk arising, and/or to reduce the impact if the risk does arise.

Using this method your project manager maintains and regularly updates a risk register compiled from the risk notification forms. Eliminate the risk when you have reduced the risk factor to less than 10 either by management, or by control, or by changing circumstances.

You can make your scales more detailed or keep them simple. This form of assessment is easy to map onto a matrix (Figure 9.8) where the vertical axis is impact and the horizontal axis is likelihood, with a high, medium, and low ranking on each. Agree with your team on your definitions of 'high', 'medium', and 'low' – they are relative to the scope and scale of your project. The matrix becomes a very powerful visual tool for seeing the big picture of risks and their relative relationships. (On Figure 9.8. the numbers are the ID numbers of the identified risks.)

Likelihood	Probability of occurring	Rank
Very high	1 in 2	10
	1 in 3	9
High	1 in 8	8
	1 in 20	7
Moderate	1 in 80	6
	1 in 400	5
	1 in 2000	4
Low	1 in 15 000	3
	1 in 150 000	2
Remote	1 in 1 500 000	1

Figure 9.9 Likelihood ranking

Figure 9.9 illustrates a more detailed ranking of likelihood. Figure 9.10 illustrates a more detailed ranking of impact (adapted from: Lewis 1998).

Second, a three-factor assessment. With this method, you make your scales more detailed and add a third ranking – prediction capability (i.e. the ease of predicting that the risk is going to occur before it actually takes place).

Some things you can predict with high certainty. For example, you can predict that your car will stop running when your petrol tank reaches empty. Other events are harder to predict – a wildcat strike, for example. When you rank the prediction capability note that the scale is reversed; that is, the more certain it is that you can detect a hazard, the lower the number. Rank the prediction capability on the scale shown in Figure 9.11.

In this three-factor approach for each risk that you have identified, multiply likelihood by impact by prediction capability. The sum of this is a risk probability number (RPN). The more critical the risk, the higher the number is. As in the two-factor analysis you then group the risks. Figure 9.12 shows the RPN ranking on three projects within the same OD programme grouped in the categories critical and high. (The risks categorized as medium or low are not shown.)

Impact	Severity of effect	Rank
Hazardous without warning	Project severely impacted possibly cancelled without warning	10
Hazardous with warning	Project severely impacted possibly cancelled with warning	9
Very high	Major impact on project schedule, budget, or performance, may cause severe delays, over-runs, or degradation of performance	8
High	Project schedule, budget, or performance impacted significantly. Job can be completed but customer will be very dissatisfied	7
Moderate	Project schedule, budget, or performance impacted some. Customer will be dissatisfied	6
Low	Project schedule, budget, or performance impacted slightly. Customer will be mildly dissatisfied	5
Very low	Some impact to project, customer will be aware of impact	4
Minor	Small impact to project, average customer will be aware of impact	3
Very minor	Impact so small that it would be noticed only by a very discriminating customer	2
None	No effect	1

Figure 9.10 Impact ranking

You may find that risk assessment is more complex than at first sight. For example, a risk may have more than one outcome if it occurs, or the same risk could occur more than once. Take a common sense view of the factors you are considering. Use more (or less) sophisticated tools if you feel your case warrants it.

Once you have assessed the risks to your project you must respond to them. That is you take action to mitigate their effect. For example, you could plan to manage high RPN risks by taking actions that would lower the likelihood or impact and/or change your prediction ranking.

Other ways you could respond to a risk include the following:

■ Minimizing the likelihood of it occurring by actively managing the sources of the risk.

Prediction	Rank
Absolute uncertainty	10
Very remote	9
Remote	8
Very low	7
Low moderate	6
Moderate	5
Moderately high	4
High	3
Very high	2
Almost certain	1

Figure 9.11 Prediction capability

- Mitigating the impact of a risk often through some kind of alert that the risk has arisen and putting a recovery plan into operation. (Read the example below of a successful risk mitigation plan by Lehman Brothers.)
- Maximizing the likelihood of a risk occurring by taking action to exploit opportunities to make good outcomes more likely.
- Avoiding the risk altogether by making a decision to abort or delay something.
- Transferring the risk, for example to a third party through outsourcing, or by buying insurance cover.

Carefully consider the way you choose to respond. At the end of the day all your risks must be addressed in a way that best fits your circumstances and situation. The choice you make will be influenced by factors including:

- your business context;
- the objectives you are trying to achieve;
- the type of risk – whether it is a negative or a positive one;
- the significance of the risk (high, medium, or low, impact and likelihood);
- the 'risk appetite' – your level of willingness to accept the risk and the organizational boundaries for risk acceptance;

PROJECT RISK BANDING			CRITICAL		
RISK REFERENCE			1	2	3
PRIORITY PROJECTS			A	B	C
PROGRAMME RISKS					
Critical	1	**Governance structure**: lack of timely and consistent decision-making	800	700	750
	2	**Ineffective sponsor**: unable to deliver with pace and resource with appropriate expertise on a timely basis	680	530	620
	3	**Lack of clear accountability at the top**: unclear accountability for projects by sponsors, Executive Director level, disturbance of multiple stakeholders	740	540	670
	4	**Organizational structure**: personal agenda, bonus, and reward structure lead to political infighting	600	810	550
High	5	**Insufficient communication planning, early enough**: poor education and engagement of stakeholders	430	590	610
	6	**Disparity**: between operating plan and strategic plan	480	520	450

Figure 9.12 RPN ranking in example project

- the cost of managing the risk versus the benefit of doing so;
- your ability to influence the outcomes of your risk management decision;
- the way your organization has handled this type of risk in the past.

An example of a well thought through risk mitigation plan was reported as follows:

One of the most resilient firms after the 11th September attacks turned out to be Lehman Brothers, an investment bank, which had

> *offices just across the road from the World Trade Centre. Thanks to*
> *careful advance planning, it was able to set up shop elsewhere in*
> *New York almost immediately. Its computer systems allowed many*
> *of its staff to work from home, and others to set up shop in hotel*
> *rooms and rented space overnight. As a result, it came through the*
> *period after 11th September better than some of its competitors*
> *that suffered much less physical damage and disruption.*
>
> *The Economist*, 24 January 2004.

Shell International (2000) guides its managers to respond to risk using one of four strategies (or a combination of them). These are shown in Figure 9.13.

Responding to the risks you have identified results in an action plan. Ensure that you have a good method of logging and tracking the risks and actions in order to monitor, on a regular and ongoing basis, the progress of your risk containment activity. Figure 9.14 illustrates how you would keep a log. (These risks were first identified in relation to an acquisition project. They were ranked on the two-factor scale, and then logged as red, amber, or green.)

Figure 9.14 illustrates one logging method. There are others that you can use. Be careful, however, not to document your risk activity more than you act on the mitigation plan. The important things are to keep track of the risks, take actions to manage them, and review them regularly. The following section discusses methods of doing this for the duration of your project.

Sustaining Risk Control

Risk assessment is carried out at the start of the project and then at predetermined points within the project life span. This activity involves appraising the whole risk landscape for your project, reviewing the risks, evaluating them again if necessary, considering any changes in the context that have occurred since the last assessment, checking that the day-to-day management of risks is working effectively and efficiently. This exercise does two things, first lets you know if your risk management

TAKE	TREAT
To some extent, there is a degree of TAKE in response to most significant risks. Many cannot be avoided, and few can be practically and affordably reduced to zero likelihood/zero impact. For example, risks which are inherent to the company's operations will often be accepted, particularly those which are reasonably predictable. Intentionally taking risk in order to pursue or sustain higher returns is clearly an option. Whenever risk taking is significant, it should be explicitly stated, understood, and approved by an appropriate level of management. The level of risk which is intentionally taken is generally referred to as 'residual' or 'net' risk	Because the response to most significant risks will be active rather than passive, there will be some degree of TREAT in response to most significant risks. Options for risk TREATment are varied; they are divided here into five categories: Organization, People and Relationships, Direction, Operational, and Monitoring. As a general rule, selective and intentional application of elements from all five TREAT categories, interlinked with particular elements described under TAKE, TRANSFER, and TERMINATE, will result in reasonable assurance of achieving business objectives
TRANSFER	**TERMINATE**
It may be possible to reduce the impact of risks through various means of risk transfer. Risk transfer decisions will depend upon the nature of the business, the criticality of the operation or service associated with the risk, and cost/benefit considerations. Explicit and detailed understanding and agreement up-front is essential for effective risk transfer or sharing arrangements. It is important to note that transfer of risk does not result in transfer of accountability; the risk owner will remain accountable. Therefore it is important to combine risk TRANSFER arrangements with risk TREATments such as contracts, performance targets, competence, and performance reviews	Risks can be avoided, for instance by ceasing a particular activity or pulling out of a specific market. It is also possible to terminate some risks by changing the business objective or process. Some risks may be terminated in part through sale or divestment; however it is important to recognize whether all of the risks will indeed be terminated or whether some will remain with the business (e.g. environmental liabilities), and to structure contracts and actions accordingly

Figure 9.13 Risk responses

process needs adjustment and second tells you whether the risks you are managing are the 'right' ones in the current context.

Usually this form of assessment involves people both within and outside your project. Get independent input to your periodic appraisal to help you maintain the diversity of input.

ID#	Risk	Impact	Likelihood	Risk factor	Mitigating action	Action leaders	Date
1	We don't have an integration strategy	9	3	27			
22	They stick together as a group	9	3	27			
5	We don't take steps to ensure they don't get deskilled	8	3	24			
11	They don't have transition from independent to team-based philosophy	9	2	18			
15	We treat them as a group rather than as individuals	9	2	18			
4	We don't leverage their skills to help us get to our ideal culture	6	2	12			
14	We won't sell them into the organization individually	5	2	10			
10	We don't retain them after they've joined	9	1	9			
12	They don't subscribe to our values?	9	1	9			
16	We position them in a lower position than they're in now	7	1	7			
21	We don't have integrated information technology (IT) systems (connectivity issues – can we connect with each other?)	7	1	7			
6	We don't transfer their knowledge effectively to our staff	7	1	7			

Figure 9.14 Risks associated with acquisition

If your project is very large and/or complex, consider a whole project assurance plan. Marks & Spencer, for example, invited internal audit teams into change projects at various points in the project life cycle to provide an independent validation of the risk and other project control processes.

Risk management is a day-to-day activity during the life span of the project. Sustain your risk management processes and actions by:

■ Getting your team members and stakeholders to support them – this involves putting risk management on the agenda at each of your team and stakeholder meetings, ensuring regular reviews and re-assessments of the risks, judging the support you receive for the actions you take to mitigate the risks, and gaining the commitment of resources to support your risk management activity.

■ Integrating risk management activity with the project work streams – teams working on their specific aspect of the project must also work on the risks associated with it. Sometimes risk assessment becomes divorced from the work of the high-level and detail-level design teams, forming a work stream in its own right. Avoid taking this approach by making sure your project manager is logging and monitoring the risks associated with each stream of work. Keep an overview of all the risks to ensure consistent approaches to managing them and avoidance of overlap or duplication.

■ Communicating the risk management process – communicate to your organization your risk management approach, why you are taking it and your rationale for taking the actions that you are. Effective communication will help people understand and support your risk management strategy and alert them to their role in giving you timely information if they see the context changing.

■ Predicting, by reviewing your plan, at what points specific risks are likely to bubble to the top. (Risks rise and fall at specific stages of a project.)

Be alert to the fact that managing risk is only one aspect of your OD project. Sometimes people go 'over the top' in managing the risks, and control too much or too vigorously. The aim of risk management is to

---

Identify gaps and opportunities: Be realistic about the extent of problems, the efforts involved, and the anticipated benefits. Think about the risk/reward relationship – in some cases little effort may be needed to result in step changes.

Clearly define changes: Specify what is to be done differently, when and by whom. Define what will be impacted by the change in your risk management process.

Agree key changes: Seek consensus amongst those who will be affected by the change.

Determine actions and assign responsibilities: Identify 'quick wins' and changes that need to be project managed. Set appropriate deliverables, milestones, and checkpoints. Establish resource requirements and get commitments.

Implement changes: Set the wheels in motion. Provide guidance and support where needed.

Follow-up: Measure effectiveness, and demonstrate or communicate the effect of the change. Be prepared to refine the approach and to 'change the change' as necessary. Hold debriefs and build learning into future change efforts/projects.

Figure 9.15 Risk management guidelines

help and support project success. If people see it as bureaucratic overkill, it is not working effectively. Avoid the tendency to over-report or over-monitor. Keep the risk management process at a fit-for-purpose level. If you see resistance to your risk management methods, adapt your processes. Shell International (2000) offers guidelines (Figure 9.15) on adapting your risk management process.

In summary, follow common sense principles for managing your OD project risks. Bear in mind that you must work through the six steps of risk management: understanding the context, clarifying the objectives, identifying risks, assessing risks, responding to risks, and sustaining risk control. The next section presents some tools to help you do this.

Useful Tools

Tool 1: Brainstorming
This technique is good for generating new, useful insights, and promoting creative thinking. Use it to help identify what risks to work on. Have between six and eight participants. Try to have one who is familiar with project risk.

Step 1: Appoint a leader and a scribe.

Step 2: Frame the question you want the team to answer (e.g. what risks does this project face in the next 6 months which will help it succeed or fail?). Note that the question needs to be specific enough to help participants focus on the intent of the session, but it must be open enough to allow innovative thinking.

Step 3: The leader states the ground rules:

- All ideas are welcome. There are no wrong answers. During the session, no judgments should be made of ideas.
- Be creative in contributions. Change involves risk taking so be open to new, original ideas. Every point of view is valuable.
- Attempt to contribute a high quantity of ideas in a short amount of time.
- Try to 'hitch hike' on others' ideas.

Step 4: The scribe writes down every idea so that everyone present can see them.

Step 5: Follow a contribution procedure, for example:

- Team members will make one contribution each in turn.
- Keep the pace to generate as many ideas as possible. You may want to give a topic change every 5 min (e.g. first 5 min ideas around demographic risk, second 5 min ideas around stakeholder risk).
- A member may decline to contribute during a particular round.
- Participants should not provide explanations for the ideas they come up with. Doing so would both slow the process down, and allow premature evaluation of ideas.
- Set a time limit for the process – usually around 25 min. Stop when there is still a buzz.
- Review all the ideas making sure everyone understands each one.
- Group and/or combine ideas into the risk list.

Tool 2: Risk Attitude Assessment

(A) Questionnaire

- Take a moment to identify a **recent uncertain situation at work** that required you to make a decision.
- Now tick the statements below that most closely describe your approach to that uncertain situation.
- You may tick as many or as few statements as you like.

Uncertain situation:	

1.	I like being dependable, and I am usually punctual
2.	I am not likely to take chances
3.	I think about the future and have long range objectives
4.	I am resourceful and prefer not to plan or prepare
5.	I like action, and I act impulsively at all times
6.	I value institutions and observe traditions
7.	I like to anticipate another person's position
8.	I work best when I am inspired
9.	I am naturally curious and often ask why?
10.	I am more self-oriented than service oriented
11.	I am responsible and prefer to work efficiently
12.	I seek excitement for the thrill of the experience
13.	I am more service oriented than self-oriented
14.	I enjoy generating new ideas
15.	I trust my intuition and I am comfortable with the unknown

(B) Scoring Key

Handout *after* delegates complete the questionnaire.

The scoring key helps to determine your relative preference for being **risk seeking** (S), **risk neutral** (N), or **risk averse** (A).

*Score one **S** point for a tick on each of statements 4, 5, 7, 10, or 12*	*Score one **N** point for a tick on each of statements 3, 8, 9, 14, or 15*	*Score one **A** point for a tick on each of statements 1, 2, 6, 11, or 13*

- Count the number of S's, N's, and A's you have ticked. The scores reflect your preferred approach(es) to risk when faced with having to make a decision when uncertain.
- You may have a **high score** in just one area – this shows your preferred way of handling uncertainty. *Or* you may be high in two or even all three areas – you have several styles of response available, and must choose the most appropriate.
- A **low score** in any area suggests a type of response with which you are uncomfortable. Being aware of this may help you to identify types of decision where you need input from another person (preferably someone with a different risk style from you!).

The three basic risk attitudes are summarized below:

- *Risk seeking*: You have a liberal risk attitude with a preference for speculative payoffs. People who are risk seeking make good entrepreneurs and negotiators. If you are risk seeking, you are adaptable and resourceful. You enjoy life and are not afraid to take action. Performing, acting, and taking risks are activities at which you excel.
- *Risk neutral*: You have an impartial risk attitude with a preference for future payoffs. People who are risk neutral make good executives, system architects, and group leaders. Risk neutral types are neither risk averse nor risk neutral, you think abstractly and creatively and envisage the possibilities. You enjoy ideas and are not afraid of change or the unknown. Learning, imagining, and inventing are activities at which you excel.
- *Risk averse*: You have a conservative risk attitude with a preference for secure payoffs. People who are risk averse are practical, accepting and have common sense. You enjoy facts more than theories and support established methods of working. Remembering, persevering, and building are activities at which you excel.

Tool 3: Society for Risk Analysis Web site
The Society for Risk Analysis (www.sra.org) defines risk analysis to include risk assessment, risk characterization, risk communication, risk management, and policy relating to risk, in the context of risks of concern to individuals, to public and private sector organizations, and

to society at a local, regional, national, or global level. It publishes a journal on risk analysis and provides resources and information on the topic.

Self-check

Check how you are doing in managing your project risks by answering the questions below. If you can answer 'yes' to the majority of them you are doing a good job. Give yourself a pat on the back, but remember to revisit this aspect of your project regularly.

- Is there a shared understanding of the business environment? Aim to get as complete a picture as possible of your internal and external business environment. Keep your eyes and ears open for signs of big changes on the horizon (internally or externally) that you must consider. Ensure your stakeholders share your understanding of the context. If they do not, your assessments of the risks your project faces will be different.
- Are the business objectives clear? Frame your business objectives SMARTly. This way you get a good grip on the risks associated with each other. If your objectives are woolly or open to miscommunication the risks will be equally difficult to handle.
- How were the risks identified and assessed? Make certain that you have a range of input to the generation of your risk list. People have very different attitudes and responses to risk. Recognize these but also get a shared view of which risks are most significant.
- Does the risk profile seem to make sense, in the context of the business environment? Get clarity on the relationship between the risks and the business objectives. Make sure your stakeholders are aware of and agree the biggest risks.
- Is there clear ownership of each risk? Every risk must have an owner who is accountable for taking the mitigating action. Risks sometimes fall between the cracks if owners are unassigned or if they do not take accountability. If this happens, you are adding another risk to project success.
- Have the risks been communicated? Everyone in your organization should know what risks the project presents and understand

the implications of this. People involved either directly or indirectly with the project must be alert to new risks arising and present these to you in a timely fashion.

- Is there evidence you are managing them effectively? Ensure you have sensible but not over the top management processes. Aim to satisfy audit requirement in your monitoring and look for evidence that the mitigation action is reducing the risk by tracking its movement on your graphic or risk matrix.

- Is there a clear understanding of what risk responses are in place, and who is responsible for what? Give your project teams sight of the risk log. If team members are not familiar with risk management approaches make sure you train them to the level they need. Where risk is accepted or taken in your project make sure the 'net' level of risk is consistent with the risk appetite of the business as a whole.

- Are risk responses monitored? Make sure people in the business can answer the 'how do I know it is working?' question. This means communicating effectively, monitoring appropriately, acting in accordance with the plan, and adapting as circumstances change.

- Are there instances of too much risk response – controls seem 'over the top' given the level of risk? Listen out for signs of manipulation or ignoring of your risk management processes. Look at the risk management method as a whole, and confirm that it is fit-for-purpose, operating effectively, and embedded in the project plan and implementation.

Do's and Don'ts

- Do take a common sense approach to risk management
- Do involve a diversity of people in helping you identify risks
- Do keep risk thinking in the front of people's minds
- Don't go overboard on bureaucratic monitoring processes
- Don't neglect to review all the risks at regular intervals during the project life span
- Don't be afraid to adapt your risk management process if it is not working effectively

Summary – The Bare Bones

- The risk management cycle has six steps: understanding the business context, clarifying the objectives, identifying risks, assessing risks, responding to risks, and sustaining risk control
- Develop as comprehensive a list of risks as you can
- Assess them using an appropriate assessment method, two- or three-factor rankings work well
- Present the risk landscape preferably graphically so you can see each risk in relation to the other
- Prepare and implement plans to mitigate the risks
- Monitor progress continuously, re-assess risk list periodically, and respond to context changes as they occur

References/Useful Reading

Lewis, J. P. (1998). *Mastering Project Management*. McGraw Hill Professional Book Group.

Marks & Spencer (2001). *Change Handbook*. Marks & Spencer.

Shell International Limited (2000). *Risk Policy and Guidelines*. Shell International Limited.

The Economist (24 January 2004). Be prepared: what companies must do to face a much-increased range of risks.

Young, P. C. and Tippins, S. C. (2001). *Managing Business Risk*. Amacom.

10

Project Management

'A project is a unique set of coordinated activities, with definite starting and finishing points, undertaken by an individual or organisation to meet specific objectives within defined time, cost, and performance parameters.'
BS 6079 – 2:2000. Project Management. *Vocabulary*.

Overview

In relation to project management, you have learned so far that:

- Appointing a project manager at the start of your project is almost essential.
- You must produce certain documents and reports within each organization design phase.
- The project manager acts to link the work of the teams and presents an overall status report to you at regular intervals.

This chapter looks in more detail at project management as it applies to an OD project and considers the role of the project manager in successful delivery of this. The chapter starts with a definition of project management.

What is Project Management?

A simple definition of a project is that it is a series of interdependent activities aimed at meeting a common, agreed objective within an agreed time and cost. (A more complex definition appears at the head of this chapter.)

Project management stages	Related organization design methodology phase
Understanding the project	Preparing for change
Defining the project	Choosing to re-design
Planning the project	Creating the high-level and detailed-level design
Running the project	Handling the transition
Reviewing the project	Reviewing the design

Figure 10.1 Project management stages and organization design phases

Organization design phase three: Creating the high-level and detailed-level design	Target completion	
	Status	Date
Step 2 – Map current state: tasks People/skills/culture Customers Interfaces Conduct stakeholder analysis	Completed	by 05/02/.. by 05/02/.. on 27/01/..

Figure 10.2 Tasks associated with a particular project

The activities cluster into tasks and these tasks group together into five stages each one associated with a phase of the organization design methodology. The project management stages describe the way in which the project is organized.

Figure 10.1 illustrates the relationship between the project management stages and the organization design phases.

You may know the stages by different labels as different project management bodies use different words. (For example, the Project Management Institute describes the stages as 'processes' and labels them initiating, planning, executing, controlling, and closing.) Getting the right label is less important than doing the right thing within each stage to achieve your objectives.

Within each stage, there are a number of tasks. Figure 8.3 illustrated the tasks associated with a particular project. Figure 10.2 is an extract from this figure to remind you.

Each of the tasks listed in Figure 10.2 is achieved by carrying out a series of activities. For example, mapping the current state of interfaces requires activities like identifying the interfaces that affect the OD project,

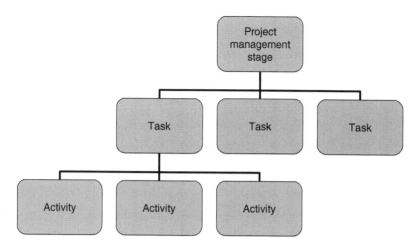

Figure 10.3 Project management hierarchy

communicating with the key people in each interface, holding a workshop to get interface data, and so on. Figure 10.3 illustrates the activity, task, stage hierarchy.

Professional project managers deploy nine knowledge areas as they work. These nine areas centre on management expertise in project integration, project scope, project time, project cost, project quality, project HR, project communications, project risk management, and project procurement (Project Management Institute, 2003).

Whether or not you employ a professionally qualified project manager, the person will need to pay attention to these nine aspects of the OD project.

Many books plumb the depths of project management. Both the UK based Association for Project Management (www.apm.org.uk) and the US based Project Management Institute (www.pmi.org) have information on some of these. The purpose of this chapter is not to go into detail on project management techniques but to encourage you to select and use those appropriate to your project to help you plan a process of activity that will deliver your required outcome in the most efficient way.

Project Management Approach

Your project is unique so there is no standard project management template for you to apply. Approach project management in a common sense

Project size	Characteristics	Approach	Example project
Small	▪ No high-level team (just line and HR manager), one small detailed-level team ▪ Upto than twenty days effort ▪ Up to six weeks elapsed time from start to finish ▪ Up to £15 k spend	▪ Project file set up ▪ Line or HR manager takes on project management responsibilities ▪ Terms of reference/ business plan informally agreed ▪ Prioritized to do list as a plan ▪ Progress monitored informally ▪ Verbal agreement at stage reviews ▪ Written de-brief at end	▪ Re-design of part of a department
Medium	▪ Small high-level team ▪ Two to five detailed-level teams ▪ Up to forty days effort ▪ Up to twelve weeks elapsed time from start to finish ▪ Up to 25 k spend	▪ Project file set up ▪ Project manager appointed (likely to be full time) ▪ Terms of reference/ business plan formally agreed ▪ Written approval/sign off ▪ Written progress reporting ▪ Written agreement at milestone reviews ▪ Written review at end	▪ Departmental or small business unit re-design (around 250–300 people)
Large	▪ Steering group ▪ High-level team of up to seven people ▪ Between five and eight detailed-level teams ▪ Up to ninety days effort ▪ Up to nine months elapsed time from start to finish ▪ Up to 50 k spend	▪ Programme office set up ▪ Programme manager plus project managers appointed ▪ Terms of reference/ business plan formally agreed ▪ Written approval/sign off ▪ Written progress reporting ▪ Written agreement at milestone reviews ▪ Formal post-implementation review by external team (e.g. internal audit)	▪ Large departmental or whole organization restructuring (up to 1000 people)
Very large	▪ Steering group reporting to board ▪ High-level team of up to seven people	▪ Programme office set up ▪ Programme manager plus project managers appointed	▪ Several departments restructuring across the organization

Figure 10.4 Aspects of project management by size of project

186

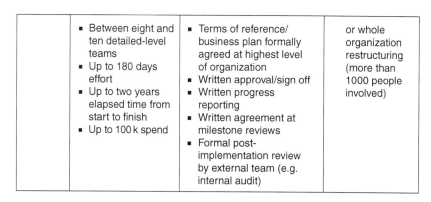

■ Between eight and ten detailed-level teams ■ Up to 180 days effort ■ Up to two years elapsed time from start to finish ■ Up to 100 k spend	■ Terms of reference/business plan formally agreed at highest level of organization ■ Written approval/sign off ■ Written progress reporting ■ Written agreement at milestone reviews ■ Formal post-implementation review by external team (e.g. internal audit)	or whole organization restructuring (more than 1000 people involved)

Figure 10.4 Continued

fashion: understand your project and what you plan to deliver, understand the business requirements and context, build a delivery process, deliver and then review and approach it logically – without this, you will create unnecessary complexity and probably a large amount of re-work.

Figure 10.4 suggests appropriate aspects of project management by size of OD project.

Regardless of the size of your project make sure you have:

■ A named sponsor commissioning the work and tracking the benefits.
■ Someone identified to lead the project, and be accountable for it.
■ A well thought through plan with targets for both costs and benefits.

But remember as you look at the size of your project this is not the only factor to consider when you are determining what project management approaches are appropriate. For example, you may have a small but complex re-design that requires formal sign offs.

One simple approach that works very well to structure the project goes by the acronym FADER (this is a generic problem solving approach that works for any problem that you are trying to solve). The links between FADER and the formal project management stages are shown in Figure 10.5.

You will see as you read a fuller description of each of the FADER steps that the questions you ask are similar in scope to the questions you ask within each phase of the OD project. This is because the project management techniques are a way of organizing the OD project – you are looking at the same thing but through a different lens and with a different purpose.

Project management stages	FADER
Understanding the project	Focus
Defining the project	Analyse
Planning the project	Develop
Running the project	Execute
Reviewing the project	Review

Figure 10.5 FADER problem solving

An analogy might be that the OD project defines the territory that you have to get through and the project management techniques you choose to use define the vehicle in which you are going to traverse it. So, for example, if you define your territory as 'mountainous and with snow' your vehicle choice would be a snow mobile. Choose the right project management 'vehicle' for your project.

The FADER steps are as follows:

Focus attention on why the project is needed, what the objectives are, what is to be included and excluded, what the financial and time constraints are, what the business risks are, and how you think you will approach the project. To do this effectively your project manager asks questions (Hallows 1998) like:

- Do I understand the project justification?
- Do I understand the background to the project?
- Do I understand the project's politics?
- Do I understand who the players are and the roles they will take?
- Do I understand the client's priorities?

Having good answers to these questions enables you to produce a robust business case or terms of reference. Write this document at the end of the first phase of the project. Use the acronym BOSCARD to structure this or use the template shown in Appendix 1. Figure 10.6 explains what BOSCARD stands for.

Analyse the current business situation, what the required situation is to be, assess the costs and benefits in detail and reaffirm how to progress the project further. During this stage ask questions like:

- Have I determined the project deliverables?

B	Background
O	Objectives
S	Scope
C	Constraints
A	Assumptions
R	Reporting
D	Deliverables

Figure 10.6 BOSCARD

- Have I established the scope, both system and project?
- Have I determined how the deliverables will be reviewed and approved?
- Have I defined the structure and organization of the client team? (In this case the high-level and detailed-level teams.)

Out of this stage comes the project proposal.

Develop your thinking by considering alternative approaches to provide the project deliverables and select the most suitable. (Here the project manager works with the high-level and detailed-level teams to help generate alternatives.) Create the main project deliverables and prepare to implement them in your business environment? Questions that will help you with this include:

- Have I defined the risks and developed plans to mitigate them?
- Have I documented the project assumptions and constraints?
- Have I defined the structure and organization of the project?
- Have I developed a quality plan?
- Have I developed a communications plan?
- Have I developed a list of detailed project activities?
- Have I defined the dependencies between the activities?
- Have I built a project estimate of the work required?
- Have I assigned resources and levelled them?
- Have I completed the schedule, complete with milestones?
- Have I aligned the schedule with the client's requirements?
- Have I developed a project budget?
- Have I prepared an overall project plan?

	RED	AMBER	GREEN
Progress (*assessed weekly*)	■ One or more key work items are/will be two or more weeks late Or ■ One or more major deliverables are not to right quality and significant re-work is/ will be required	■ One or more key work items are/ will be one week late Or ■ One or more major deliverables are not to right quality but significant re-work is not required	■ Work items are on target or have slipped by less than one week And ■ Key deliverables are to the right quality
Issues (*assessed weekly*)	■ Serious issue(s) are affecting the work stream and good progress cannot continue unless they are resolved quickly	■ Major issue(s) is threatening the work stream (i.e. delivery or cost) and probably need to be escalated to the steering group or other external entity, to get resolved	■ Issues are within the ability of the work stream or project to control
Risks (*assessed fortnightly*)	■ Severe risk with high probability and no risk reduction or contingency plans in place	■ Severe or major risks with medium probability have no risk reduction or contingency plans in place	■ All severe or major risks are of low probability, or of medium probability but with risk reduction or contingency plans in place
Costs (*assessed monthly*)	■ Costs year to date are more than 20% over budget Or ■ Total costs forecast are more than 20% over last approved budget Or ■ Costs 10% or more over budget (as above) and likely to escalate further unless action taken	■ Costs year to date are 10–20% over budget Or ■ Total costs forecast are 10–20% over last approved budget Or ■ Costs less than 10% over budget (as above) but likely to escalate further unless action taken	■ Costs year to data are on target or less than 10% over budget And ■ Total costs forecast are less than 10% over last approved budget And ■ Costs are unlikely to escalate to 10% over budget (as above)

Figure 10.7 RAG definitions

From this work comes the detailed project plan (the stages, tasks, and activities related to each task with timeline, milestones, and success factors). Tool 1 suggests criteria for a good project plan. Tool 2 gives some guidance on how to break down the tasks into activities.

Execute by putting project deliverables into place and creating the working environment that enables you to realize the business benefits of your project. The questions you want answers to during this stage include:

- Am I building an effective team?
- Do I know where I stand against the schedule estimate and budget?
- Am I managing risks?
- Am I solving schedule problems?
- Am I managing requests for scope changes?
- Am I managing for quality?
- Am I micro-planning when needed and not elsewhere?
- Are my sub-contractors delivering on their commitments?
- Do I understand the expectations of my client and can I meet them?
- Am I conducting regular team meetings and are they effective?
- Do I report project status and outstanding issues regularly?
- Am I taking the time to reflect privately on progress?
- Do I and my team celebrate our successes?

During this phase you are regularly producing status updates. These take a number of forms. One that works well is RAG (red, amber, green). This is a guideline for monitoring and assessing project progress as you go through the implementation phases.

The RAG status of each work stream is defined by the highest ranking RAG colour under any of the areas outlined in Figure 10.7. The RAG status is defined on a 'realistic' as opposed to 'best case' basis, for example if a work item is considered green in three of the four areas, but amber in the other, the overall status is considered amber.

Figure 10.8 gives an example of a completed RAG status form for an OD project. As you complete your form bear in mind that it is a factual and informative document designed to serve three objectives:

- First, to check progress so be able to quantify:
  - What work has been done versus what work should have been done

● R. Urgent, remedial attention required   ● A. Warning – corrective action required   ● G. Progressing in accordance with plan

Key	Previous status	Current status	Commentary	Planned action
Delivery – work streams attraction and recruitment		G	Paper sent to steering group for approval 15 February	
Benchmarking		G	Benchmarking visits completed. Appropriate information fed into other work streams	
Communications		G	Plan confirmed	Video confirmed. Detail announcement and leaving piece being confirmed. Longer-term communication approach for Head Office being prepared
Communities (culture)		A	Work commenced with Management team within Head Office	
Conduct review		G	Approach agreed with steering group on 12 February. Detail implementation work being progressed ready for Business Unit Managers take on 6 March	

			Completed	
Customer proposition		G	●	
Customer survey		G	◐	Revised questionnaires implemented, new reports produced through to March	Waiting Business Review over the future of Customer surveys
Reward		A	○	Being progressed	To be presented at March steering group meeting
Structures		G	◐	Structure proposals prepared (including Change Manager)	To be agreed as part of the Operating Plan
Induction training		G	◐	Work and research started	
Union risks		R	●	Paper for Legal department late. Some union unrest evident	
Working patterns		A	○	Detail analysis completed. Time scales and resource to be agreed	Implementation plan being prepared

Figure 10.8 Completed RAG status form

- – How long the work has taken versus how long you scheduled it to take
- – What it has cost versus what the estimates and budgets were.
- ■ Second, to justify the progress made so consider:
  - – Why you are where you are
  - – What problems have occurred and why
  - – What resources have been available or with held
  - – The extent of any re-work
  - – The number of OSINTOT's (oh s***, I never thought of that)
  - – Your understanding of what is really going on.
- ■ Third, to assess the impact of the project to date so assess:
  - – Whether you are still working to the original objectives
  - – The impact so far on time scales and budgets
  - – The impact on resource usage
  - – The increase or decrease in risk
  - – The impact on other projects.

Review at the end of the project when there has been sufficient time lag to ascertain whether the project deliverables have 'stuck'. Usually a review done between six and twelve weeks after closure gives you a good handle on whether the project has achieved its goals and whether you should consider taking further actions to get the new status embedded.

The review also serves to consolidate learning, capture project statistics, and provide a narrative so that future projects can benefit. (Reviewing is discussed in more detail in Chapter 13.)

Question to ask in reviewing include:

- ■ How effective and efficient was the project management method?
- ■ How useful, valid and reliable were the techniques and tools used to support the project?
- ■ How far did the deliverables actually produced by the project match the planned deliverables?
- ■ How far has the project achieved the intended benefits?
- ■ What are the business lessons learned that can be applied in future situations?

Include in your project management approach one other element – quality control. A quality plan helps ensure that the way you manage and deliver your project is 'fit for purpose' – that it has the characteristics that will deliver project success. If you want more detailed information on quality management, look at the Institute of Quality Assurance web site (www.iqa.org). Here you can find useful fact-sheets on quality management.

Tailor your quality plan to suit your project. The elements that are usually included in all but the smallest projects are:

- Project description
- Critical success factors
- Summary of risks (see Chapter 9)
- Roles and responsibilities of project team
- Project structure
- Change control process
- Quality gates (sometimes called decision points or go/no-go)
- Communications plan (see Chapter 6)
- Interfaces
- Training and development requirements.

The next paragraphs discuss change control and quality gates.

Changes are inevitable and can severely impact the project manager's ability to deliver successfully. Changes happen in any one of the project elements:

- Sponsor change
- Project team members change
- Objectives and scope change
- Deliverables change
- Project approach changes
- Time schedule change
- Budget changes.

To keep the project on track follow a change control process (but keep it simple). The five-step approach shown in Figure 10.9 works well.

A typical change request form looks like the one shown in Figure 10.10.

Quality gates or go/no-go decision points (sometimes also called stage reviews) appear at the end of each stage of the project. Figure 10.11 illustrates the quality gates.

Using this gate process allows project funding and resource to be progressively committed, as the requirements and benefits of the

Document the change	Find out who originated the change and write up as much detail on the degree of it as you can
Justify the change	Get the originators of the change to provide the reasons they see the change being necessary. Ask them to assess whether they really need to instigate it
Assess the impact of the change	Look at the project schedule and budget and think how the change could be accommodated with minimum impact Look at other ways of dealing with it. Whatever impact does exist make sure it is quantified and justified
Recommend any actions arising from the change	Based on the steps above go to the project sponsor with a recommendation: ■ either reject the change or ■ put the change on hold and deal with it at some future point or ■ accept the change and manage its implications
Agree the recommendation and communicate it	Communicate the decision and its implications to the all of those who need to know about it

Figure 10.9 Change control process

	Input required
Title	Short description of the change request, used to identify the request in summaries
Project	The name of the work stream which will be impacted by the change request
Priority	This is used to grade the relative priorities of change requests. Select from the options: ■ High ■ Medium ■ Low
Requested by	The name of the person who is requesting and/or documenting the change request
Request date	
Description of proposed change	Detailed description of the change request, including work effort required, tasks and deliverables. Also, where necessary, what gave rise to the change request
Status set by	Name of the person logging the change request

Figure 10.10 Change request form

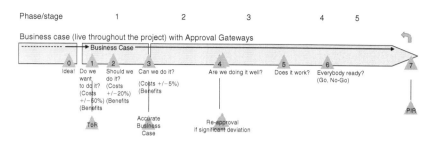

Figure 10.11 Quality gates

project are progressively understood. Additionally the process offers a degree of protection for the sponsor and the business by giving them the opportunity to validate the project and thus assure themselves at each stage of its continued viability.

At each quality gate the project steering group or sponsor has the authority and the capability to:

1. approve for continuation the project if it has met the standard criteria;
2. agree their priority on continuation of this project versus other projects (where there is a conflict);
3. stop the project if they deem it necessary;
4. speed the project up or slow it down.

They do this by checking the same acceptance criteria at each gate, typically – ownership, scope, cost, benefit, plans, resources, risks and issues, impact, business priority, evaluation, and expenditure. At each gate, there is usually a set of standard deliverables, for example at gate one it is terms of reference, project plan, risk assessment, and communication plan.

Roles and Responsibilities

You have already learned about the role of the sponsor in your project and the advisability of appointing a project manager to keep your project on track and under control. You have also come across mention of a steering group.

All of these roles are part of a full governance structure that you should bring into play if your project is to run any longer than six weeks, (usually a medium- or larger-sized project).

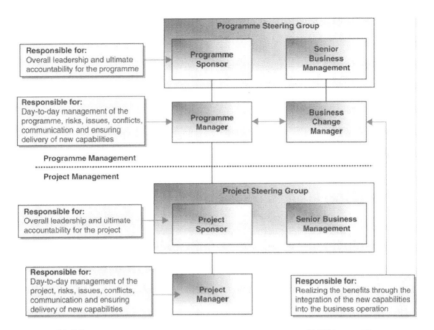

Figure 10.12 Program management governance structure (CCTA 1999)

This book has referred throughout to 'project' rather than 'programme'. The difference between the two, explained briefly, is that a programme is a collection of projects which may or may not be interdependent.

A project is a series of interdependent tasks and activities aim to meet specific objectives within an agreed time and cost boundary.

The scale and scope of what you plan to achieve determine whether you set it up as a programme or a project. Whichever you do the governance structure requires similar components – a 'champion' of the work (the sponsor), a group monitoring progress and making decisions on continued viability (usually called a steering group or project board), someone managing the day-to-day delivery of the work. Where it is a programme of work, the programme manager will have project managers reporting in. Figure 10.12 illustrates a typical programme management governance structure. In this graphic you can see the relationship between a programme and a project.

Each role within the governance structure has certain responsibilities attached to it. These are comparable within programmes and projects. Figure 10.13 describes each of the roles and the types of responsibilities associated with them.

Steering group	▪ Steering the project team with respect to the needs of the steering group members' areas and the wider business ▪ Challenging the contents of the terms of reference and business case to ensure the project is set up for success ▪ Questioning, and validating, the conclusions and recommendations made ▪ Reviewing project progress at key quality gates ▪ Taking action to remove barriers to successful delivery of the project ▪ Supporting communication across the business about the benefits successful delivery of the project will bring to the organization
Sponsor	▪ Ensuring that the project or programme meets its overall objectives and delivers its projected benefits. (This should be included in their personal objectives.) Ideally the sponsor should be a senior member of the organization with the most to gain from the success of the project and the most to lose from its failure (see Chapter 3 for a more detailed discussion of the sponsor role)
Project manager	▪ Achieving the benefit of the project through the day-to-day leadership of the team by: ▪ Ensuring the project has a clear outcome, and that the whole project team understand it and remain focused on it ▪ Ensuring each team member has clear accountabilities and their time on the project has been agreed with the line manager ▪ Being responsible for drawing up and gaining approval for key project documentation, for example terms of reference and business case ▪ Managing a full project plan and co-ordinating activities of team to meet that plan ▪ Dealing with changes systematically ▪ Managing a strong internal communications programme to communicate to stakeholders and managing key stakeholder relationships ▪ Monitoring progress against plan, including critical path and key milestones ▪ Managing the project budget ▪ Communicating clearly to sponsor, steering group (if applicable) and team members
Project team members (typically specialists accountable for one element of the project with the skills and knowledge needed to achieve the project goals)	▪ Communicating their specialist knowledge in a way that is easily understood by the rest of the team ▪ Representing their 'home department' when part of the project team, and the project when back in their home department ▪ Creating a realistic plan for their part of the project ▪ Co-ordinating activities to meet that plan and deal with changes in a systematic way ▪ Resolving issues that arise, either alone or with the support of other team members ▪ Communicating clearly to other team members ▪ Working with other team members

Figure 10.13 Program governance roles and responsibilities

199

Useful Tools

Tool 1: Criteria for a Good Project Plan

For simple projects with little resource required you could get away with a prioritized 'to do' list but most OD projects are complex, risky, and resource consuming. Whatever software or methods you use to develop your project plan when you think it is complete check it against the following criteria.

	Linked to clear business objectives
	Flexible
	Realistic
	Adequate resources to achieve the plan
	Identified resources (who is required to do what)
	Skills required to do the work
	Capable of evaluation
	Time bound
	Comprehensive and comprehensible
	Achievable
	Prepared by (owner/creator of plans clear)
	Complete (no activities missing)
	Practical

Tool 2: Work Breakdown

1. For each stage of the project list that stage's deliverables.
2. Think through the main tasks involved in delivering each.
3. For each task identify what activities (units of work) are needed to complete the task. As you do this consider: (a) Complexity of the activity (b) Skills, experience, and attitude required to carry out the activity

(c) Availability of people to carry out the activity

(d) Tools available to make the job easier

(e) The general working environment

(f) Past experience/learning in carrying out this (or similar) activity.

4. Factor in the dependencies that impact completion of the activity. These fall into three categories:

(a) Mandatory inter-activity dependency. That is activities within the project which cannot possibly start until another activity within the same project has completed

(b) Optional inter-activity dependency. That is activities within the project which could start at any time but which the project manager would prefer to undertake in a particular sequence

(c) Inter-project dependency. That is the activity within the project which cannot possible start until an activity within another project has completed.

5. If your project is large enough to warrant it draw a critical path to get the activities in logical order (www.mindtools.com tells you how to do a critical path analysis).

6. Estimate the time it will take to do the work.

7. Document the work breakdown as a table (or use Microsoft Project or similar software). A simple table looks like the one below.

Stage/task/activity	Time estimate	Dependency	Deliverable

8. For each activity listed check that is conforms to the following criteria:

(a) Clearly named with a verb and a noun

(b) Performed by a single resource

(c) Produces one single deliverable component

(d) Is achieved within a reasonable time scale.

Self-check

This chapter is a brief overview of project management and you should think of it as such. If you want more help on project management there are all sorts of courses of varying durations available. The Association of Project Management or the Project Management

Institute will point you in the right direction on these. However, use the questions below to check your current thinking on project management and its application to your project:

- Are you clear that your project is a project and not a programme? If the work you are doing is focused on achieving specific objectives within certain constraints, you are initiating a project. If your work is a more broadly spread piece with less certain objectives and across a range of complexity then you are more likely to be initiating a programme of work.
- Is your management team supportive of your project organization? Kerzner (1998) suggests that successful projects result from a set of senior management attitudes that exhibit as a hands off but supportive/concerned style where authority and decision-making are at the lowest possible level.
- Is your project structured for effective project management? Using the organization design methodology means that your project teams are in effect 'task forces' set up on a temporary basis to work on the project. Once the project has been delivered the task forces will disband. Mostly the team members work on a part time basis. This task force structure brings challenges to the project manager who has to deliver the project through people who may have conflicting pulls on their time and interest. Make sure you appoint a project manager who can handle this sort of situation.
- Are you clear that the phases of the organization design method run in sync with the stages of project management? Look back at Figure 10.1 which shows the linkages between the organization design phases and the project management stages. They harmonize well and should be orchestrated together, the organization design phases giving you the 'what' you want to deliver and the project management stages giving you the 'how' you can get successful delivery.
- Do you know what you are looking for in a project manager? Project managers have a difficult role to play mainly because they have no reporting control or authority over the team members. They have to deliver using a strong set of interpersonal skills combined with technical skills and professional characteristics. When you are selecting someone for the role make sure that they are

decisive, organized, and determined (but in an engaging and participative way).

- Are you familiar with the documentation that you should produce at each stage of the project? Producing documentation often seems like a chore you could do without. Keep project papers to a minimum but do keep them. They serve as an audit trail when you come to review the project and as a reminder to yourself and others of where and why you are doing the project and the progress it is making. Sometimes you feel you are running around in ever-decreasing circles getting nowhere – well kept records can show you if this is an accurate perception or if you are just having a bad day and you have achieved more than you recognize.

- Do you have a mechanism for coping with changes that occur as your project proceeds? Changes to plan are inevitable as you progress. The trick is to not let them derail you. Make sound decisions (based on agreed processes) regarding the impact of changes on your project. One of the more frequent mistakes is deciding to continue with the project when changing circumstances suggest that you should pull the plug on it. It is a much braver and more difficult decision to stop something than to continue with it. Your change control process should include a 'stop' option.

- Do you have quality assurances procedures in place? Quality thinking should pervade your approach to the design challenge. Right the way through be confident that you are making sound decisions and exercising good judgement. Post-implementation reviews frequently highlight a lack of quality assurance as a reason for less than optimal project results.

- Are you drawing on the project management learning from elsewhere in your organization? Ask around to find out how project managers would do things differently if they could start their projects again. You may find, for example, that their projects suffered because team members were not familiar with project management techniques and disciplines in which case you could consider training programmes if your team members were similarly unfamiliar. Other learning is worth drawing on. Do not be afraid to ask.

- Do you know how you would measure the success of your project management approach? Too often projects are measured by 'to time/within budget' types of metrics. The organization design must deliver the promised benefits – measure your success against these aspects too (not only against the mechanics of the project management approach).

Do's and Don'ts

- Do remember that project management is a method of organizing the delivery of your project – use it wisely
- Do look at the variety of tools and techniques associated with project management and see where you can usefully use them in your project
- Do learn from other projects' experiences – avoid their pitfalls
- Don't think you can manage without some project management techniques
- Don't go overboard on the techniques – keep things simple
- Don't neglect the review and decision points

Summary – The Bare Bones

- Use project management techniques and use them wisely
- Be clear about the roles and responsibilities in your project organization structure
- Keep good documentary records of the progress of your project
- Ensure you include change control and quality assurance processes
- Hold regular reviews of project progress and make tough decisions on continuing viability
- Select a skilful project manager

References/Useful Reading

CCTA (1999). *Managing Successful Programmes*. The Stationery Office.

Hallows, J. (1998). *Information Systems Project Management*. Amacom.

Kerzner, H. (1998). *In Search of Excellence in Project Management*. John Wiley & Sons, Inc.

Taylor, J. (1998). *A Survival Guide for Project Managers*. Amacom.

Wysocki, R. K. et al. (2000). *Effective Project Management*. John Wiley & Sons, Inc.

11

Phase Four – Handling the Transition

'Neither fit nor commitment is sufficient by itself; both are needed.'

Jay R. Galbraith (1995).
Designing Organizations. Jossey-Bass.

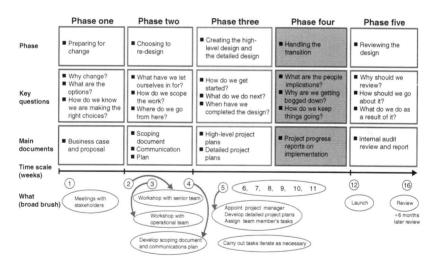

Figure 11.1 Phase four – handling the transition

Overview

The transition phase of an OD project is when things are most likely to go wrong. People have lived through the excitement of visioning, and the detail of planning, and now have to get to grips with transitioning to the new design and the new ways of working it brings. They find this much easier said than done.

However, if your teams have been working well and you have thoroughly planned the change, you should be able to deal with the usual problems that arise during the transition. Transition is about placing people in the right jobs, putting new processes into place, making sure you have aligned the systems to deliver the outcomes you have specified, and so on. Doing this successfully means having the right answers to the three questions shown in Figure 11.1:

- What are the people implications?
- Why are we getting bogged down?
- How do we keep things going?

What are the people implications? The people implications of transitioning are significant and are more fully covered in Chapter 12. Briefly, your aim in relation to people in the transition stage is twofold: first, to help them manage any changes in their work roles, and second, to ensure that collectively they reach high performance as quickly as possible. (Remember that in nearly all cases, one of the objectives of re-design is to improve performance.)

Beware of the phrase 'high performance'. People often use it without defining what it means. Ensure that everyone involved with your project has a common and agreed definition. Figure 11.2 lists common characteristics of high performing organizations.

Having agreement on what high performance is, helps you focus the transition stage on getting to this. Even with a target and a project plan, it is easy to get stuck – which gives rise to the second commonly asked question in this phase.

Why are we getting bogged down? Although there are many reasons for getting bogged down, one of the most common ones is that people lose energy and enthusiasm. Liken it to moving house – you have arrived at the new location having spent months planning the

High business performance depends on the following criteria:

- Financial and market performance
- First, second or third position in market sector
- Earnings per share
- Sustained and sustainable financial performance
- HR initiatives that have changed the organizational culture for the better

Frequent invention of new strategies for success. (Through clarifying and energizing strategic direction, honing and refining leadership skills, increasing and improving communications both to and from employees)

A values driven culture that:

- Recognizes, and celebrates, people's need for meaning in their working lives and their desire to make a positive difference to the world around them
- Is based on mutual trust and respect
- Develops efficient, secure, engaged and motivated employees with the expertise and the energy to provide enthusiastic and exemplary levels of customer service

Strong delivery on organizational promises

Continuous investment in the competencies and commitment of the people

The customer at the centre of everything

Figure 11.2 Characteristics of high performing organizations

move, packing your goods, and now it is time to start living in the new place. You look around at everything boxed up, heaped rather randomly, and you quail at the task that lies ahead. You realize that the move presages a start-point not an end-point. You have to galvanize yourself into the unpacking, rearranging, and getting to know the new location. You have to build up new and effective routines, and generate confidence that the move was absolutely the right thing to do for you.

The transition phase of the re-design project is very much like this except that many of the people you are working with would not have willingly chosen to 'move' if the choice had been made available. Thus, it is over to you to jolly people along, motivate them to keep going, and encourage them on the journey.

A second common reason for getting bogged down is that leadership attention gets diverted. The excitement has been in the initial whipping up of enthusiasm and selling the project in the right places. Once they have achieved this, many leaders feel their role is complete. However, successful re-design projects require leadership commitment and focus from start to finish. If other things prevail on leadership attention, the project is very likely to flag at this stage.

Project delivery status	Key status indicators						
STATUS SUMMARY [one-line summary of overall status]	**Progress**	**Scope**	**Resources**	**Comms**	**Issues**	**Costs**	**IT**
Status for each element current period **(INDICATE AS Red, Green or Amber)**							
STATUS RATIONALE [rationale for each non-green indicator]							
Status for each element previous period **(INDICATE AS Red, Green or Amber)**							
KEY ACHIEVEMENTS THIS WEEK							
SLIPPAGE AGAINST PLAN THIS WEEK: IMPACT & ACTIONS							

Figure 11.3 Example project progress report form

A third common reason for the project flagging is to do with the sheer weight of custom and practice which can drag down your re-design as you try to transition to the new model. You hit unexpected barriers – most often because you have done insufficient work with the interface departments, systems, and processes – and the time and effort needed to overcome these means that there is a slow reversion to business as usual.

To avoid getting stuck, plan regular and systematic progress checks. Figure 11.3 illustrates a typical project progress tracking form. Back up this form of assessment of progress with more qualitative and anecdotal assessments – asking people how things are going, listening carefully, and 'taking the temperature' of the project. Often you get a good feel for project status simply by being observant and picking up on clues (or what is not said rather than what is said).

Robert Shaw (1992) suggests further things that bog down implementing the re-design effectively.

Priority stress:

- you have too many things to do, with no clear view of the top items versus the other forty (you do not know what to do)
- your re-design conflicts with other strategic initiatives (your competing and conflicting priorities)
- you have insufficient resources to do everything (you have too much to do and cannot do it all).

Going for activity rather than results:

- you work more on processes than results
- you focus on tasks that drive current measurement systems
- you are risk averse – sticking to known ways of doing things.

Feeling powerless to implement your plan because you have:

- unclear accountability
- over-control by your boss
- inadequate resources.

If you find you are getting bogged down ask yourself the third question.

How Do We Keep Things Going?

Bear in mind that you can go a long way to keeping things going by communicating in a vital and inspiring way. In his book 'Who Says Elephants Can't Dance?' Lou Gerstner has a wonderful appendix of memos that he sent to staff during his 9 years at IBM. All demonstrate his enduring focus on turning the organization around. Figure 11.4 is an example of one of these memos.

Good communication however is not always enough to combat loss of energy and enthusiasm, distraction of leadership focus, or the weight of the way you have always done things. Each requires a bundle of activities to help you keep the project on track.

The remainder of this chapter guides you through some of the things you can do. It considers the roles you play in this transition phase, discusses

---

Subject: Stock Milestone

Dear Colleague

Today we reached a major milestone in the history of our company. Our stock price hit 177⅛ during trading this morning, passing our all-time intraday high of 176⅛ on August 20, 1987. This is obviously good news for our shareholders – and, importantly, more than half of all IBM employees are shareholders, too.

But records are meant to be broken and milestones to be surpassed. In fact, I believe this is an early milestone in the long, long life of the new IBM. And other milestones are probably as important – achieving customer satisfaction second to none, accelerating revenue growth (we've posted record revenues two straight years, but we can do better), reaffirming technology leadership.

The next milestone I am looking forward to very much is just ahead when the total number of IBM employees will be larger than when we began building the new IBM in 1993.

In my eyes you stand tall. You did all this – the milestones passed, the victories just ahead, and those far down the road.

Thank you. Take a bow. You've earned it.

And, of course, I can't resist: Let's all get right back to work because we've just begun!

Figure 11.4 Letter from Lou Gerstner to staff 13 May 1997

handling the informal 'shadow' side of the organization, and talks about the importance of getting some quick results in this phase. Then, following the format of previous chapters, it presents a self-check, some do's and don'ts, and a bare bones summary.

Your Roles in the Transition Phase

Remember as you work through the transition, that for everyone who sees the changes as beneficial there will be someone who sees the changes as detrimental. Simultaneously some will see a muddle erupt and others will see clarity emerge. Everyone's experience of what you are doing to change the design of your organization will be different. Your roles are to manage these diverse responses to reality by being aware of them, understanding them, and treating them appropriately. This requires the manager to be fully in the leadership seat, driving people through the transition, and making tactical decisions swiftly. It requires the HR practitioner to operate across the full spectrum of

	Manager activity (strategic management moving towards tactical management)	HR practitioner activity (facilitator to expert)
Handling the transition	- Leading the transition process - Motivating people to work with the changes - Projecting confidence and optimism - Adjusting plan appropriately	- Surveying responses to change and relaying to manager - Recommending actions as needed to maintain progress - Supporting and guiding people into new state - Determining policies and practices

Figure 11.5 Your roles in the transition phase

activity. (Refer back to Chapter 2, Figure 2.2: The role of the line manager, and Figure 2.3: The role of the HR practitioner). Your respective roles in this phase are summarized in Figure 11.5.

The key activity of the line manager is to lead people through this transition. To do this effectively means asking yourself why anyone should follow you. Goffee and Jones (2000) discuss this question in their article 'Why should anyone be led by you?'

They suggest that inspirational leaders exhibit four specific qualities (as well as the commonly mentioned ones of vision, energy, authority, and strategic direction). People follow leaders who:

- Selectively show their weaknesses: this means showing that you're not perfect but have the normal human frailties. It helps people relate to you on a human rather than a hierarchical level. Of course, you have to pick your frailty with caution. Exposure of something that may damage your standing is not a good idea.
- Rely on sensing and intuition to gauge the appropriate timing and course of their actions. This means noticing cues, clues, and symbols, and being able to 'read' a situation accurately from intangibles. This skill is one to cultivate and learn to work with. If you are not confident about your perceptions find someone you can validate them with before you take action.
- Manage employees with tough empathy. This can be difficult. You have to care greatly about your people yet also care about what you

are trying to achieve. The two may be incompatible. You will not always be able to give people what they want in a situation, but you will be able to keep people's commitment and motivation if you behave and act in a way that they respect and trust.

■ Reveal their differences. Keep in mind that you are the leader and dare to be different. Again a word of caution – be different in a way that is motivating. Pick differentiators that people admire but cannot always emulate themselves. Ivy Ross, Senior Vice President, world-wide, girls design, and development, at Mattel, Inc is a case in point:

> *For years, Mattel has worked to grow beyond Barbie. One strategy was growth through acquisition. Ivy Ross's strategy is to inspire innovation – to reinvent how the world's number-one toy company designs its toys. To do this she successfully set up Project Playtpus. In many ways, Ross can be seen as Mattel's original playtpus. Like the beaver-tailed mammal with the duckbill and webbed feet, she is an uncommon creature, a hybrid leader. She's an adventurous entrepreneur who started her own jewelry business shortly after graduating from New York's Fashion Institute of Technology and for years continued working on the side as a designer while rising through the executive ranks; she's a 20-year veteran of big companies such as Avon, Calvin Klein, Coach, and Liz Claiborne. An ingenious right-brain designer and an effective left-brain executive, she defies conventional labels – with obvious pride.*
>
> Salter, C. (2002). Ivy Ross is not playing around.
> *Fast Company*, November.

The HR practitioner has a range of activities to work on in this phase. The primary one is getting the right people in the right roles at the right time. (Methods of doing this come in the next chapter.) Complementary activities include:

■ steering the line manager through all the people implications and consequences of the design
■ ensuring good management of people's feelings

- watching for signs of stress in the manager and staff and then acting to handle these
- supporting the manager in keeping the business going
- challenging the manager and his team to keep on 'walking the talk'
- being alert to warning signs that things are going wrong and helping the manager deal with this
- reminding people of the milestones that have been achieved and celebrating these.

Together present a unified front and demonstrate the desired behaviours and changes in performance for the future organization. You are the role models as you transition to the new design so your approach should reflect leading standards of behaviour. (If practical constraints get in the way of this, the reasons why should be made clear.)

During the transition, be flexible and responsive to the changing situation. People will appreciate you being sensitive to their needs and responding appropriately to these. When you have to make difficult decisions be honest and clear about your reasons. At this stage it is your style and approach that will carry the project forward as much as it is the planning you have put into it.

Handling the 'Shadow Side'

Organizations are designed to be power networks, through which influence is exerted and results achieved. 'Legitimate' power is overtly recognized and/or reinforced through formal authority networks and codified in the formal organization charts.

However, there are sources of power in organizations other than formal authority, many of these holding more power than that of 'legitimate' power. Your organization is a minefield of informal systems, processes and interactions that frequently contravene sometimes contradict and often over-rule the formal policies, instructions, organization charts and so on (Chapter 1, Figure 1.4). The fact that this is the case is widely known but not often acknowledged or brought out into the open by people.

Although you are the formally designated leader of your OD project anyone who works in an enterprise involving people and interactions knows that despite the way things are 'supposed' to be, in practice people continually jockey for power, position, turf and resources. It is an organizational fact that organizations consist of competing political coalitions of people engaged in legitimate and illegitimate conflicts to define the agenda of the organization and in doing so shape its course of action. Your success in your design project depends on your ability to handle this 'shadow side' – the part of your organization that Egan (1993) describes as those 'realities that often disrupt, and sometimes benefit the business but are not dealt with in the formal settings of the organization.' More often than not, these realities remain publicly undiscussed and undiscussable but everyone is aware of them. They are the unwritten rules of the game.

To ensure a successful transition from current state to planned state you must align the unwritten rules of the game with the written rules. This means having the courage to put on the table what one organization called 'the bleeding rhinoceros head'. Unless you do this, you are likely to encounter defensive behaviour, blocking, non-compliance, and other potential showstoppers. You will not be able to force through a change. You must get the informal and shadow aspects of it on your side. Of all the organization design phases, it is in the transition phase that these are the most powerful.

How you get the shadow side working with you this depends on your style, your willingness to confront underlying issues, and your organization. One way of doing it is to ask the survivor question. To do this you ask a number of people the question, 'If you were leaving this organization tomorrow and I was joining it a few days after you left, what would you say was key to my survival here?' (You have to assume that they are going to give an honest response.) Reflect on what they say – does it square with what you are trying to achieve? If not, decide what you can do to get better alignment.

Getting Results

Assessors of change projects suggest that unless you deliver measurable results quickly your project is likely fail or have 'ambivalent success' (Pettigrew 1998). Key to building your design is specifying exactly what impact it will have on business performance in terms of things like

Performance area	Current performance	Target performance	Reason this is achievable (+ or – change)	When this will be achieved
% Cost of sales				
% Market share				
% Customer complaints				
% Employee absence rates				
% Call handling				

Figure 11.6 Example matrix to measure impact of re-design on business performance

customer service, increase in sales or revenue, increase in employee satisfaction, decrease in waste or rework.

As you start the transition process, confirm once again that you have clear deliverables in mind and know why you expect your new design will achieve these. Complete a simple matrix as shown in Figure 11.6 to remind yourself of what you have to do and date stamp it. Aim to have 'quick wins' within the first two weeks of the start of the transition.

Achieving transition plan milestones and results is crucial to maintaining momentum and avoiding cynicism. The old adage holds true – nothing succeeds like success.

Success in aligning the informal and shadow side of your organization with your goals and plans is not of itself sufficient to bring quick wins and early results. Even given optimum conditions, your project is not necessarily going to be successful. The unforeseen might strike – a sudden change at the top, a crisis that hits the whole organization or something else diverts attention. Your risk planning will help you keep your eye on a range of factors that might derail your project. To secure results you have to:

1. Maintain sustained support from your stakeholders and your sponsor over the transition period. If this fades away for whatever reason, then the energy to change may flag, momentum falter, and a return to status quo set in.

2. Aim to institutionalize the changes, doing so in a way that gives you early results and improves the traction of your project. As you do so manage expectations carefully and make sure you realize them. Failure to show evident onward progress to the end state or goal is a frequent cause of regression or withdrawal of support.

3. Recognize local conditions and do not try to impose a corporate model on a local entity without due consideration. A stark reminder of this comes from an information technology (IT) project.

Corporate has sent a team of people to help us re-organize as they introduce a new global accounting system. We don't want this system as we have very good relationships with local suppliers which will be disrupted if the centre takes over our supplier list. We won't be able to guarantee good levels of customer service.

Worse than that is the fact that they didn't check whether we have the right equipment to run the new system and haven't budgeted for new hardware. It's no good saying that the system will be up and running from 1st July when my 'computer' is actually a fax machine and it frequently breaks down!

---

4. Spend as much time on the cultural and behavioural aspects of your project as you do on the design of systems and processes. Again, IT systems implementations often fall foul in this respect, neglecting to design in the people aspects from the initiation of the project.

5. Keep both a short and a long-term perspective as you aim for results. It is easy to lose sight of one or other and both are essential. Quick wins are what is going to maintain support from stakeholders, but keeping the end-game in mind is what will determine ultimate success.

6. Avoid exclusive project team membership – cycling people through the teams brings new thinking and encourages feelings of participation. There are some risks in bringing new people into project teams. However, the new team member brings 'fresh eyes' and these generally outweigh the risk of newness. A greater risk is sticking with the same team all the way through. Members can form exclusive 'silos' which sometimes sidelines the project rather than keeping it mainstream.

7. Minimize bureaucratic support structures around the implementation of the re-design. Ensure good project governance with the minimum of bureaucracy. You have seen many different forms through this book. Use them judiciously. You may not need all of them.

8. Cascade re-design work to the lowest possible level in your organization to get maximum involvement and ownership. As said earlier (Chapter 8) involve people who do the grass roots work in the organization in the project design teams. Their experience is valuable to your project.

9. Delegate and give accountability to others. Reduce your stress levels by letting go of some of the work. Your role is to lead and to get results through other people. Sometimes it is tempting to roll up your sleeves – particularly if you think you will achieve results more quickly by doing something yourself. But stop and think whether this is in the best long-term interests of the project.

10. Balance trade offs between quantity, quality, and pace in achieving the results you want. Organization designs are not static creations formed in isolation. They are a dynamic part of a wider ecosystem. Aim for 'good enough' and what works rather than getting things perfectly right. A pragmatist stands a better chance of success in organization design than a perfectionist.

11. Think carefully about the type of transition you think will work best in your situation. For example, you may decide to phase the changes to ensure minimum disruption to the customer by rolling out certain processes first, or changing certain jobs first. Or you might decide to go 'big bang'. There are pros and cons to each approach. It really depends on your own situation and context.

12. Communicate the timing of the transition actions so that people are prepared and ready for new roles, new locations, or whatever. Do this as much in advance of the change over as possible and then stick with the dates. If you have to miss them, give people adequate notice and clear reasons for any changes. 'No surprises' is the rule during the transition phase.

13. Communicate what is not part of the transition plan so that people know there are some things that will continue in relative stability. It is unlikely that everything will change as you transit. Reassure people that some of the familiar ways will continue. Show that you value the legacy and heritage of the past and the part people played.

14. As stated earlier maintain a close watch on the politics of the change and prepare yourself to influence, lobby, and negotiate if you start to see things slide. Part of this includes constructing forums for addressing top down or bottom up concerns.

15. Ensure new reward and recognition systems are in place very early in the transition phase, so they start to reinforce the desired new behaviours and ways of working from the start of the move from old to new. Leaders of change often underestimate the part reinforcing organizational systems and process play in the success of the project.

16. Remind people of the part the re-design plays in the strategic direction of the organization in both the short-term and the long-term. Let people know that you are not changing things for the sake of it. You are changing things to achieve business results as determined by the short and longer-term strategies. In doing this you are helping to answer the questions, 'why re-design, why now, why us?' which pop up in every phase of the project.

17. Demonstrate how your re-design works with other change projects. Clarify how these work to develop the business and are part of a coherent strategy to keep the organization moving effectively into a planned future. Too often people have a cynical view of 'change for change's sake.'

18. Provide honest, open and regular feedback regarding changed behaviours. Deal swiftly and constructively with negative behaviours and disengagement. Your task is to get the organization moved from the current to the new state. Letting things go may feel easier at the time but will rebound on you in the future.

19. Implement feedback mechanisms to track performance changes. You already have some suggested metrics and measurements – review these to check that they cover all four aspects – people, formal organization, informal organization, and work. Put in metrics (quantitative and qualitative) for any missing areas.

20. Adjust the design if it becomes apparent that this would be the best course of action. It may well be as you implement that a gap between design and actual use emerges. If you find this is the case aim to understand why and then review the design. Use your design principles to guide any changes so that you retain the overall integrity of the project.

Useful Tools

Tool 1: Team Audit: How are We Doing?

You can use this with the implementation team(s) and/or with the work teams you have created in your new design.

Use this audit periodically to gather data from each team member to create a group profile, the team can use as a focal point for discussion about, 'How well are we doing as a team?' The discussion provides an opportunity to compare points of view objectively, and if need be, to get back on track and move forward more productively. Each team member can complete the audit. Individual responses should be kept confidential. Compile the individual responses into a group profile for the team to share in a team meeting.

Team's goals/purpose

Rate your opinion of the team's effectiveness on the dimensions listed below with '1' being an ineffective area in need of improvement to '5' being an area of effectiveness and strength.

Aspect/dimension	Rating					Comments/examples
	1	2	3	4	5	
Goals/purpose						
Meetings						
Ground rules and norms						
Communication						
Leadership						
Workload						
Distribution of work						
Energy level						
Commitment level						
Adequacy of resources						
Availability of resources						
Management of stress						

Aspect/dimension	Rating					Comments/examples
	1	2	3	4	5	
Decision-making						
Respect for differences						
Management of conflict						
Level of participation						
Comments						

The biggest challenge we face as a team is:
Our greatest strength as a team is:
The one thing I would most like to see the team do is:

Tool 2: How are We Doing on Change?

Use this tool to measure the success of your transition plan. You can administer it at the start of the transition phase and at intervals as it proceeds. You can use it with various stakeholder groups and/or across the whole population

Success	1	2	3	4	5	6
Focus and clarity of direction and communication. Everyone understands where we are going, how, and why.						
Clarity of objectives, roles and accountability. Everyone understands and owns what they are expected to do.						

Success	1	2	3	4	5	6
Team-working across the business is based on trust and support. Everyone feels able to share ideas and work with other groups and functions.						
Motivation, confidence, and commitment are obvious and aligned with reward. People want to come to work and feel proud to be here.						
Customer focus and meeting customer needs is the driver of everything we do.						
HR policy and process is consistent and clear, creating a leading standards working environment.						
People feel willing to challenge, to be open and honest, and demonstrate a 'can do' attitude.						
We are measurably and increasingly successful. People are determined to deliver results.						

Self-check

If you have decided to go for a 'big bang' transition (that is on a certain day there will be totally cut-over from current state to future state) then conduct this self-check a month or so before the cut-over date (depending on the size of the project).

If you have decided to go for a phased transition, do this self-check a month or so before the transition starts and then at intervals as it proceeds.

Answering 'yes' to all the questions suggests that you have a good chance of getting through the transition phase successfully.

■ Have you allocated sufficient resources to support the change over? Sometimes it is difficult to judge how much resource you will need. Time, money, and headcount are what people usually say they have too little of. Your project plan should help you work out the ebbs and flows of your resource requirement.

■ Have you phased the transition appropriately? This becomes a particular issue if your phasing is dependent on things happening in a particular order. For example, if you are doing an IT implementation you have to phase the training just as system use is planned to begin. Either holding the training too far in advance of the implementation or after it is running is a barrier to success. Early in the project, you should have completed a critical path analysis that will help you get things phased correctly.

■ Have you considered what barriers might affect the change and planned methods of overcoming them? Review your risk analysis and check that you have mitigation plans in place. Even if different obstacles present by reviewing in this way you will have the right mindset to tackle whatever does come up.

■ Have you considered what staff need to know to feel fully informed of the transition timetable? Try putting yourself in the position of each level of staff and viewing the re-design from their perspective. Again it is not unlike a family moving house. Each family member will want to be told different things about the new house and location.

■ Have you identified all the stakeholders and agreed the transition process with them? No matter how good your original stakeholder analysis, review the stakeholder position again as you start the transition process. Things may well have changed in the period. New stakeholders may have emerged while others will have left the scene.

■ Have you informed all the stakeholders of changes in personnel and process? Many projects have difficult transition phases because key stakeholders are not kept in the communications loop. Unfortunately, sometimes the people most impacted are the last to know what is going on – for example, when employees hear about significant organizational changes on the television news. Make sure this does not happen on your project.

■ Have you updated all necessary service level agreements (SLAs)? If you have not had SLAs with interface departments and customers think about introducing them as part of the transition process. If you have got SLAs check that they are renewed and that they reflect the organization design changes you are making.

- Have you revisited what customers need to know about the changes and planned communications accordingly? Customers most want to know that they will have uninterrupted service as the project transits, and improved service as the benefits are delivered. Ensure that you have measures of this and can track service levels. Keep the customer informed at all times.

- Do you have contingency plans in place to manage teething problems with new roles and processes? Accept the fact that things will go wrong. Be prepared to handle whatever comes up. Strikes, breakdowns, and slippages are among the range of contingencies you will meet. Keep calm and keep going through these rough patches.

- Have you identified the training and development needs of all staff and planned accordingly? Hopefully you will have budgeted for the necessary training at the start of the project. Be realistic about what staff need to know and when. A 'sheep dip' approach may be quick and easy but it may not be the right response. Use a variety of training and development tools and methods so that you match everyone's learning styles.

- Have you scheduled face-to-face meetings with all staff whose roles are impacted so that they are prepared well before the event? Check that you will be meeting with everyone (including contracted, part time staff and staff on your payroll who may be on leave). Chapter 12 outlines the type of conversation to have with staff and presents a template for you.

- Have you adjusted performance measures and the business scorecard to reflect the new organization's deliverables? As you transition from current to new state the way you measure business performance is likely to change. Make sure you adjust the metrics at the appropriate time in the project rollout.

- Have you identified the work you still have to do to ensure sustainability and effectiveness of the new design? Successful transition is not the end of the project. You need to do a certain amount to ensure sustainability, continuous improvement, and renewal. Breathing a sigh of relief and even celebrating transition success are good things to do, but remember transition is just another milestone in the life of your organization.

▪ Have you brought into the open the informal and shadow side issues of the design? If not, do so before you go any further. Unmarked undercurrents could well bring down your project.

Do's and Don'ts

▪ Do balance short-term wins with long-term gains. You need both
▪ Do make deliberate and understandable decisions about your transition phasing plan
▪ Do communicate the transition plan timings and impacts regularly to all stakeholders
▪ Don't underestimate the power of the informal and shadow organization
▪ Don't evade the problems of successful transitions
▪ Don't forget that you are human and subject to stress in difficult times

Summary – The Bare Bones

▪ Maintain a high level of trust and co-operation throughout the transition phase to minimize disruptive currents
▪ Address the issues upfront of keeping the business running effectively as you handle the change
▪ Lead and drive the project – make sure you know why people will follow you
▪ Describe and reach milestones on the transition path – communicate achieving these
▪ Plan for contingencies and accept that things will go wrong
▪ Take regular soundings on progress and adapt your plans as necessary

References/Useful Reading

Egan, G. (1994). *Working the Shadow Side.* Jossey-Bass.
Goffee, R. and Jones, G. (2000). Why should anyone be led by you? *Harvard Business Review.* September–October.

Pettigrew, A. in Galliers, R. D. and Baets, W. J. R. (eds.) (1998). *Information Technology and Organizational Transformation.* John Wiley & Sons Ltd.

Schaffer, R. H. and Thomson, H. A. (1992). Successful change programs begin with results. *Harvard Business Review.* January–February.

Scott-Morgan, P. (1994). *The Unwritten Rules of the Game,* McGraw-Hill.

Shaw, R. B. (1992). The capacity to act: creating a context for empowerment. In David A Nadler et al., *Organizational Architecture: Designs for Changing Organizations.* Jossey-Bass.

Stacey, R. (2000). *Strategic Management and Organizational Dynamics,* 3rd edition. FT Prentice Hall.

12

The People Planning

'Nothing is more crucial to the success of your transition than how you select and treat people.'

David van Adelsberg and Edward A. Trolley (1999).
Running Training Like a Business. Berrett-Koehler Publishers.

Overview

Your project's success is largely dependent on how you plan and implement people's transition from their current role to their new role. Handling this sensitive and demanding aspect requires all your technical HR and management skills and all your interpersonal and leadership skills.

If you do not have technical skills related to workforce planning, job design, skills audits, developing role descriptions, recruitment, and consultation seek advice and support from the Chartered Institute of Personnel and Development in the UK (www.cipd.co.uk) or, in the US, from the Society for Human Resource Management (www. shrm.org).

As a foundation for your transition plan, you must have completed the following:

- Developed and articulated a vision of the new organization.
- Clearly described the business objectives.
- Designed a high-level organization structure to deliver the business plan.

- Mapped the business processes/workflows.
- Defined the units of work that make up roles and jobs.
- Described the jobs and person specifications.

Once you have these elements your task is to assess the number and type of staff required over an agreed period for the new organization and to develop a resourcing and selection strategy with an appointment process.

In your transition plan detail exactly how you are going to assess, select, and communicate with your staff. State what you are going to do to manage the role changes (induction, training, and other development activity). Figure 12.1 lists the main elements of a transition plan and typical actions to take in relation to each element.

You shape strategy for selection by the degree of openness and choice you want to offer. The more open you are the more likely you are to retain the goodwill and motivation of your staff. People who have been through a transition process involving things like applying for 'their' job find the experience painful and difficult. However, if you treat staff sensitively and with empathy, ensure their self-esteem remains intact, and they fully understand what is happening then the process is on the right track.

The benefits of adopting a strategy of choice and openness are that involved employees understand the new organization and the role they could play in it. They understand the logic behind decisions even if they find the decisions unpalatable. From an individual's perspective, it is the difference between 'being done to' and having 'no say' to being able to 'contribute to or influence the outcome'.

I was frightened that I would lose my job in the reshuffle. A lot of people got stressed and there were negativities and hostile attitudes to the whole idea of applying for new jobs. But management said from the beginning that no one would be put out of work, and that people would be matched as far as possible to their preferred role. There was a lot of communication on the process. Over a few weeks, the scepticism and anxiety gave way to more positive feelings. In the end things turned out fine for people – some opted to leave and got good support to do this. Everyone felt valued and cared for even though they did not necessarily get what they wanted.

Element of transition plan	Activities
Define organization structure	▪ Review the new design and develop an appropriate workforce plan
Workforce plan	▪ Identify required critical skill by level/family against different scenarios ▪ Assess the population against the requirement (skills audit) ▪ Define the skills gap ▪ Define what is trainable ▪ Define transition skill requirements

	Numbers
	▪ Identify headcount targets for Yr 1, Yr 2, and Yr 3 against different scenarios (e.g. Scenario A: re-engineer/automate; Scenario B: relocate; Scenario C: outsource)
	▪ Identify future flexible resourcing requirements (e.g. part-time, annual hours)
	▪ Identify workforce flows:
	(a) Natural flows (historical)
	    Natural was wastage
	    Internal staffing flows
	(b) Identify induced flows required against each scenario and skill requirement.
	    – Number and skills to shed (e.g. induced exit, redeployment, termination of temporary contracts)
	    – Number and skills to acquire (e.g. based on volume, performance)
	    – Numbers to reskill/train
	(c) Identify workforce transition requirements including change programme resourcing
	▪ Develop resourcing plans for new locations (if appropriate)

Consultation plan	Involvement ▪ Decide level of involvement required and involvement principles ▪ Develop mechanisms to deliver involvement Communication ▪ Define all stakeholders ▪ Identify a communications strategy for each group ▪ Develop communications plan and processes Industrial relations ▪ Develop consultative mechanisms ▪ Develop dispute processes ▪ Identify agreements that need to be changed ▪ Review future bargaining arrangements

Figure 12.1 People transition plan: elements and activities

Element of transition plan	Activities
	Legal • Identify how Transfer of Undertakings will occur if required • Identify possible changes to contracts and implications
People support	• Identify support required and mechanisms for giving it • Communicate what support is available
Job profiles and roles	• Identify jobs that remain unchanged • Write and agree job profiles • Evaluate jobs • Finalize a list of available positions and position descriptions • Communicate outcome • Identify numbers of people available for possible redeployment and potential target areas • Assess the probability of redeployment with the potential receiving area • Identify and design options to meet requirements and associated costs to build into budget and reflect in business case • Identify who to retain and who to let go • Identify and develop support mechanisms for staff leaving or moving on a redeployment basis (e.g. counselling) • Identify approaches to Transfer of Undertakings scenario • Identify legal implications of terminating staff
Reward and recognition	• Identify boundaries/fit with other areas of organization • Determine what to reward/recognize • Consider current and future state • Agree what to keep/change • Identify options for reward and recognition • Develop incentive mechanisms for retention • Identify requirements for future reward processes (e.g. what will align with future business objectives) • Develop recognition mechanisms • Agree approach • Communicate approach
Selection and recruitment process	• Define selection criteria • Determine approach to selection into jobs • Communicate the selection process • Appoint an interview team • Appoint/select managers • Clarify selection process for vacant positions • Identify external recruitment by skill and level

Figure 12.1 Continued

Element of transition plan	Activities
	▪ Identify internal movement through career development processes/selection ▪ Identify possible redeployment flows into project delivery area ▪ Review contract types required for now and for the future depending on the nature of future work ▪ Identify resources required to deliver the change programme ▪ Develop a clear, detailed resourcing plan with built in recruitment lead times (e.g. twelve weeks to offer) ▪ Ensure that critical roles have sufficient succession cover
Training and development	▪ Conduct a skills audit as part of the workforce plan ▪ Identify opportunities to retrain staff to meet needs ▪ Assess and design management and other training and development to support change ▪ Develop appropriate training budget to meet requirements
Performance management **plan**	▪ Discuss and agree key performance indicators for all roles ▪ Discuss teamworking principles/impact on KPIs* ▪ Determine implications of new roles on grades of staff ▪ Communicate KPI process ▪ Agree KPIs with job holders ▪ Identify performance measures to deliver and track the change ▪ Develop KPI and capability targets in line with targets
	* Key Performance Indicators

Figure 12.1 Continued

In addition, the more open the process and the more influence they bring to bear, the fairer people feel it is. The more autocratic and closed the process, the more likelihood the process will feel unfair, and will be open to comments of 'stereotyping', 'subjectivity', 'jobs for the boys', 'personal views', and so on.

Some of your choices about the openness of the selection process have to do with your organizational culture and/or the culture you are aiming for. If you are trying to move from a command and control culture to a collaborative culture then your people transition plan and selection process should reflect this.

Bear in mind that the more open the process the more time it takes to operate it, but the chances of maintaining motivation and performance are good. A closed-door system while quick usually results in performance drops and damaging emotional stress.

ORGANIZATION	MATCHING	INDIVIDUAL
Develop business plan ■ Purpose/Objectives ■ Long-term-based strategic ■ Short-term operational detailed	**Integrated matching process** ■ **Organization's employment strategy** What kind of employer do we want to be? ■ **Resourcing strategy** Acquire, shed, transform staff? What contracts are needed? (e.g. annual hours/homeworking). Do we need to outsource/integrate with our partners?	**Individual needs** ■ Occupational choice ■ Employer choice ■ Lifestyle requirements ■ Career plans ■ Self assessment ■ Expectations
People plan ■ Organization & culture ■ Volume of activity ■ Processes ■ Impact of IT ■ Workforce plan (roles, capabilities & numbers)	■ **Capabilities** What will future capability need to be? ■ **Training and development** What development and training will build required capabilities? ■ **Career management** How will people move through the organization? What are the career paths? How do processes need to be improved? What are the individuals' aspirations? ■ **Performance management** How can we achieve effective performance management processes? ■ **Management style** What should managers spend more/less time doing? How can consistency be achieved?	
Organizational action plans ■ Develop, acquire, shed or transform skills ■ Address an organizational weakness ■ Revise people processes	■ **Reward and recognition** What do you want to reward? How are people recognized? ■ **Participation** To what extent do you want employee involvement? ■ **Culture** What is your desired culture and how will you achieve it. How can you achieve it? ■ **Industrial relations** How effective are your industrial relationships?	**Individual outcomes** ■ Individual feedback on realism of aspirations ■ Revision of individual plans
Organizational outcomes ■ Productivity ■ Flexibility ■ Level of service ■ Unit cost improvement	Assess resources and philosophy against business requirement Action plan	**Individual outcomes** ■ Job satisfaction ■ Motivation ■ Personal development ■ Sustained/enhanced performance optional integration of work and family

Figure 12.2 A people planning framework

People Planning Framework

Figure 12.2 illustrates a framework for thinking about people planning. Briefly, your aim is to match with a close as fit as possible the needs of the new organization design with the individuals in the workforce.

To apply the framework to your situation, answer the questions in the middle column of Figure 12.2. Check that your answers match the organizational requirements that informed your design and as far as possible the individual's requirements. If the people processes do not support the design then it will not work. When you have satisfactory and agreed answers to the questions you are ready to move on to the nitty gritty of developing job descriptions and person specifications, and then going through the selection process to fill the available roles. If at the end of the matching process you have jobs that are unfilled, you recruit either internally or externally.

Selection Options and Consultation Processes

Essentially, there are five selection options available to you.

Make Appointments Through an Involving Bidding Process

How you do this:

- Create the new organization and develop the new structure.
- Publish full job descriptions, criteria, and person specifications together with the vision, the new organization chart, the mission, and goals.
- Invite employees to consider the published jobs in relation to their career development plans, their match to the criteria, their skills and abilities.
- Hold 1:1 manager–employee discussions on options and possibilities.
- Ensure each staff member completes a bidding form for the jobs they are interested in.
- Recommend that they attach supporting documentation to the form, indicate the preference order of the jobs, and nominate one or two referees to be contacted when the bids are considered.
- Collate bids.
- Convene a series of management meetings by grade. Each level of management selects the lower level of staff making a team decision on appointees.

- Use information collated from the bid, current manager, performance data, career development data, and referees to inform the decision.
- Give everyone a feedback on their applications and the reason for the decision (the current manager holds these discussions).
- Have an appeals process available.

Figure 12.3 is an actual example of a bid process timetable in Xerox (names have been changed). In this particular case, the bid process was open to people whose current jobs were lost in the new design. They bid for the new and different jobs that had been created. Current incumbents kept jobs that were the same in the new design as in the previous design.

Comprehensive Selection Process

How you do this:

- Publish the new organization and the jobs.
- Make available full job descriptions and person specifications and essential criteria.
- Communicate a summary of the selection process that you will use to assess suitability and potential for each role.
- Invite staff to apply for the jobs using a standard application form.
- Screen the applications to identify staff who meet the essential criteria.
- Call those who do meet the criteria for interview with the new owning manager and an independent representative.
- Give everyone a feedback on their application and the reason for the decision (the current manager does this).

Management Appointments

How you do this:

- Create the new jobs as you create the new organization.
- Lead the management team through a process of matching jobs to people in the organization.
- Offer jobs to individuals as you make the decisions.
- Publish the new organization chart with jobs allocated and names attached.
- Have feedback available to support the appointment decisions you make.

Date	Activity	Notes	Action
8th October a.m.	Confirm organization meets numbers target. Confirm individual appointments can be discussed	If this has not been achieved – individual discussions with Branch Heads	Susan
8th October p.m.	Discussions with individuals to be placed in re-proposed jobs. Brief individuals whose job is disappearing and explain next steps in process	Individuals should be given week-end to decide. Ensure that jobs being offered for preference bidding are different from any individuals current job unless desire to move has already been indicated by individual. To provide proper levels of support. All displaced people should be allocated to People Leadership Team (PLT), if Senior Manager or SM if Manager. This will normally be line manager unless line manager has been displaced	Purchasing Leadership Team (PLT)
11th October	Finalize job titles for second level in organization	Any suggestions to Penny Friday p.m.	Susan/Penny
11th October	PLT Meeting 0900–1000 to finalize placement decisions and jobs to be offered for preference bidding	*Brief meeting Monday a.m. with PLT to ensure we have ducks in a row. (0900–1030)*	PLT
11th October	Appointment process finalized Brief descriptions completed for all roles	Job Description format attached	PLT Penny
11th October	Communication plan completed		Helen/Penny
12th October	Breaking the news on the new organization. Face-to-face briefings	Venues to be booked and presentations prepared. Timings to be agreed	PLT

Figure 12.3 Timetable for bid process

Career Development Appointments

How you do this:

- Create the new organization.
- Write the job descriptions and person specifications.
- Use succession plans and career development data to match staff to jobs (staff may not know the range of jobs available, management judgment drives the appointments).

Move with the Job

How you do this:

- Move people who are currently in jobs allocated in the re-design with the job.

In practice, there is a combination of these five approaches. Some jobs being bid for, others being allocated, and other jobs moving with incumbents. Decide what will work best for you. Then design a robust and fair selection process that people understand and feel is fair and respectful.

Consultation processes depend on your situation and may well require specialist advice and expertise. Trade Unions and Works Councils are key stakeholders in any re-design project. Check that you have included them in your transition plan and that you keep them fully informed as your people planning progresses.

If you feel confident to manage without specialist advice, work through four areas:

Consult or negotiate? Ask yourself if the people plan requires consultation, negotiation, or both. If an agreement needs changing then you have to negotiate this. Check that you are aware of all the agreements in place. It is very easy to overlook some. If there are no agreements in place then consultation is appropriate. Your decision now is who should be consulted, when, and where?

Understand the context for the consultation or negotiation. If appropriate, assess the existing state of industrial relations at both the local and corporate level. Ascertain the current level of employee involvement, communication processes, and style of consultation.

Whom should you involve? Which categories of staff are involved? Which are the bargaining groups? Who are the main players (e.g. officials/lay representatives)? Representatives tend to be key influencers and their potential to provide either support or opposition may be a critical factor in your transition. Is this a highly unionized area?

Legal considerations. What are your company's contractual obligations for the affected staff? Will there be redundancies or surpluses? What are the notice period requirements? What is the length of the consultation period? What impact does the negotiation/consultation process have on your implementation plan?

As you approach these questions, be aware of options you can present, the risks these might raise, and the advice you may require. Aim to keep your workforce and any unions on your side. Plan realistic time scales for your transition – consultation and involvement take longer than you think, particularly where there is significant change for employees.

The Difficult Conversations

You are likely to be familiar with a number of thousands of books and articles on helping people manage through change and transitions. Models and approaches compete although most seem to have a similar concept that people have to say farewell to the past, look with optimism to the future and in between is some sort of neutral state (see Figure 7.1).

Bearing in mind that your staff members will be going through this transition process at different rates and with individual responses, consider why some of them may find it more difficult to work through to feeling confident about the outcomes of the transition. Kanter (1984) has distilled a list of ten common reasons why you may find individuals resisting your people transition proposals. These are summarized in Figure 12.4.

Part of the process of organization re-design involves having discussions with displaced people or people having to take on new and different roles/jobs/responsibilities. Much has been written about the 'survivor' syndrome and people will measure some of the success of your re-design by the way you conducted these conversations with themselves and their colleagues.

Loss of control	People want to feel they have a say, not that they are being 'done to'
Excess uncertainty	People do not know what is going to happen next
Surprise, surprise	People do not like decisions or requests coming 'out of the blue'
The 'difference' effect	People are required to question and challenge familiar habits and routines
Loss of face	People are not comfortable if they have to accept or think that the way they did things in the past was wrong
Concerns about future competence	People want to feel they are competent to do the job. A potential change may threaten this
Ripple effects	Any change has a ripple effect and/or unintended consequences. Be sensitive to these
More work	Transitioning from one state to another means a heavier workload and takes time
Past resentments	People who are aggrieved with the organization over a past issue may resent you telling them things are changing again
Sometimes the threat is real	People know that change creates winners and losers

Figure 12.4 Reasons for resistance to change (adapted from Kanter 1984)

Prepare yourself well to handle the difficult task of talking to people about job changes. Be sensitive to people's stage of transition. Understand the reasons why they may resist changing. With this baseline, it is your job to help them leave the discussion with you feeling clear about the reasons for the changes in role, about the specific impact on themselves, about dates, next steps, and available support. If they are leaving the organization they must also be clear about notice, working arrangements till their notice period ends, and finance.

Additionally, ensure the person you are talking to feels supported and valued. You want them to leave a discussion with you able to think rationally and objectively about the change, able to manage their emotions, able to talk about things to colleagues, able to trust in and use the available support. Help individuals keep their dignity and self-esteem intact. Those you talk to should leave the discussion feeling they have been treated empathetically, with honesty, and constructively.

Having these discussions is likely to leave you feeling drained and you may feel distressed at times. If you feel you have covered everything with the staff member and done the best you can it will help you handle your own feelings effectively.

Handling your own feelings may be hard if the staff member is difficult to manage. There are three types of hard-to-handle behaviour commonly evident in job changes related to organization re-design – confusion, rigidity, and withdrawal.

A staff member demonstrates confusion by talking in a disjointed way, not taking things in, appearing oblivious to the realities of the situation, and using phrases like 'I don't understand', or 'can you say that again'. In these cases remain empathetic but focused. Help with specifics. Take the person back to the key points that you have made – these provide signposts in the discussion. Summarize the conversation frequently, and support the person in feeling that it is all right to have feelings of confusion at this point.

If staff members take a rigid (or entrenched) stance to you and to what you are saying they are likely to be expressing things in black and white terms. They may well be angry and inflexible (or they may be in very strong control of their emotions). Their body language is probably tense. Aim, with these people, to loosen up their thinking and/or attitudes – ask them questions on the lines of 'How else …?' or 'What else?' Challenge them to have a positive perception of the situation and of themselves by suggesting that they reflect on their knowledge and/or experience and the ways this will help them through the current situation to the new situation.

Noer (1996) describes withdrawn people in terms of being 'overwhelmed'. They feel frustrated, powerless, and anxious. They seek approval, reassurance, and stability. Generally, withdrawn people have a low comfort level with change and a low capacity for managing it. Their tactics include avoidance of confronting the real issues, thinking about the future, and planning for it. Managing discussions with people who withdraw from change means you have to provide help. Specifically help them deal with their stress, fear, and frustration. Show them the future in terms of a supportive environment. If possible, help them locate a role where their benefit is in their knowledge and experience of the organization's history and legacy.

People who approach change positively and who come to the discussions with you in an optimistic, grounded, and open-minded way are a joy to talk with. However, remember that they too need support and reinforcement in achieving their goals.

Useful Tools

Tool 1: Checklist for a Successful Job/Role Transition Discussion

Clarity of objectives	
Are you clear what the objectives are for each discussion? (Each discussion may have a different objective.)	
Is the staff member clear about the objectives of the discussion?	
A good process	
Have you prepared carefully for the discussion? (Have to hand employee details, knowledge of their situation, and perhaps some information on their likely reaction to what you are discussing.)	
Have you allowed enough time for the discussion? Include time for questions and reflection.	
Do you have a clear structure for the meeting?	
Are you clear and informed about the situation? Have you got answers for the questions that might arise?	
Do you have a method for addressing the issues that might come up?	
Are you clear how you are going to wrap up and close the discussion?	
Logistics	
Have you booked a suitable room for the discussion?	
Have you got back-up information with you?	
Have you turned off your mobile phone and any other phone?	
Have you ensured that you will not be interrupted?	
Have you got water and tissues to hand?	

Behaviour	
Are you able to demonstrate integrity and respect?	
Are you in control of your own emotional state?	
Have you determined to listen actively and genuinely?	
Are you willing to conduct the discussion at the staff member's pace?	
Are you able to adjust your message for each person appropriately? (Use simple, clear language. Match your speech with your body language.)	
Will you remember to check their understanding of the conversation?	
Are you confident you can stay focused on the topic?	
Are you determined to cover all the bases and not be tempted to short cut?	

Tool 2: GROW Model for Structuring Job/Role Transition Discussion

Goal	Outline and agree expectations for the meeting. Log the issues to be addressed before the meeting closes. Take account of the intellectual and emotional aspects. *How to say it* 'My goal is that at the end of the meeting you will be clear about outcomes and next steps'. 'My goal is that you should continue to feel valued and supported, and have confidence going forward'.
Rationale and review	Recap or explain the business context and the specific rationale on which judgments have been made and outcomes based. Explain the impact on the employee. Have back-up information in hand in talk through the detail. Ensure employee understands each element of the discussion.

	How to say it 'These are the things we had to consider very carefully in the light of your capabilities and what you said you wanted to do.' 'Let me turn to the details of the terms which will apply in your case'.
Options	Explore possible options for the person. Depending on the circumstances this may be a combination of internal and external things to consider. Options may include the following: ▪ Training and development ▪ Alternative jobs/roles ▪ Support and help ▪ Who to go and talk to ▪ Where to get more information *How to say it* 'You have great strengths in terms of … have you thought how these might be applied?' 'What help do you think you'll need in the longer term?'
Wrap up	Summarize the key points of the discussion. Ensure the staff members understand what you have said. Invite questions. Ask about thoughts and feelings. Offer further support. Make sure the person is committed to at least one action. Provide any informational material to consolidate your message. *How to say it* 'What else can I do to help?' 'Next week, when you've had a chance to think this over, I'll arrange for us to have a follow-up discussion'.

Self-check

The movement of people as you transition from the current organization to the new organization is complex, time consuming, and emotionally draining. Prepare yourself for the ups and downs of this process by checking that you have things in place to maximize a smooth flow.

If you can answer 'yes' to the majority of these questions you are on the right track.

- Have you identified the core competencies of your business (or your part of the organization)? A core competency is the fundamental knowledge, ability, or expertise on which an organization trades. Companies with specific strengths in the marketplace, such as commercial air travel, have a core competency in that area. The *core* part means that the company has a strong basis from which develop other products or services. If you cannot identify your core competence, you will have a hard time finding the right skill sets amongst individuals to deliver your business plan.
- Do you know what you most want your organization to achieve over the next one to three years? To develop an effective workforce plan that ensures bench strength and pipeline over a given period you must know what you are in business to do. You will not be able to supply the organization with capable people if you are not clear what it is aiming to achieve.
- Have you clarified the styles, values, and culture of the organization you want your staff to subscribe to and demonstrate? It is not enough to select people solely on the basis of their skills and expertise to do a job. People's behavioural attributes and mindsets must match the style, values, and culture that you want to embed and sustain in the new organization.
- Have you forecast the capabilities and behavioural attributes you will need to deliver your business plan? Have you matched these to what you currently have? To get a line of sight between what you forecast you will need and what you currently have, you will need to do some form of skills and capabilities audit. This will help you identify areas of under or oversupply from which you can develop a workforce plan that addresses these issues and ensures continuity of supply to meet demand.
- Do you have clear sight of the way to organize your business processes into meaningful units of work for job design? Business process analysis enables you to examine the end-to-end workflows in your organization and 'package' the work units that enable the work to be done. These units of work form the basis of jobs and

roles from which you design the jobs and develop job descriptions and person specifications. You must know what the workflows are before you design jobs and create roles.

- Are you taking steps to align your performance management system with the new organization design? Having a performance management system that reinforces the behaviours, skills, and operating style that characterize your new organization is critical to its success. Often there is a time lag between transitioning to the new organization and getting the HR systems aligned to support it. Allowing a time lag encourages your project to fail. Introduce reinforcing HR systems in line with the phases of the transition.
- Are you taking steps to align your reward and recognition system with the new organization design? As it is for performance management systems, so it is for reward and recognition systems. If people are still being rewarded in the new organization for 'old' behaviours and skills there is no incentive for them to change. To make a successful transition to the new organization you must have in place the carrots and sticks that will support it.
- Have you developed a complete people transition plan? A people transition plan must be complete and detailed. Figure 12.1 lists the majority of the areas to cover, but check it for completeness in relation to your organization. You may want to add other aspects to the plan – for example if your re-design involves relocating you will have to organize a geographic move and relocation incentives, both will feature on your transition plan.
- Have you started communicating your transition plan to the organization? As the plan firms up, communicate it appropriately. Even if you know very little, it is worth telling people that you have no information at this stage. When people are feeling anxious and stressed, they are much more likely to attribute lack of communication and information to conspiracy than to cock up.
- Do you have support mechanisms in place for people who are changing jobs/roles or who are leaving the organization? As well as managerial support, it is a good idea to have other sources of support available to staff. These may come from internal or external agencies. Your organization may have an employee assistance programme, or you may be able to offer counselling, mentoring,

or other help (e.g. from an outplacement firm). Make these possibilities known to the workforce.

- Are you confident that your managers have the skills to handle difficult discussions? Managers are people too, and in many cases, the organization re-design affects them. Managers whose own jobs are changing are in the difficult position of having to present effective messages, and hold supportive discussions with their staff when they may be feeling many similar emotions themselves. Prepare your managers to handle the discussions and recognize their own job related issues and concerns.

- Do you have a robust and agreed process for matching individuals to the new organization's requirements? Whatever method you decide to use to match individuals with jobs, you must either negotiate or consult on it with the appropriate stakeholders in your organization. These may be Trade Unions and Works Councils representatives or your own business involvement groups. Holding these discussions takes time, so factor this into your plan's time scales.

Do's and Don'ts

- Do have support mechanisms for helping individuals manage their own transitions
- Do get expert help and advice on the technical aspects of your people plan
- Do give people information and do it again and again
- Don't neglect to look after yourself in this phase
- Don't be surprised at 'over reactions'
- Don't underestimate the time it takes to negotiate, consult, and get people into new roles

Summary – The Bare Bones

- Develop a detailed, agreed, and communicated people transition plan
- Implement it with sensitivity and care. At all times treat people with respect and in a way that preserves their self-esteem

- Match people to jobs in a fair and defensible way. Give feedback to individuals on the reasons for your decisions
- Remember to hold negotiations and consultations with the relevant employee representatives in your organization. If possible, involve these representatives in the design of your transition plan
- Recognize that people experience transitions in different ways and at their individual pace. Recognize too that you and your managers are going through your own transition experiences
- Enter 1:1 discussions on new roles well prepared, with the information you need, and your own emotions in check

References/Useful Reading

Bridges, W. (2003). *Managing Transitions: Making the Most of Change*, 2nd edition. Perseus Publishing.

Caplan, G. and Teese, M. (1997). *Survivors*. Davies-Black Publishing.

Johansen, R. and Swigart, R. (2000). *Upsizing the Individual in the Downsized Organization: Managing in the Wake of Reengineering, Globalization, and Overwhelming Technological Change*. Perseus Publishing.

Kanter, R. (1984). *Managing Change: The Human Dimension*. Goodmeasure Inc.

Noer, D. (1993). *Healing the Wounds*. Jossey-Bass.

Noer, D. (1996). *Breaking Free: A Prescription for Personal and Organizational Change*. Jossey-Bass.

Pfeffer, J. (1998). *The Human Equation*. Harvard Business School Press.

13

Phase Five – Reviewing the Design

'One of the most common reasons that re-designs fail, is the all too common assumption that the job essentially ends with the announcement of the new design.'

David A. Nadler and Michael L. Tushman (1997).
Competing by Design. Oxford University Press.

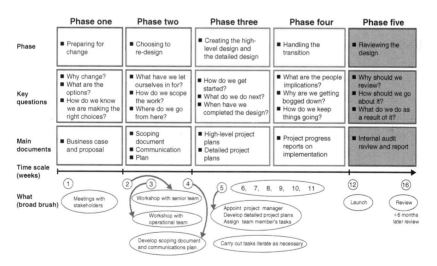

Figure 13.1 Phase five of the design (shaded)

Overview

Reviewing your project is usually a much overlooked part of the project plan – if, indeed, it ever appeared on your project plan. But neglect this phase and you risk your project falling at the last post, because you will not know the aspects that need amendment. Neither will you get the most learning from the experience to pass on to future organization design teams. Do two reviews – the first an informal review (primarily with your project team) four weeks after you have accomplished the transition. Three to six months later, do a formal review – or if you have an internal-audit department, ask them to do a full post-implementation review (PIR). Undertake the reviews to verify and validate that:

- You correctly identified the purpose of the project.
- The objectives set will deliver that purpose.
- The design chosen will achieve those objectives.
- The design will achieve its purpose within the boundaries and to the principles established.
- The information on which you based the design is reliable.

Figure 13.1 illustrates the timing of the two reviews and lists the three questions to start you off in phase five of your project – Why should we review? How should we go about it? What do we do as a result of it? This chapter answers the three questions and gives more information on the review phase.

Why should we review? There are four good reasons for reviewing your design. First, it enables you to evaluate your success in achieving your objectives. You can start to find out how successful you are being, about four weeks after you have implemented your plan. Reviewing at this point will give you early warning of anything that is not working towards meeting your objectives.

If your design shows signs of not meeting plan it may be that the objectives themselves need revisiting – particularly if the context in which you are now operating has changed since your plan was conceived.

Second, reviewing enables you and your team to reflect on the OD project and learn from your experience. Ask yourselves some basic questions at this point:

- What happened as things unrolled?
- Why did they happen?
- How should we do it differently next time?
- What should we do about things now?

A four week review point provides the opportunity for personal learning (how you operate, your strengths and weaknesses), team learning, and learning for the organization (six months later in the formal review, you get more information on this).

Third, reviewing at both points gives you information and knowledge to share with other project teams and with your stakeholders. Most large organizations describe themselves as 'siloed' or 'smoke stacked' and have difficulty learning from their own members. Many organizations are much better at benchmarking other companies than learning from their own experiences. If you are able to share your knowledge effectively, you can avoid re-inventing the wheel and also avoid other people making the same mistakes that you have just made. Publishing what you have learned can help spread good practice and develop common values and consistent approaches.

Fourth, reviewing four weeks after launch (or full transition to the new state) gives you a formal opportunity to debrief and disband your implementation team(s). The end of the transition phase marks the end of the project. People working on the project are likely to view its closure with mixed feelings. They may look forward to future opportunities or face their own job loss because of the new design. This was the result for a project manager of a British Airways re-organization. She project managed herself out of a job.

I knew fairly soon after I was asked to take on the project management role that a likely outcome would be that I would be jobless when the project closed. The thing we were doing was so radical and the effect on jobs, roles, and the organization structure so significant that I was frightened at the potential outcome for me, but honoured that the MD asked me to manage the project.

> *In one way, it was good – I had enough time to plan what I wanted to do when I left British Airways, and I was able to empathize with people in the same position as me (though I did not publicize my own situation until it was announced along with every one else's). I learned a huge amount about project management and about myself. I found that I was adventuresome and courageous. May be the project enabled me to take the leap and move to Australia to start a new life!*

Debriefing meetings fulfil five purposes. They identify any task yet to be completed. These may be things on the list or they may arise out of the discussions you have. They identify the impact of change so far – using the measures and metrics, you have in place to track success. They provide a forum for agreeing the method of transferring ownership from project managers to line managers. They provide the opportunity to recognize and reward the achievement of project team members and others involved. They celebrate the end of the project.

Reviewing three to six months after the project ends, gives you a much more in-depth look at the success or otherwise of your new design in achieving its objectives. In large organizations, an internal-audit team using a standard reporting format generally does implementation reviews. An example of a standard form appears later in this chapter (Figure 13.4).

How should we go about it? At the informal 4 week review, use the basic questions listed above as a start-point. At this stage, also do the following:

- **Re-do the alignment exercise**: The alignment exercise that you undertook when you had finished the design (Chapter 8, Tool 1), made sure that all the elements in your plan, dovetail to produce the critical skills and behaviours necessary to achieve your objectives. Re-doing the exercise, a short while after you have implemented the plan, will highlight both the elements working well and the elements that need more work.
- **Decide the criteria for judging progress and success**: Ask yourself a number of questions, for example, how will you know whether your re-structuring is working? What is the appropriate amount of

time before you see results? How will outsiders judge whether you have 'won' or 'lost'? How will your staff judge this? Answers to these questions give you the foundation for doing the more formal review within three to six months.

■ **Develop metrics that will measure what you are doing now, not what you measured in the previous state. Get the new measures recognized by your staff and the wider organization**: A problem with aiming to do something differently is that existing measures may not support the difference. Negative assessments of progress or failures of the re-design to deliver are often a consequence of inappropriately applying traditional metrics.

■ **Develop a plan for maintaining and improving the new design**: Implementing your transition plan will take time. For at least a year, after you have made the transition you need to be measuring and monitoring your progress towards achieving your objectives. Check that your plan is operating as part of the three to six month audit.

When you get to the three to six month point, do a formal audit (also called the PIR). Do this for five reasons:

1. To check whether everyone is aware of your purpose, goals, strategies for achieving goals, and critical success factors.
2. To check whether everyone understands the purpose of his/her job, where it fits in, and has sufficient information to do it effectively.
3. To check whether everyone has felt involved appropriately in the re-design process.
4. To check whether each person is able to establish an effective dialogue with his/her customers and suppliers.
5. To check whether an appropriate culture and management style is being supported and maintained.

A later section gives you more detailed information on the conduct of a PIR.

What do we do as a result of it? As a result of the review and audit, there are a number of things to do:

■ **Monitor progress**: Do this, both quantitatively and qualitatively. If people are expressing concerns on progress, listen to them. Their concerns are almost always valid. Quantitative measures will provide different information from qualitative measures.

- **Leverage your ability to manage expectations**: Significant change takes time. Encourage stakeholders to take a realistic time horizon for realizing the benefits of the re-design. Stop them from trying to pull-up the radishes to see how they are growing. There is often a 'results gap' between expected results and actual results. This gap drives negative assessments of projects. You need to manage these expectations to avoid people undermining the credibility of your work.

- **Challenge (or at least question) traditional metrics if they are inappropriate for your use**: If the re-design does not quickly produce the expected results, senior management often jumps to the immediate conclusion that the project was poorly conceived. Encourage assessment of the metrics by those who control them. Raise awareness of the many types of measurement possible, and of the most appropriate ones to measure what you are trying to achieve.

- **Recognize the progress you have made and are making**: One department in Marks & Spencer carried out a review four weeks after transition to the new organization and was pleasantly surprised to see how much they had accomplished in such a short span of time. People quoted 'getting some benefits already', 'better focus on single activities', 'team working improved'. You can help recognize progress by establishing interim goals, noticing unanticipated achievements, and recording shifts in people's views.

- **Be prepared to change track or acknowledge mistakes**: Re-designing your organization is a major change effort. There are bound to be areas where you have made mistakes or had problems. Rather than ignoring these, recognize what you can learn from them and take steps to recover the ground.

- **Stay committed**: You have committed yourself to this re-design because you believe it is what you have to do. If asked the question 'Can you prove to me that what you propose will work?' Your answer must be no. There is no way of knowing and there is a chance you will fail. Your re-design is an act of faith. The essence of faith is to proceed without any real evidence that your effort will be rewarded. Whatever the outcome you are responsible. If <u>you</u> do not keep things going things will not keep going.

Roles in Phase Five

In phase five, you are working towards project closure, and embedding the new design. The manager in this phase is taking a strategic role – commissioning the reviews and then planning the strategy for acting on their findings. The HR practitioner is taking a facilitative role supporting the manager (Figure 13.2).

In phase five, the leaders of the reviews have a significant part to play. In effect, they are managing this phase of the project and your roles are on the side. Once you have commissioned the reviews you can handover the work to the review teams until they present their report. Your role almost reverts to keeping the day-to-day business running but now it is on its new track.

Consider asking an external facilitator or consultant to handle the four week informal project review. If you do this, you can contribute on the same terms as other team members.

Commission a full PIR from an independent party. This may be an internal-audit department or an external-auditing body.

Phase five	Manager role	HR practitioner role
Reviewing the design	■ Commissioning a PIR about eight weeks after project closure ■ Assessing the findings against the intended project outcomes ■ Taking action to address issues and concerns to ensure benefits of change are delivered ■ Transferring knowledge, skills and learning, gained in the OD project ■ Strategic management	■ Ensuring PIR is thorough and reliable ■ Guiding and supporting manager to understand, communicate, and act on the findings ■ Following through on the agreed actions and recommending a second review about six months after project closure ■ Advocate ■ Facilitator ■ Objective ■ Process counsellor

Figure 13.2 Roles of manager and HR practitioner in phase five

What and How to Review

The purpose of the audit is to ensure that the new design enables you to conduct the activities of the organization in an efficient way, to deliver your objectives, and to avoid waste, loss or theft. Additionally the audit will check that there are no mistakes in the design of the activities. Figure 13.3 illustrates the process for conducting the review. To get the utmost value from the reviews conduct them in an open manner. Encourage participants to make constructive criticisms. It is only in this way that you will learn real lessons or be in a position to make improvements to business processes and supporting infrastructure.

Be aware that an audit should not become another project – your role is to see that auditors undertake it as a quick and simple exercise.

Identifying Scope and Stakeholders

Your business case largely dictates the scope of the PIR. It would have identified the rationale for the re-design and the objectives you aimed to achieve. As a minimum, the PIR will usually assess:

- the achievement (to date) of business case objectives;
- costs and benefits to date against forecast, and other benefits realized and expected;
- continued alignment to the business strategy;
- the effectiveness of revised business operations (functions, processes, staff numbers, etc.);
- ways of maximizing benefits and minimizing cost and risk;
- the sensitivity of the business service to expected business change;
- business and user satisfaction.

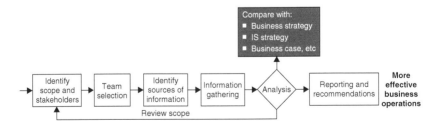

Figure 13.3 The PIR process (OGC 2004)

Team Selection

Team members conducting the review typically include some or all of the following:

- members of the audit department or other agency conducting the review;
- people with working knowledge of the business area under review and its processes;
- people with relevant technical knowledge;
- strategy planners with knowledge of the organization's business strategy and the organization design contribution to it;
- people involved in meeting the objectives of the project.

Identifying Key Sources of Information

The views of stakeholders and customers form the basis for information gathered at review interviews and workshops. The main sources of documented information will include:

- the business case
- information kept to track costs and benefits
- any previous PIR report(s)
- data collected on a regular basis as part of the normal working process
- questionnaires directed at a pre-determined audience, or a sample.

Information Gathering

You have identified issues for addressing in the scope of the PIR review. Business cases should include provision for PIRs and for the collection of information that supports them. The first task is to gather relevant information that will help you answer specific questions related to the complete design, and to its effective achievement of objectives. Goold and Campbell (2002) discuss nine tests of a well-designed organization that make an excellent basis for a PIR.

- Does your design direct sufficient management attention to your sources of competitive advantage in each market?

255

- Does your design help the corporate parent add value to the organization?
- Does your design reflect the strengths, weaknesses, and motivations of your people?
- Have you taken account of all the constraints that may impede the implementation of your design?
- Does your design protect units that need distinct cultures?
- Does your design provide co-ordination solutions for the unit-to-unit links that are likely to be problematic?
- Does your design have too many parent levels and units?
- Does your design support effective controls?
- Does your design facilitate the development of new strategies and provide the flexibility required to adapt to change?

Analysis

Analysis of the information gathered involves comparing what actually happened against that predicted to happen (e.g. in a business case). It will examine what you did well and what you did less well; this forms the basis for recommendations. It is at this stage that the data obtained from the information gathered is brought together and coherent, useful, and supportable recommendations are formulated.

Reporting the Results

The PIR is concerned mainly with maximizing the effectiveness of the business change. The PIR report you commission is yours. You decide who else should have a copy. Figure 13.4 illustrates the content areas of a typical PIR report.

Recommendations for improvements should add value to the business and you must implement them to make the reviews worthwhile. This could involve you doing something major such as changing the way the business system or process operates in some way, or it could be doing something minor. Either way, recommendations must be sufficiently robust for you to be able to act upon them. Importantly, good practice in project management and business operations should be included in recommendations for incorporating in your organization's good practice guidelines.

Check list item	Description
Reference:	
Project title/reference:	*Project name*
Project manager:	*Project manager(s) of the project*
Project sponsor:	*The sponsor for the project*
Review conducted by:	*Who conducted the review? (Usually it is someone independent of the project team).*
Review dates:	*When was the review actually conducted?*
Date project completed:	*When was the project completed or terminated?*
Outcomes:	
Outcomes of the project:	*Were the objectives of the project clearly defined and measurable? Were the objectives of the project met overall? If so, where is the proof? If not, why not?*
	Were the objectives met in terms of quality? If so, where is the proof? If not, why not?
	Were the objectives met in terms of cost? If so, where is the proof? If not, why not?
	Were the objectives met in terms of time? If so, where is the proof? If not, why not?
Reason for variance:	*What were the main reasons for not meeting the project objectives? What can be learnt from this for the future?*
Scope:	
Scope of the project:	*Was the scope of the project clearly documented and agreed?*
	Were changes to the original scope clearly documented and approved?
Scope delivered:	*Was the planned scope actually delivered by the project? If so, where is the proof – if not, why not?*
Benefits:	
Expected benefits of the project:	*The project financial case included values and measures for financial benefits. Was this accurately completed?*
	Were the benefits adequately described, bought in to by the sponsor and measures adequately defined?
Direct – financial:	*Were the latest agreed estimates of direct financial benefits, the project would deliver, achieved? If so, where is the proof? If not, why not?*
Direct – intangible:	*Were the latest agreed estimates of direct intangible benefits, the project would deliver, achieved? If so, where is the proof? If not, why not?*
Indirect:	*Were the latest agreed estimates of indirect benefits, the project would deliver, achieved? If so, where is the proof? If not, why not?*
Unexpected:	*Were there any unexpected benefits arising from the project? If so, where is the proof and why were they not identified earlier? Did any unexpected negative impacts to the business occur?*
Reasons for variances:	*What were the main reasons for not delivering the project benefits? What can be learnt from this for the future? Was the justification or benefit review process ineffective or given adequate attention?*

Figure 13.4 Template for a PIR report

Costs: Costs review:	Was a project budget established at the start of the project accurate? Were costs adequately reviewed throughout the project? Were changes to costs adequately controlled and authorized?

Financial summary:
Project costs (£k)

	Authorized	Actual	Over/under spend
Capital			
Revenue			
Total			

Project benefits (£k)

	Original	Revised	Variance
Income			
Staff costs			
Other costs			
Total			

Project returns

	Original	Revised	Increase/decrease
IRR (%)			
NPV (£k)			

Project time scales

	Authorized	Actual	Variance (+/− mths)
Start date			
Completion date			

Customer comments: Customer satisfaction	Is the customer satisfied with the project outcome? If not, why not?
Team performance development review (PDR's)	Please confirm that all team members have had a PDR before leaving the project.
External consultants or other professional advisors	Did they perform to expected standards? Were agreed benefits delivered? Were costs and time constraints met? Would you recommend them for future work? What were the main strengths and weaknesses? If there was a partnership agreement, how successful was it?
Lessons learnt: Things that worked: Things that did not work:	What went well with regard to managing the business benefits and why? What did not go well and why?
Further actions:	Are there any actions arising from the review which need to be addressed? Who needs to address them and when?
Agreement: Sponsor: Project manager: Customer: Finance:	

Figure 13.4 Continued

PIR Caveats

The use of auditors to check the design ensures that the design produced and implemented meets requirements. However, because the auditors' job is to undertake a detailed, methodical examination and review and then report on this they may tend to over-zealousness. The design may well be adequate though not perfect.

From the auditors' perspective, the Office of Government Commerce (OGC 2004) reports that there are a number of common problems that may be encountered in carrying out PIRs and the review team needs to be aware of these (although they may not be able to solve them). These include:

- More than one organization involved, where there is no common standard for measuring and recording the benefits and costs.
- *Lack of documentation*: Much factual information will come from project documentation, especially the business case.
- *Lack or inadequacy of baseline measures*: For a PIR, measures of success can only be made accurately by comparing the level of performance before the project implementation against that at the time of the PIR.
- *Sensitivities*: Examining the performance of project teams, or current operations against a predicted level may lead to feelings of insecurity or grievance for those who were involved with the project, or in the business area supported by the change.
- *Management of expectations*: Although the use of reviews will improve the effectiveness of the organization, the review team should ensure that they do not raise expectations of system enhancements or business change. They may cost more to implement than the value of the benefits they would deliver.
- The organization is too busy to do a PIR and never gets it done. There should be policies to ensure that reviews are carried out as part of the organization's normal practice.
- Lack of co-operation from the service provider.

Review teams can take some action to avoid or reduce these problems such as:

- rigorous investment appraisal
- reviews of project plans

- careful selection of the project team members to ensure independent review
- formal agreements with providers to participate in the review process.

The Common Issues that PIRs Find

Be reassured that all reviews find issues and concerns for addressing. Your project will not be different and it is not a failing on your part if the reviews highlight these. The purpose of the PIR is to assess whether the changes you have made have improved effectiveness and to make recommendations for further improvements. Having this pointed out now gives you the opportunity to get things on the right track for ongoing successful achievement of your objectives. Without a PIR, you cannot demonstrate that your investment in the organization re-design was worthwhile.

You will find that the reviews you do will highlight some of the following most common and frequent implementation problems:

Implementation took more time than originally allocated: If you do a phased transition it is sometimes difficult to know when you have reached a point where it is clear that you have reached the new design. Phased transitions often drift towards their goal rather than march to it decisively reaching agreed milestones as they go. To avoid drift have clear markers of the end point you want the project to reach so that you know when to 'stop the clock'. Even with these, projects often take longer than you anticipate. Build contingency time into your plans.

Major problems surfaced during implementation that you had not identified beforehand: These can be internal or external and either way will have an adverse impact on implementation. However good your risk analysis you may leave-out something that you could not anticipate. Catastrophes and about turns occur out of the blue. If this happens re-do your risk planning and be flexible enough to change course and respond appropriately. Derailment is extremely traumatic for people so remember to address emotional responses sensitively.

Co-ordination of implementation activities was not effective enough: This talks about your project and programme management abilities. Good skills here are essential. Where you have a number of streams of work progressing simultaneously you must have a governance structure that keeps clear over-sight of all of them and provides a coherent framework for them to operate within. Reminders about collaboration, boundaries, and principles all help the project teams stay in touch with each other's progress.

You do not define key implementation tasks and activities in enough detail: Check the detail of your project plan. Imagine that your project manager leaves halfway through implementation. If this happens, you will find out that high-level descriptors are insufficient. Your test of having enough detail is that a newcomer could pick up and run with the project without a hitch. The cliché 'the devil is in the detail' holds true in re-design projects. However, the trick is to get enough detail without becoming bureaucratic and prescriptive.

Competing activities and crises distracted attention from implementing this decision: Day-to-day running of the business has to happen even through the re-design process. People's tendency is to work on the urgent rather than the important. Design work usually falls into their 'important' category. To offset this have at least one person (depending on the size of the project) who is charged with working on it full time or with full focus. This person must have the authority to keep people on track with the project time scales and milestones.

Capabilities of employees involved were not enough: When people move to new roles or responsibilities they must have the skills to deliver quickly in these. Make sure you time training and development activity to match the milestones of the project. This is particularly important if it is technology training. Too often people try to do new things without adequate preparation and instruction. Budget enough time and money at the start of your project for the training aspects.

Training and instruction given to lower-level employees was not adequate: Remember front-line staff are the people delivering your business. Unfortunately, they often come last in the pecking order of communication, training, and support in new processes. Put them as much in the spotlight as other grades of staff to ensure parity of treatment. Where lower levels of staff need more help give it to them or your customers will suffer.

Leadership and direction provided by departmental managers was not adequate: You are the conductor of the re-design and have to keep everyone together on it. This is a difficult task and before you embark on it take thorough stock of your skills and abilities to lead and manage through the long haul. If you get wobbly en-route, get help and support from external or internal sources. Do not struggle with issues alone. Make sure people can trust your judgement and integrity in leading them through to the new state.

Information systems used to monitor implementation were not adequate: Use systems that are quick, simple, and transparent to monitor implementation. A balanced scorecard approach works well. Getting all the information on one sheet weekly and paying attention to this week's progress compared with last week's is helpful. You do not need a 'magilla' of an information system to keep your project on track, but you do need metrics that give you relevant, progressive, and actionable information.

People resist the change, try to shift the burden, and/or become accidental adversaries: The people issues that reviews uncover are often significant. Traditional operational metrics do not monitor people's responses to change. However, these usually untracked responses act against the project. You can tell if there are these kinds of behavioural barrier when:

- You have announced the changes but implementation does not get under way.
- Change is taking longer than you could reasonably expect.
- Old ways are cropping up and people have gone back to doing what they used to do.
- You have to keep reinforcing the change – it does not run by itself.
- When the same problem pattern repeats.
- When people still have an investment (or are rewarded) for doing things the old way.
- When no one seems aware or involved with other parts of the organization that interact with your area.
- When you have 'enemies' or there is an 'us and them mentality', or 'in-groups and out-groups'.
- You have to work harder to achieve the same results you got a few weeks or months ago.

Pay attention to these symptoms and look for the underlying causes. They will not go away without conscious action on your part. If you can see these sorts of issues arising, try to understand why people are behaving this way, bring it out for discussion, and work with them on solving the problems.

More major issues: If you have done the work outlined in each of the phases, your reviews should offer up no real surprises. In some instances, reviews come up with major problems that may call in question, the whole rationale for doing the re-design. These types of findings include:

- Making organizational changes that are unrelated to any desired business benefits.
- Re-structuring to fix yesterday's problems, not recognizing that the world has changed and moved on.
- Implementing a re-design of generalized, organizational concepts (or current management fad) rather than one tailored to your specific needs and objectives.
- Fiddling with the organization chart instead of re-structuring.
- Politics rather than business benefit and customer requirements decide the shape of the organization.

Useful Tools

Tool 1: OGC Web-based Product, the Successful Delivery Toolkit
OGC's successful delivery toolkit (SDTK) describes proven good practice for procurement, programmes, projects, risk, and service management. The toolkit brings together policy and best practice in a single point of reference. It helps you to ask critical questions about capability and project delivery; it gives practical advice on how to improve. This free product is to spread OGC's best practice as a single electronic repository, in a way that allows any organization to easily adopt, adapt, and embed the guidance within the toolkit, into their own processes and business models. It is aimed at the strategic (board) level and senior management level within an organization. To get to the practitioner level guidance that underpins every aspect of it, there are links to OGC's various publishing partners where OGC's practitioner guidance (which is chargeable) can be purchased.

A free copy of the OGC SDTK as a CD, either as a single user version or an Intranet version, is available. The SDTK is a dynamic web-based product which is on a six month (or sooner) update cycle. The only real restriction upon its usage (as defined by its embedded 'shrink wrap' licence) is that you cannot make money out of it. The licence builds in all necessary permissions as regards Crown Copyright reuse. The SDTK was developed with Central Civil UK Government Departments in mind, but has much wider organizational value and usability. The address is http://www.ogc.gov.uk/sdtoolkit/index.html.

Tool 2: Radar Chart (adapted from Brassard & Ritter 1994)
The radar chart (an example is given in Figure 13.5) shows in one graphic the size of the gaps among a number of both current organization performance areas and ideal performance areas. It makes concentrations of strength and weakness visible, clearly displays important categories of information, defines full performance in each category, and captures the perceptions of team members about organization performance. Use it to track progress through your implementation and/or during the review phase to highlight where you need to do more work.

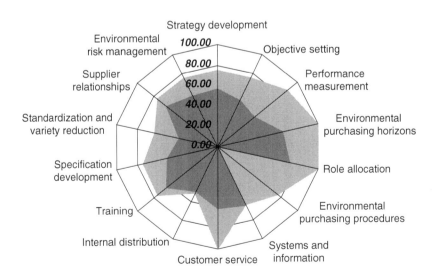

Figure 13.5 Radar chart

How to use it

■ Assemble the review team.

■ Select and define the categories you want to rate. Name the categories at the end of each spoke. The categories you choose are those that form the focus of your organization design objectives.

■ Define non-performance and full performance within each category.

■ Draw a large wheel with as many spokes as there are categories to rate.

■ Mark each spoke on a zero to 'n' scale with zero at the centre equal to 'no performance' and the highest number on the scale at the outer ring equal to 'full performance'. You measure performance, either objectively or subjectively.

■ Rate each category. Through a consensus or an average of individual scores get a team rating for each category.

■ Connect the team ratings for each category.

■ You can add gap scores. These are the differences between the rating score and the highest number. In Figure 13.5, customer service within the inner band had a score of 60.00. The full-performance score was 100.00 – thus the gap score was 40.00.

■ The overall ratings identify gaps within each category but not the relative importance of the categories themselves. Work on the biggest gap in the most critical category.

■ Post the radar chart in a prominent place, and review progress regularly. Figure 13.5 has the results for two periods. The inner shading is period one and the outer shading is period two. The difference between the two periods reflects the work done to address issues.

Self-check

The review phase is critical to the ongoing success of your new design. Doing effective reviews soon after the transition is finished and again approximately six months later gives you sound information on which decisions to make for going forward. If you miss out this phase, you will not reap the benefits of the new design or learn much from your work. If you can answer 'yes' to the majority of the questions below you are on track for completing a good review.

■ Do you have ongoing plans for breathing life into the new design? It is not enough to have reached the end of your transition phase and to disband your team. You must have a further plan to sustain and embed the changes, adjusting course as necessary. If you do not have a 'benefits realization plan' you are in danger of slipping back to the old ways. People often do not trust the new systems or processes and work the original way as an insurance policy in parallel with the new way. This leads to overlap and duplication. Help people trust the new ways by making them trustworthy and reinforcing their use by various methods.

- Is your business case still valid? As you move on from the transition phase confirm that the business case still fits with strategic objectives and departmental priorities, and is achievable and affordable. Confirm ongoing stakeholder commitment. Revisit the business strategy to check that assumptions about current business priorities are correct and that the key objectives are unchanged. If fundamental aspects of the business strategy have changed, the plans for ongoing service improvement must reflect those changes.
- Are the business benefits you forecast, starting to be realized, as set out in your business case? Have you already achieved more than you anticipated? The key consideration is to focus on the benefits in terms of successful outcomes for the business rather than delivery of (say) systems or new buildings. PIRs are an essential input to the review of the post-transition operating phase. Findings from these reviews should feed into further improvement plans.
- Have all the stakeholder issues been addressed? Your reviews should highlight areas of stakeholder concern. These typically include some of the following: the statutory process, communications, external relations, environmental issues, personnel, etc. Once you have these on the table, update or renew your stakeholder map, and develop communication and action plans to manage stakeholder concerns.
- Have the project documentation, training materials and training programmes been delivered and kept up to date? Most organization design implementations require you to train staff in the new ways of doing things. Your training programme should be matched with requirements for delivering new services and/or working in new ways, and be visible in the development plans of your people. Keep good training records including tracking the outcomes of the training in terms of productivity enhancement.

- Are plans for ongoing risk management up to date? The end of the project transition is not the moment to abandon your risk register, business continuity, or contingency plans. As part of your new day-to-day operation, ensure you continually update your risk management practices. Include in your work the ongoing operational health and safety aspects of your organization.
- What is the scope for improved value for money? Doing a PIR, six months into the new design, is a good point to assess the potential for further improvements. You do not want to do another full-scale re-design, but you may well want to get good answers to the following questions:
  - Can more be done for less?
  - Could any of your providers deliver better service quality at the same price?
  - Can maintenance costs be driven down?
  - Why have you not achieved some of the forecast benefits/ objectives? Can you take remedial action to achieve them or must they be foregone?
  - If targets have been met, should they be increased?
  - Is there any pattern to the success/failure that you can use to inform other organization design work or further exercises/programmes?
  - Did you achieve any unexpected benefits? If so, can you get further value from them?
- Have you benchmarked the performance of your new design against comparable departments or organizations? Benchmarking can offer new insights and ideas that will help you identify ways of improving processes such as demand management, service planning, and development. However, use benchmarking with caution. What produces high performance in one organization, may not produce it in yours. The value of benchmarking lies less in comparison purposes and more in ideas generation.
- Do you have a well-defined, implemented, and effective process for embedding improvements based on the lessons learned from the project? You should have well-defined processes for capturing lessons learned and taking action on recommendations for improvements. Too often, OD projects fail to work through methods of getting improvements working and then improving on these

improvements. Make sure you track your progression to improved performance. Use key milestones and realistic targets for continuous improvement in your new design. Remember that targets should be specific, measurable, agreed, realistic, relevant and time related or trackable (SMART). Organizational performance measures should relate to:

- Economy: minimizing the cost of resources used for an activity, with regard to appropriate quality.
- Efficiency: the relationship between outputs, in terms of goods, services, or other results and the resources used to produce them.
- Effectiveness: the extent to which you have achieved objectives, and the relationship between the intended impacts and actual impacts of an activity.

Do the selected performance measures offer clear and demonstrable evidence of the success (or otherwise) of your new design? For ongoing operational services, you should be concerned with service delivery and outputs, using conventional service level agreement approaches and related measures of aspects such as volumes and quality. Performance measures and indicators need to be:

- Directional: to confirm that you are on track to reach the goals.
- Quantitative: to show what has been achieved and how much more is to be done.
- Worthwhile: adding more value to the business than they cost to collect and use.

Your performance measures that relate to delivery or capability improvement should be tracked against an existing baseline. Remember that in phase three, you established your baseline for performance measurement. Check that the baseline measures still apply in the new design and re-agree if not. Your performance management strategy must link key departmental objectives to operational outcomes.

Do's and Don'ts

Do conduct more than one review – one soon after transition, and one, six months later

Do work on the recommendations of the reviews

- Do capture what you have learned and disseminate it to others
- Don't skimp this phase of your project. It is essential to success
- Don't neglect to review the behavioural as well as the operational aspects of it
- Don't forget to recognize and celebrate what you have achieved

Summary – The Bare Bones

- Informal and formal reviews that pick up both operational and behavioural issues are an essential part of your design success
- The review process, done systematically, will give you good information on the problems and issues you must solve or work as you embed the new organization design
- No design is perfect in its conception and implementation, so be prepared to learn from your experiences and pass on your learning to others
- Measurement of progress from a baseline, coupled with regular management information is critical as you seek to sustain the new design
- Your roles in the review process are to commission the review(s), facilitate their progress, and act on their recommendations
- Reviews tend to highlight deficiencies rather than good work. Do not take this to heart, as it is the nature of an audit process. However, make sure that you and your teams know what is praiseworthy and admirable in their work

References/Useful Reading

Goold and Campbell (2002). Do you have a well-designed organization? *Harvard Business Review*, March.

Block, P. (1997). *The Empowered Manager*. Jossey-Bass.

Brassard, M. and Ritter, D. (1994). The *Memory Jogger*. GOAL/QPC.

Office of Government Commerce (2004). *Successful Delivery Toolkit*. http://www.ogc.gov.uk/sdtoolkit/index.html.

14

Trends in Organization Design

'There is a melt down of all traditional boundaries. Products and services are merging. Buyers sell and sellers buy. Neat value chains are messy economic webs. Homes are offices. No longer is there a clear line between structure and process, owning and using, knowing and learning, real and virtual. Less and less separates employee and employer.'

Davis, S. and Meyer, C. (1998). *Blur: The Speed of Change in the Connected Economy*. Warner Books Inc.

Overview

You have read all sorts of predictions about the opportunities, constraints, influences, and future trends relating to organizations. At any business conference you will hear the same list of 'drivers for change' being cited as giving rise to all sorts of business challenges. You have identified them in relation to your own project as you started to think about re-design.

Looking at these from a slightly different focus – as trends rather than drivers you can see more patterns emerging, for example:

- There is a certain destabilization of management characterized by a rapid turnover of CEOs and senior executives. Related to this is a diminishing public trust in executive leadership and some private sector organizations.
- There is massive continuous change described in various terms – explosive, turbulent, disconnected, chaotic – just look at some popular business book titles. These sorts of adjectives imply a high degree of unmanageability.

- There is cut-throat competition in various dimensions, one of the results of which is exporting work to offshore locations.
- There is a notion of 'Digital Taylorism' – the view that technology can and will solve productivity problems. People in many jobs are under constant pressure to ratchet up performance knowing that their e-mail, telephone calls, computer files, Internet logs, even keystrokes can all be monitored.
- There is a move in the UK to intensify and develop human capital and to report on this to shareholders, accelerated by the Government's interest in this.

> 'The Government agrees that companies should provide more qualitative and forward looking reporting. ... It recognizes that companies are increasingly reliant on intangible assets such as the skills and knowledge of their employees, their business relationships and their reputation. Information about future plans, opportunities, risks and strategies is just as important to users of financial reports as a historical review of performance'
>
> Department of Trade and Industry (2002). *Modernising Company Law, Command Paper CM 5553.* Stationery Office.

There are similar trends appearing in the US. Identifying the trends to act on in your organization design is tricky. It is difficult to know where the trend hype ends and the valid trend prediction begins – so what can you do?

First, be aware that a design is not for life or even for very long. Static designs do not work. There is a need to keep on creating the right conditions for your organization to remain competitive. This means continuously asking yourselves questions about the best way to design your organization. Learn what you can from other company's experiences of re-designing – a good way of doing this is to join an organization design network or special interest group.

Second, keep your organization design skills honed. If you want to design a speedy, flexible, integrated, and innovative organization, make sure you are developing yourself and your colleagues in line with your context. If you have the skills and capabilities to get the design right, your organization is likely to be high performing.

Third, notice that much of the 'noise' around the future of organizations is about the people, relationships, and processes that glue them together rather than the structural, operational, and technical aspects that keep them in the marketplace. Predict that it will pay to you focus as much on the human, softer, side of the enterprise as on the harder elements as you re-design. If your design optimizes the capability, processes and work arrangements of your employees you are well placed to deliver the business strategy and to meet stakeholder expectations.

Fourth, recognize that new organization designs will run alongside, or be nested within, traditional organization designs (unless you are starting from scratch). For this reason familiarize yourself with the organization design history, trends, and current theory so that you can make informed trade-offs between old and new organizational models. Figure 14.1 summarizes these.

Currently theorists seem to be talking of organizations as part of an ecosystem that is a network of organizations including, for example, suppliers, distributors, technology partners, service centre partners, and other stakeholders. Embedded in this ecosystem is another system, embedded in another system – much as the Russian dolls. The challenge is to sustain a dynamic, changing, evolving, self-organizing, self-entailing, adaptive ecosystem realizing that the health of one member of the ecosystem has an impact on the health of other members of it. Technology is the enabler of ecosystem opportunity, integration, and new organizational forms. In organization as ecosystem thinking, the focus is less on core operations, and more on market and industry opportunity creation. This, in turn, shifts competitive strategy towards new forms of corporate leadership and structure.

What this means for organization design in practice has yet to emerge but there are some threads and thoughts. This chapter presents some of the trends and predictions in organization design. Remember, however, the prediction of 'the paperless office'. What follows, although interesting, may be as wrong as that prediction has so far proved to be.

New Organizational Designs

Whittington and Mayer (2002) make the point that current global trends have spawned numerous new models of organizations. They note that

Traditional view of organizations and change	Emerging view of organizations and change
Organization can be <ul><li>Managed, changed and controlled</li><li>Restructured and re-engineered</li><li>Fixed – causes for problems identified and solutions implemented</li></ul>	Organizations are socially constructed – we create our own reality in organization through relationships and dialogue. Conversation leads to rules and regulations that may be in place too long and stifle innovation. Organizations are seen as a culture
Change happens as a rational process where we can discover, diagnose, design, recommend, and implement solutions to rational problems	Change is a natural process that will evolve and unfold. Possibilities for transformation and difference are available within a system. The challenge is how to access it, unleash it and contain it (bounded instability)
Emphasis on analysis and digital information and objectivity	'We cannot communicate' We are engaged in constant analysis, interpretation and meaning making
Organizations exist in an environment that can be mapped, plotted and quantified	All organizations have the innate capability to grow, change and adapt in response to changing environmental circumstances
Strategy is a rational, conscious positioning of an organization within an environment or market	We can choose what we pay attention to and notice in organizations. This lens affects our way of being and acting in any given scenario
Energy for the change can be external to the system. Change is a thing to be driven, cascaded, managed, and rolled out	Control is a myth – at best, all we can perceive is a perspective (usually incomplete) on the patterns of connectivity
Change is seen as a fixed state from A to B (Lewin – Unfreezing, changing and re-freezing)	Change as flux, unfolding process, inevitable, potentially chaotic, and discontinuous
Emphasis in change is in selling, cascading, overcoming resistance, achieving buy in; getting skilled up to achieve change. Change is something to be delivered against fixed, clear objectives	Change through participation, co-creation, unfolding process and dialogue

Figure 14.1 Traditional and emerging views of organizations and change

common to the new models are the notions of knowledge and change capability, which they suggest, may compromise operational efficiency. However, they also state that traditional organization design models are not good at coping with knowledge flows and dynamic change. Practitioners

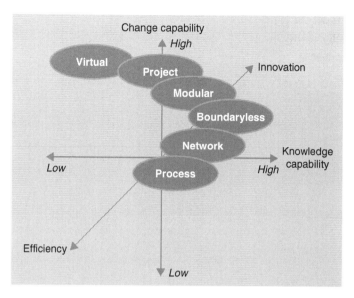

Figure 14.2 Mapping the new models of organization (Whittington and Mayer 2002)

and theorists have not yet come up with organizational forms that resolve knowledge, change and efficiency tensions. Figure 14.2 illustrates the common new forms mapped against their respective knowledge, change and efficiency capability.

Each of the organizational models in Figure 14.2 is different from the other. Each one has upsides and downsides. Going back to the notion of an organization as part of an ecosystem there is no doubt that the dynamics are complex. That is they are not deterministic. They have a degree of unpredictability, and exhibit phases of rapid change and even catastrophic change. They are continually evolving and going through a birth, growth, death, renewal process in different temporal and spatial scales (Kay, 1994). For this reason any organization design model is appropriate only in particular circumstances – in other words, there is no one new organizational form that works for all, and there is no guarantee that what will work for you now will work for you for very long.

The following section describes emerging organizational models. Some of these appear in Figure 14.2 and others do not.

The boundaryless organization: Ashkenas et al. (2002) describe the boundaryless organization in their book of the same name. They argue

increasing pace of change, organizations have to think
the four boundaries that characterize most traditional

....aries: those between levels and ranks of people.
- Horizontal boundaries: those between functions and disciplines.
- External boundaries: those between the organization and its suppliers, customers, and regulators.
- Geographic boundaries: those between nations, cultures, and markets.

Instead of thinking of these boundaries as being fixed, inflexible, and unyielding (resulting in 'silos'), think of these boundaries as being permeable, flexible, and organic membranes in a living and evolving organism/organization.

Organizations that start thinking in this way see four things start to happen:

- Employees start to share information throughout the organization resulting in a sense of common purpose and knowledge of organizational goals.
- Whoever has leadership skills and technical skills use and develop them regardless of their level in the organization. Organizational systems and processes encourage this.
- Authority and decision-making appear at appropriate points in the workflow. This demonstrates trust in employees and allows fast response to customers.
- Reward becomes based on results and achievements.

Debra's Natural Gourmet store established in 1989 is a good example of a boundaryless organization.

> *No question, Stark owes much of her loyal customer following –
> and her 11 consecutive years of double-digit revenue growth – to
> her 26 employees. And no wonder, for Stark has assigned every
> employee a management role. Staffers benchmark sales against
> regional and national averages. Others closely monitor product
> turnover. For her part, Stark prominently posts daily and monthly*

> *sales reports, highlighting the figures to show big advances or*
> *troublesome declines. And in a radical departure from most*
> *retailers, each quarter she distributes 20% of her after-tax profits*
> *among everyone – 'divided,' she says, 'according to each person's*
> *number of hours, salary, and how I see they're interacting with*
> *customers, each other, and me.'*
>
> Osborne, D.M. (2001). *The Store that Stark Built, Inc.*
> Magazine, August.

The atomized organization: In a reissue of their classic book *Corporate Cultures*, Deal and Kennedy (2000) talk about the atomized organization where the work of the corporation is done in small, autonomous units linked by technologies to a corporate nerve centre. Similarly to Ashkenas et al. they argue that the vertical organization will cease to exist, replaced by webs of social influence and strong cultural ties.

Where Ashkenas describes the organization in terms of a living organism, Deal and Kennedy describe organizations in terms of atoms and molecules bonding together. Critical to keeping them from flying apart are those who perpetuate and develop the values, beliefs, rituals, myths, symbols, and ceremonies; that is, the culture and cultural ties of the organization that give people something to identify with and thus keep the organization strong and cohesive.

The adaptive organization: Fulmer (2000) describes an adaptive organization that, like the boundaryless and atomized organization is fairly decentralized, it has a powerful technology based information system, and it is constantly evolving. Fulmer notes that an adaptive organization also has high spans of control that facilitate fast, effective decision-making.

In his description, adaptive organizations maintain flexibility by using a variety of temporary structures (similar in nature to project teams or communities of practice), alliances, and partnership arrangements. Using these means that the organization can keep changing shape, as an evolving organism does, in line with the emerging business strategy.

Theory on organizations as complex adaptive systems is a rapidly growing field of academic interest. Ralph Stacey (2000) is a significant writer in this field. Theory posits that organizations co-evolve with the environment through people, self-organizing as they navigate market opportunities and competitive dynamics. Self-organizing occurs when people are free to mix, network, and cross-internal and external boundaries.

The *Horizontal Organization* written by Frank Ostroff (1999) takes the vertical boundary (similarly described in the *Boundaryless Organization*) and makes the case for re-designing vertical organizations as horizontal organizations. He describes these as centred on the cross-functional end-to-end work, information and material flows known as core processes. These three or four processes are the 'catalysts which transforms an organization from the traditional vertical to the horizontal'. In his analysis horizontal organizations demand an empowered workforce and to get that requires changing training and development interventions, performance measurement systems, and information systems and flows. Changing the systems is not the only way of achieving an empowered workforce. Members must be motivated and enabled (through multi-skilling) to take the initiative and make decisions at any stage of the workflow. (Horizontally organized businesses are also known as process based.)

Other newer forms of organization include virtual, networked (cellular), modular, and project based. Chapter 1 briefly describes these forms.

Reading the descriptions and theories on the emerging shape of organizations reveals there are 10 consistent trends across them:

1. Organizations are constantly evolving organisms in a wider eco-system.
2. The health of the ecosystem depends on the health of the organisms.
3. The boundaries between the organisms are permeable.
4. Within each 'organism' (organization or department), there are small autonomous work groups, 10–20 people.
5. Group members are undifferentiated by job title or level in the hierarchy – ideas and results count.
6. There are no direct reporting relationships. 'Management' is by self-organization. Leadership rotates to task competence.
7. The people who do the work have authority and decision-making power.

8. Members of the work group are accountable.
9. Technology links contacts and information flows between groups, the wider organization, and the ecosystem.
10. A strong value based culture bonds the work groups.

Meeting Your Design Challenge

Whether you are the line manager or the HR practitioner you are also the organization designer. You have to make sense of the various design possibilities open to you now that will carry you into the future. Those of you in a large, traditional, bureaucratic and hierarchical organization probably feel that you have no chance whatsoever re-designing the 'oil-tanker' to become the state of the art Americas Cup winner. You are right. But that does not mean ignoring the emerging trends. Far from it. Do what you can to bring the best and most appropriate trends to your organization. Whatever your business it will not survive in it if it does not keep pace with change.

Work out how you can move towards being an organic, adaptive organization, with permeable boundaries. Here, the biggest challenge facing most traditionally designed organizations is breaking down functional thinking. Think cross-organizational co-operation, co-operation, and integration – your design must facilitate this but you do not have to take a giant leap into a new organizational form. The predominant facilitators of these are technologies and social interactions.

Lars Groth (1999) talks about the technologies related to integration. He discusses ways to design, build and develop organizations with the assistance of information technology (IT) but as he does so is careful to point out, as well as the immense opportunities, the inherent limitations of IT. Technology allows real-time coordination and integration of information regardless of amount of data and geographic location. Retail banking is an industry sector making good use of the opportunities of IT in re-designing. Think of the way the banks have reorganized (and continue to reorganize) to develop on-line services, ATMs, and point of sale information.

Some of the limitations of IT relate to operationalizing the theories of ecosystems. Groth points out that standardization issues are huge even within an organization. Challenges multiply when you try to standardize across organizations. He warns us to beware using terms like 'networked' or 'virtual' organizations too lightly as they downplay the effort it takes to establish them and the risks and costs involved in opting out of a mutually dependent relationship once it is established.

Hesselbein et al. (1998) are provoking on the social interaction aspects of integration. The chapter written by Dave Ulrich (Six practices for creating communities of value, not proximity) argues that, aided by technology, communities based on values are replacing communities based on proximity. Therefore, organizations must seek ways of creating and operating communities of value if they are to integrate and co-operate effectively.

If you subscribe to this argument, your designs must pave the way for this and Ulrich offers six practices:

1. Forge a strong and distinct identity that presents internally and externally the distinguishing features of your organization. This is more than a brand image. It is centred on the values and purpose that the brand image represents.
2. Establish clear rules of inclusion. Make clear the 'price of membership' of this community. It may be a particular level of expertise (as in a professional institute) or other qualifying characteristics.
3. Share information across boundaries. Permeable boundaries allow information sharing. Web-based discussion groups are an example of this. Work out how you can develop rapid social transmission of usable information across your organization. (Many organizations have the technology for rapid transmission but not the commitment of the people to transmit and use the information.)
4. Create serial reciprocity. This is a kind of 'bartering' idea. You may give Joe some information or help but he will not return the favour to you, instead giving support to Jane. At some stage you will receive help from someone but it may not be Jane either.
5. Use symbols, myths, and stories to create and sustain values. Storytelling is a powerful way of building community feeling and experience. Myths and symbols work in this direction too. Use them prudently – as inclusion devices, not exclusion devices.
6. Manage enough similarity so that the community feels familiar. Predictability is important to a community. As this story illustrates:

> *I am a member of Weight Watchers. Every morning I log on to a discussion database to talk to about 30 other people who have somehow formed into a community. None of us know each other face-to-face. We have something in common in that we all have a significant amount of weight to lose. None of the 30 of us wants to lose less than 90 lbs. We share our ups and downs. Some mornings about five of us are present. Other mornings there are more. This informal and ad hoc support group has really kept me going over the last year and I've lost over 60 lbs.*

Building communities into your design thinking is a powerful move into a future state organization where cooperation, collaboration, and integration across permeable boundaries produce business results. As Ulrich points out establishing such a community requires planning hard work and good management. Nevertheless, when they work they are productive and supportive.

Developing Your Organization Design Skills

Whittington and Mayer (2002) report that

> *'Organization design is more critical than ever in the success of contemporary organizations, with the potential both for large-scale value creation and value destruction' and 'human resource professionals have a central role to play in the new processes of organizing.'*

Assume from the statements that line managers and HR practitioners must be alert and responsive to emerging trends in this field and then reflect on what you do to keep your skills and knowledge up dated. If your performance and development review is looming now is a good time to plan for the coming year and review what you have learned about organization design in the past year. Make a habit of regularly recording your development activity. If you are an HR practitioner, remember it is a requirement for members of the Chartered Institute of Personnel and Development to keep a continuing professional development (CPD)

Advantages	Disadvantages/issues
▪ It gives people a good basis for performance review discussions ▪ It proves to yourself and others that you are continuing to learn in a variety of ways with an all round increase in skills, knowledge and experience. ▪ It helps you improve your performance when you meet a similar situation again. ▪ It provides a rich source of information you can reflect on to learn more about yourself, and your ways of operating giving you confidence and a sense of direction.	▪ It is time consuming and perhaps feels bureaucratic to compile ▪ It is hard to recognize what activities or situations have resulted in learning something actionable or of significance ▪ It is difficult to remember what has been a learning experience if you are not recording on a regular basis or almost as it happens ▪ It is usually considered an important rather than an urgent task and in the day-to-day drops down the priority list as urgent tasks take over.

Figure 14.3 Advantages and disadvantages of reviewing and recording development activity

record. If you are a line manager, take this opportunity to evaluate the pros and cons of recording your organization design development activity. Figure 14.3 gives you a start-point on this.

Make a decision to record what you are learning as your OD project proceeds.

Following the 10 guidelines below will make it easier for you do this.

■ **Make it a habit**: Plan to record regularly what you have learned under the headings you have chosen. Do this weekly. Your appointments diary and e-mails are good reminders of what you have been doing. Picking out the organization design aspects that lead you to reflect on what you have learned in relation to the event or situation.

■ **Keep it simple**: Try not to make heavy weather of the recording. A simple format usually works best. Figure 14.4 is an example of the form in action.

■ **Collect the evidence**: You'll find that it's easier to think through the week's learning if, on a daily basis, you put in a folder (either hard or soft) things which you think have contributed to your development – an e-mail with some feedback for example.

Learning method	What did you do?	Why?	What did you learn from this?	How have/ will you use this? Any further action?
Key internal meetings	Led the communications team meeting	As part of my role of organization design consultant	The value of having a structured agenda. Skills in facilitating debates around tricky items. Managing push-back from participants. Keeping things flowing and tracking progress.	Will bear in mind the need to verify information that comes my way for action before acting on it. Will do more lobbying ahead of time with participants.

Figure 14.4 CPD record form

Do you measure new hire satisfaction with the hiring process?	
January–December 2003	Yes = 28.1%
	No = 71.8%
January–March 2004	Yes = 35.6%
	No = 64.4%

Figure 14.5 New hire satisfaction

■ **Think it over**: Some things may not immediately strike you as a development activity, but take the piece of information in Figure 14.5 extracted from a survey on hiring.

Think about a requirement to hire people into your new design. How important is it to the success of your implementation that new hires feel good about your hiring process? If this is a question that causes you to reflect and then take action, it is worth recording in your CPD log.

■ **Look for patterns**: It may be that you find you are recording the majority of your development which takes place within a specific type of activity, for example book reading or external meetings. It is worth noting these types of patterns as you may find you have a particular learning style that is better suited to some methods than others which could help you select development activity which is right for you.

■ **Make it work**: Knowing you have learned something is good but making it actionable and then applying it is better because that way you are able to continuously improve your performance. One of the more well-known theories of experiential learning is Kolb's (1984) learning cycle which suggests four phases running in a continuous circle: reflective observation, abstract conceptualization, active experimentation, and concrete experience.

There are critics of this theory but it is worth familiarizing yourself with it and forming your own view of its applicability to CPD.

■ **Get feedback on improvements**: It is often worth telling people that you are trying out something you have learned or are practicing in order for you to get feedback (hopefully constructive) and support in what and how you are doing. Only by trying things out and then trying them out again in an improved way will you develop yourself.

■ **Extend your range**: What and how you learn is unique to you, but it is easy to get stuck in the same type of learning rut and talk yourself out of valuable new experiences from which you can learn. A great instruction to follow is to 'Do something every day that scares you.' Only by extending your boundaries can you learn new things and develop yourself.

■ **Make the most of yourself**: You may think that you are not in a position where you can develop yourself. This is not the case. Every role has potential for providing development opportunities – it is up to you to exploit these and recognize that you are acting in your best interests if you do so.

■ **Learn what works for you**: What works for you in terms of development activity may not work for someone else. Experiment with your learning styles and aim to use a variety.

Following the tips listed above becomes easier if you:

■ think of CPD as something helpful to yourself;
■ remember learning is a lifelong activity – the CPD record just recognizes this;
■ aim to enjoy the reflection on what you have learned.

Useful Tools

Tool 1: CPD Self-assessment

Your development record needs to reflect a range of all the learning and development opportunities that you have undertaken. The CIPD recommends a minimum of thirty-five hours per year, but this is only a guide. They also recommend that you concentrate on the activities that have made the most impact on you and your role. Anything can count as evidence as long as you show, or know, that you have learnt something from it. Remember, it is the outcome that is important and how it impacts on you and your role, rather than what you did.

Record your development activity for the past week using the list below – with any additions of your own – and the template (Figure 14.6). When you have done this, decide whether it was valuable enough to do on a regular basis. If so, timetable yourself to do it:

- Key internal meetings
- Key external meetings
- Networking activity
- Web sites
- Journal reading
- Book reading
- Formal training (short courses or qualification programmes)
- Informal development, for example coaching sessions
- Community activity

Learning type	What did you do?	Why?	What did you learn from this?	How have/will you use this? Any further action?
Key internal meetings				
Key external meetings				
Web sites				

Figure 14.6 Template for CPD

- Work experience
- Social or interest activity (e.g. a film that sparked reflection on high performing teams)
- Work experience/on the job training.

Tool 2: Web site

www.organizationdesignforum.org The Organization Design Forum is an inclusive not-for-profit international professional association created to link practitioners, organizational leaders, academics and students in continuous learning about the field of organization design.

The Forum believes that organization design you learn best by surrounding yourself with the broadest possible perspectives. Its services benefit:

- Organization design practitioners, both internal and external.
- Executives and line managers who are themselves leaders of organization design efforts.
- HR and training practitioners.
- Academics involved in research and teaching.
- Students in graduate level programs with an organizational focus.

Self-check

You are well on the way to understanding and keeping up to date with emerging trends in organization design if you can answer 'yes' to the following questions.

Are you challenging the assumptions on which your business has been traditionally organized and led? The prevailing wisdom is that future organizational success (innovation, productivity, and performance and competitive survival) depends on a fundamentally different view of organizational form.

Are you championing the view that the need to adapt or change radically is urgent? If you are not you are lagging behind the most bureaucratic machines in the world. Both the UK and US Government are sponsoring extensive e-gov initiatives aimed at transforming the way government and citizens interact. If they can do it, so can you.

Has your organization started to respond to customer pressure to deliver more efficiently, faster, and in a more tailored way than you did even two years ago? Customer requirements for service, customization, and swift response are putting tremendous pressure on organizations to adapt to meet these.

Are you making best use of your IT systems in working towards a collaborative, cooperative, cross-functional organization? Technology enables innovative organizational forms and responses. The majority of systems are under-used partly because people do not trust them, partly because people do not understand their capability, and partly because organizations are not designed to make best use of them.

Are you introducing new forums for organizational information exchange and learning? The way you exchange information in your organization is key to performance outcomes. The quicker expertise and information travels and is used to organizational effect the more benefits will accrue in performance. The ability to transform learning into action gives competitive edge.

Does your organization recognize and reward innovative individuals regardless of their hierarchical position? Trend setting organizations are open to ideas from anywhere in the organization – the well publicized GE initiative is an example of this.

Jack Welch's order to GE execs to 'destroy' the business and rebuild for the Internet during a now-famous managers' meeting in January 1999 was a shot heard around GE's world. The idea was to figure out where the Internet could cut costs, boost customer service, and improve the productivity of every GE business unit before dot-coms could encroach on the company's territory.

Focused may be an understatement. Over the last several months, GE has evaluated the 'analog,' or human, touch points of all processes across GE's business to get as many of them on the Web as possible. For instance, GE Capital's mortgage business eliminated 60% of the 200 analog steps in its mortgage application-approval process by moving much of the work to the Web. This let GE reduce the number of employees needed to process mortgage applications and redeploy them in more critical posts. GE expects to reduce costs in manufacturing processes (the 'make' side of GE) by about

> *15% over the next two years through productivity improvements gained by using the Web.*
>
> > *Marianne Kolbasuk McGee Information Week,*
> > *27 November 2000.*

Are you promoting co-ordination of activities? You should be moving your organization away from centralized command and control, vertical, structures towards one of the more organic forms where authority and decision-making sit with the people who do the jobs.

Are you fostering systems and processes that encourage free movement of people and ideas? Where people mix, network, and are able to self-organize you will find strong motivation to perform and innovate. Your challenge is to inculcate a strong value set that develops bonds working for organizational success.

Does your organization design develop people's abilities to discuss and share ideas, to talk to each other, to reflect and converse? Too many organizations operate through managerial diktat and control. This does not work in favour of dialogue, exploration, and improvement.

Does your organization have a strong value set and clear purpose? Where this exists success is likely to follow. Johnson and Johnson is an example of an organization that has created a strong and successful culture embedded in a value set introduced more than sixty years ago (in 1943).

> *At Johnson & Johnson there is no mission statement that hangs on the wall. Instead, for more than 60 years, a simple, one-page document – Our Credo – has guided our actions in fulfilling our responsibilities to our customers, our employees, the community and our stockholders. Our worldwide Family of Companies shares this value system in 36 languages spreading across Africa, Asia/Pacific, Eastern Europe, Europe, Latin America, Middle East and North America.*
>
> ### Our Credo
>
> *We believe our first responsibility is to the doctors, nurses and patients, to mothers and fathers and all others who use our products and services. In meeting their needs everything we do must be of high quality.*

*We must constantly strive to reduce our costs
in order to maintain reasonable prices.
Customers' orders must be serviced promptly and accurately.
Our suppliers and distributors must have an opportunity
to make a fair profit.
We are responsible to our employees,
the men and women who work with us throughout the world.
Everyone must be considered as an individual.
We must respect their dignity and recognize their merit.
They must have a sense of security in their jobs.
Compensation must be fair and adequate,
and working conditions clean, orderly and safe.
We must be mindful of ways to help our employees fulfill
their family responsibilities.
Employees must feel free to make suggestions and complaints.
There must be equal opportunity for employment, development
and advancement for those qualified.
We must provide competent management,
and their actions must be just and ethical.*

*We are responsible to the communities in which we live and work
and to the world community as well.
We must be good citizens – support good works and charities
and bear our fair share of taxes.
We must encourage civic improvements and better health and education.
We must maintain in good order
the property we are privileged to use,
protecting the environment and natural resources.*

*Our final responsibility is to our stockholders.
Business must make a sound profit.
We must experiment with new ideas.
Research must be carried on, innovative programs developed
and mistakes paid for.
New equipment must be purchased, new facilities provided
and new products launched.
Reserves must be created to provide for adverse times.
When we operate according to these principles,
the stockholders should realize a fair return.*

Do's and Don'ts

- Do keep up to date with trends in organization design.
- Do think through which of these you can appropriately apply to your project
- Do aim to design your organization towards being adaptive and perhaps boundaryless
- Don't adopt trends that are not right for your organization
- Don't take a theory and try to make it a practice without careful consideration
- Don't go too far too quickly in trying to be an organization design trendsetter

Summary – The Bare Bones

- Organizations are changing at a rapidly quickening pace
- Technologies are enabling new organizational forms to emerge
- New organizational forms are boundaryless, evolving, and adaptive
- New forms cannot be adopted wholesale into traditional organizations
- Strong values and purpose appear to bond new organizational forms
- Collaboration, integration, and cross-functional networks are the direction to go in

References/Useful Reading

Ashkenas, R. et al. (2002). *The Boundaryless Organization: Breaking the Chains of Organizational Structure*. Jossey-Bass.

Davis, S. and Meyer, C. (1998). *Blur: The Speed of Change in the Connected Economy*. Warner Books Inc.

Department of Trade and Industry (2002). *Modernising Company Law, Command Paper CM 5553*. Stationery Office.

Drucker Foundation, Hesselbein, F. et al. (eds.) (1997). *The Organization of the Future*. Jossey-Bass.

Drucker Foundation, Hesselbein, F. et al. (eds.) (1998). *The Community of the Future*. Jossey-Bass.

Fulmer, W. E. (2000). *Shaping the Adaptive Organization*. Amacom.

Groth, L. (1999). *Future Organizational Design*. John Wiley and Sons Ltd.

Goold, M. and Campbell, A. (2002). *Designing Effective Organizations: How to Create Structured Networks*. Jossey-Bass.

Haekel, S. H. (1999). *Adaptive Enterprise: Creating and Leading Sense-And-Respond*

Organizations. Harvard College.

Hock, D. (1999). *Birth of the Chaordic Age*. Berrett-Koehler Publishing.

Iansiti, M. and Levien, R. (2004). Strategy as ecology. *Harvard Business Review*, March.

Kay, J. and Schneider, E. (1994). Embracing complexity: the challenge of the ecosystems approach. *Alternatives*, 20 (3), 32–38.

Kennedy, A. A. and Deal, T. E. (2000). *Corporate Cultures*. Perseus Publishing.

Kolb, D. A. (1984). *Experiential Learning: Experience as the Source of Learning and Development*. Prentice Hall Inc.

Morabito, J. (1999). *Organization Modeling: Innovative Architectures for the 21st Century*. Prentice Hall.

Ostroff, F. (1999). *The Horizontal Organization*. Oxford University Press.

Routledge Tapscott, D. et al. (1998). *Blueprint to the Digital Economy*. McGraw Hill Professional Book Group.

Ridderstrale, J. and Nordstrom, K. (2001). *Funky Business: Talent Makes Capital Dance*. BookHouse Publishing.

Stacey, R. et al. (2000). *Complexity Management: Fad or Radical Challenge to Systems Thinking?*

Whittington, R. and Mayer, M. (2002). *Organising for Success in the Twenty-First Century*. Chartered Institute of Personnel and Development.

Appendix 1: Business Case Template

Overview

A compelling business case, developed and presented in the right way, will

- Convince people that change is necessary (by reference to hard facts).
- Help engage people.
- Enable you to build and sustain commitment to the changes you are proposing.

It has two characteristics:

- To provide a sound justification for why the project or activity needs to happen.
- To strongly motivate people to undertake the change.

Business Case

Project Title

Draft xx.x Date dd/mm/yy

Contents

Executive Summary

- Specify the end goal (high-level outcome) you are shooting for.
- State the compelling reasons why the change is a business imperative, not just a 'nice to have'.

- Highlight how the change fits into the overall organizational pro-gramme and contributes to achieving the business goals.
- Convey a sense of urgency with a clear (but brief) explanation of why the benefits of the proposal make the costs and effort of it worthwhile.

Background

Use the opportunity to motivate the readers, build commitment and create ownership. Ensure you have sound justification

- Give an overview past state, current state, and desired state.
- Clarify the presenting problem/challenge/dilemma.
- State why you are presenting the proposal at this stage and what the high-level outcomes will be.
- Balance negative with positive messages. Explaining clearly how serious the situation is, the dangers inherent in not supporting the proposal, and articulating the benefits of supporting it.

Project Objectives

- Describe SMART objectives this project will achieve (stretching, measurable, attainable, relevant, and time bound).
- Limit the number of objectives to five.
- Ensure the objectives are soundly justifiable and positively motivating.

Scope

- Define the boundaries and scope of the project.
- Include a brief assessment of the implications of these.
- Note the exclusions from the project and the methods of addressing interface complexities.

Methodology/Approach

- Describe how you are going to involve stakeholders.
- Clarify the roles of the project sponsors.

- Outline the structure and operation that will deliver the proposal (e.g. steering group, programme manager, project co-ordinators, project stream leaders).
- State the style and phases of designing and delivering the proposal.

Key Deliverables and Milestones/Time scale

Deliverable (by objective)	Milestone	Start date	End date

Success Criteria/Measures of Success

- State the success criteria or how you will measure success for each deliverable by milestone.
- Ensure the measurements are realistic, valid, and actually measurable.
- Use the measures chosen to support your justification for the project.
- Identify measures which will increase motivation and support for the project.

Issues and Risks (Including Dependencies and Assumptions)

- Note the basis for identifying risks and issues (which usually relate to dependencies and assumptions).
- Include the issues which are outstanding at this point and need to be resolved before proceeding.
- Identify the key risks at the start-up stage of the process (further risks can be identified as the project proceeds.
- Recommend methods of addressing the issues and mitigating the risks. (Briefly.)

Costs and Resources

- Put a best guess here as things may change as the project is firmed up.
- Bid for more than you think rather than less to allow for budget cuts.

- Be realistic in the other resources you need (time, people, skills, etc).

Benefits to be Delivered

- Clearly state the benefits that will be delivered by this business case.
- Identify who will be responsible and accountable for realizing the benefits on an ongoing basis.
- Describe the method of evaluating and reporting on the benefit realisation after project completion.

Sign Off

(As agreement for the project to run and to the content of the business case)

Stakeholder xxxxxx   ....

Stakeholder yyyyyy   ....

Stakeholder zzzzzz   ....

Index

Printed in the USA/Agawam, MA
April 9, 2014

587769.024